THE TRADES OF
MARCH 2020

THE TRADES OF

MARCH 2020

A SHIELD AGAINST UNCERTAINTY

ALEX GUREVICH

THE TRADES OF MARCH 2020
A Shield against Uncertainty

ISBN   978-1-5445-2515-0   *Hardcover*

          978-1-5445-2513-6   *Paperback*

          978-1-5445-2514-3   *Ebook*

My first book was about a sword. This one is about a shield. Unlike swords, shields are rarely sung in fiction and they don't get glorious names like Stormbringer or Daystar Clarion. Yet without survival, there is no victory, and even the most brilliant portfolio manager can't function without food and electricity.

I dedicate this book to medical researchers and to frontline workers in healthcare, food distribution, and critical infrastructure, who were our shield in the pandemic crisis.

CONTENTS

INTRODUCTION

In March of 2020, a few days after shelter-in-place was ordered in the Bay Area, my wife woke up in the middle of the night when she heard me collapse on the bathroom floor. I didn't quite pass out, but I was experiencing shortness of breath, palpitations, chills, and severe sweating. I was certain I didn't have COVID. It was stress.

The path that led me to that point in my health and personal life is inseparable from my journey in financial markets.

Have you ever wondered what is going on in the command center of a sophisticated hedge fund? Have you ever wanted to be a fly on the wall of a CIO's office when the markets are melting down?

When I finished my first investment book, *The Next Perfect Trade: A Magic Sword of Necessity* (henceforth, TNPT), I hoped to call my next book *The Next Perfect Portfolio: A Magic Shield of Sufficiency*. COVID-19 interrupted this plan.

However, in a sense, a book about trading during a pandemic is a natural sequel. In the introduction to TNPT, I compared formulating a trading strategy to preparing for a battle.

> If you think of investing as a battle, you need to prepare for it thoroughly. Get in proper shape. Learn your moves, acquire your armor, your shield, your helmet, and your battle horse. A magic formula (or magic weapon in this context) will be wasted if you get killed by the market's first arrow. But with proper training and equipment this weapon may give you a devastating advantage.

It is only natural to next recount what happened in battle.

Winston Churchill once said that history is written by the victors. So here is a spoiler: this is not a story of how we failed and lost a fortune in the pandemic. Few can truly be considered winners in 2020, but from a financial perspective, this thriller has a happy ending.

This is the story about how HonTe Investments, LLC (HonTe) navigated the pandemic successfully.

A SHIELD AGAINST UNCERTAINTY

We named our investment company after a Japanese strategic term applied to the game of Go. *Hon* stands for *truth* and *Te* in this context stands for *move*. A "true move" or an "honest move" is one that applies a patient strategy, which may appear slow but is the best at delivering long-term results.

In the chaos of the pandemic, it was difficult to decide what would be a *perfect portfolio*. I had to deal with so many unprecedented developments and uncertainties that betting on short-term outcomes was virtually impossible.

I had my weapon, though, my Magic Sword of Necessity, which allowed me to select trades with odds skewed in my favor. But I also had to avoid being destroyed by wild market fluctuations.

My approach was to exclude variables of which I didn't have expert understanding. I didn't speculate on epidemiological peculiarities of COVID-19, the effectiveness of mitigation measures, the timelines for vaccines, or the details of policy response.

It was enough to know just two facts:

- Eventually, the pandemic would pass.

- The monetary and fiscal policy response would continue building until it overwhelmed any lack of liquidity.

By focusing on trades, which capitalized on these simple concepts, I avoided being blindsided by price swings. This was my *Shield against Uncertainty.*

It may sound too easy: "just put on the trades which will work eventually and wait till they work." That was indeed the *true move,* but the wait was often long and painful. The year 2020 was long and weird. I recall someone tweeting, "Do you remember Australian wildfires? That was 2020."

Back in the spring of 2020, I made my own joke: "Every trading day in March felt like a month, so on this scale, the bear market we experienced was of average duration." We'll get to the duration of the bear market later, I promise. I also quipped that a book should be written about just that one month in the financial markets, when things really came unglued. By the time I had embarked on this project, it was no longer a joke.

I felt a little strange starting to write the story while living through it and not yet knowing how it would end. As I was writing, COVID cases were on the rise, the timing for vaccines was uncertain, and macro analysts were divided in their predictions regarding inflation and growth. On top of everything else, the United States experienced unusual election jitters leading into November 2020.

In the two previous crises—9/11 and the global financial crisis (GFC)—we lost our sense of security and some measure of innocence. We moved on from those events with a new understanding and new concerns, which were there to stay. We got used to taking off our shoes at the airport and distrusting collateralized debt obligations. Yet, the perception of stability did return gradually in both cases. It was a "new normal" but a "normal" nonetheless.

I believe that in two or three years, we will look back at the time of the pandemic in the same way: as a brief but intense episode, followed by normalization to a somewhat altered world.

MY STORY

There are many different kinds of books that could be written, have been written, and no doubt will be written about the COVID pandemic.

I tell the story I know: my own financial and emotional journey. Although I am providing just one narrow viewpoint, I hope it will illuminate a shared experience of money managers.

My goal in writing this book is to present readers with a view of what was actually happening "in the trenches" of financial markets during the first month of the pandemic. It is designed to be a vivid replay of those few fateful weeks, as well as a strategic and psychological guide to surviving an extraordinary crisis.

I discuss investment strategies and I expect many of my readers to be interested in making money in financial markets. At the same time, I hope the account of coping with the tremendous psychological pressure created by market volatility will appeal to any reader.

I pride myself on having an exceptional recall of price action. I claim, albeit with exaggeration, that I can recall principal price-level dynamics of any asset class with which I was involved during my two-plus decades in financial markets. But the memories of March are not clear in my mind. There was just too much. Too much then and too much since. I can no longer recount the sequence of the silver crash, the stock market bottom, the Treasury funding crisis, or the Federal Reserve actions without first looking at the charts.

Fortunately, I have more than charts: I have my trading log. Furthermore, when our entire team had to abandon our San Francisco office and retreat to our homes, we had to establish new communication routines. Luckily, remote work was not entirely new to us; a manager on a business trip or on a vacation always stayed connected.

We had already adopted Slack for internal chats. We had established channels for subjects such as trade orders, operational issues, general market info, risk management, planning and scheduling, and so on.

During the lockdown, Slack became our main form of communication. Reviewing our chat on the trading channel, I can reconstruct not only the flow of transactions but the flow of thinking as well. Of course, a lot happened on video and phone calls, Bloomberg chats, and emails. There were longer discussions and market analysis happening on other channels as well. I decided to publish the entire trading channel transcript from March of 2020 because this is the most concise and faithful way to convey the zeitgeist of that remarkable month.

It is a minute-by-minute commentary on most actions we took; an account of every insight and every screw-up; of every second thought, reconsideration and persistent folly. The sheer volume of transactions testifies to how busy we were. And the time stamps attest to our sleepless nights.

Because this book is intended for a broad audience, I want to emphasize something that might not be obvious to readers without experience in the hedge fund business: The communications you see below are just my company's (HonTe Investments) internal chatter. When I say, "buy this" or "sell that," those are not official orders. A team member, myself included, will convey an actual order electronically, through Bloomberg chat or a voice call to our execution agents and counterparties, such as brokers or banks.

This Slack channel is neither official nor complete. It doesn't cover all the transactions, and it is not used for operational reconciliation. It also, as you will see, includes very little economic discussion or trade analysis. Those happen on different channels as well as via emails, forwarded research pieces, and Zoom conferences. However, in going over it, I find the trading Slack channel sufficient to reconstruct our short-term focus and long-term strategy.

The book's narrative unfolds as if we were trading a single portfolio; in fact, we have several accounts under management. The reader will see references to allocating trades and risk between the accounts to keep them properly balanced. Portfolio names and some other identifications were redacted for privacy and compliance reasons.

I retained all the repetitions, typos, symbols, and acronyms. There are also multiple references to operational issues such as credit, margins, and order limits. Those might be confusing, but I don't expect you to decipher every line of the Slack chat. I want to convey the sense of our process and the general frame of mind and flow of activity, while highlighting some of the crucial decision points.

As I began to pore over the trading records, I immediately faced surprises. My memories did turn out to be faulty.

I can no longer deceive myself with stories of being more prudent or more prescient than I actually was. The trading records and the daily P/L[1] don't lie. We traders are always naked in the face of scrutiny.

CAST OF CHARACTERS

I am writing this book purely from my perspective, and I use "I" statements throughout: "my trade," "my portfolio," "I decided," "I made a mistake," and finally, "I made (or lost) money." Don't take this as me disregarding the HonTe team's value and the importance of my coworkers' contributions.

---

1 P/L stands for profit and loss.

My colleagues stayed up many nights executing orders and ensuring smooth operational flow amid unprecedented market upheaval. They conducted trade analyses and provided a forum for discussing ideas. They negotiated margins and maintained the dialogue with our external counterparties to ensure continuous liquidity. Many of them did this while managing the challenge of distance learning for their children.

The main distinction of my position as the Chief Investment Officer (CIO) is not that I have to work harder or know more but that I bear the final burden of decision making. When all the discussions are over, all the research is read, and all the charts are studied, someone has to decide what trades to execute.

My goal here is to expose the reader to the thought process and emotional state of a CIO, with full recognition that everyone else on my team had their own poignant journeys.

This is not the acknowledgments section. Acknowledgments are due, as my colleagues have been working hard not only to push HonTe and its investors to financial success but also to help me produce this book. Here, however, I want readers to become familiar with our firm's structure and the jobs of all participants in the trading chat transcribed in the chapters to follow.

Chris Lutton (CL), Co-founder and CEO of HonTe Investments

I'd rather manage money than people. Hence, starting a new firm was contingent on me finding a trustworthy partner to run the business side. Chris and I go back to 2004 when he started to cover me (then a prop trader at J.P. Morgan) from the Foreign Exchange Desk at Bank of America. Over the years, we developed a relationship and talked of doing something together. A few years ago, the time was right, and we launched HonTe.

As CEO of HonTe, Chris generally focuses on business development and managing the firm's operations. His background in FX sales, however, makes him knowledgeable about macro markets. You will see him pitch into the discussion on the trading chat.

Qin Zhu (QZ), Chief Risk Officer

Qin and I met in 2000, when I came to Chase (soon to be JPMorgan Chase) to run basis swaps. She joined me as a junior trader to help run the franchise. She has always been a reliable partner, and I was pleased to have her join in the early days of HonTe. Her knowledge of trading markets and software code and systems helped us bridge the gaps between models, trading, and operations.

Her main job as Chief Risk Officer is to analyze portfolio exposures and establish position limits. She also contributes diligently to the analysis of future trades and participates in the execution thereof. In her area of expertise—asset swaps—her input was so valuable in March of 2020 that without it, I might have been forced to abandon that instrument.

Chris Kelley (CK), Head of Markets

He was the most recent hire at HonTe, pre-pandemic. In his previous jobs, he researched a broad range of financial instruments and efficiently executed a wide variety of transactions. When he first came on board in August 2019, I had no idea how beneficial it would be to have a colleague dedicated to following all the widely gyrating markets and maintaining the dialogue with Prime Brokers and other counterparties.

* * *

Two more employees didn't participate directly in the trading chat but were very much a part of the effort.

Joann Shie-Chen (JSC), Head of Operations

The pandemic disruption made her job extra challenging. She manages booking and reconciling all the portfolio transactions and cash flows through multiple accounts and custodies. She faced a considerable increase in volume right when the shutdown forced her to work away from her usual technological setup.

Tony Peng (TP), Quantitative Analyst

He runs quantitative models at HonTe both as an independent way to allocate capital and as a way to inform discretionary decision processes. He dealt with the pressure of the disruption in the historical levels of volatility and correlations caused by the pandemic.

Many more people supported HonTe internally and externally. Okay, it's starting to sound like the acknowledgments section, so I'll stop here and leave my thank-yous for the end.

CHAPTER 1

THE FATEFUL CONTRACT

I AM AN INVESTMENT MANAGER SPECIALIZING IN LONG-HORIZON, discretionary, global macro trading. What do all these adjectives mean? Essentially, I look for opportunities around the world in every category of financial markets. My trades often take years to pay off. And although I may use assistance from computer models, it is I who make all of the decisions, not an automated system.

One of my goals here is to provide an underappreciated perspective on the pandemic crisis. The books *Liar's Poker*, *The Bonfire of the Vanities*, and *The Big Short*, to mention a few, have introduced to the broad audience the importance, the complexity, and the very existence of the bond market. There is also some awareness of currency and commodity trading. Still, too many people I speak with, even those with "money in the market," equate the words "market" and "stock market." In fact, stocks are only the tip of the iceberg, carried by the currents of more powerful and fundamental financial flows.

Almost everyone was aware of that tip melting in the month of March, but few had any sense of the boiling water underneath the iceberg.

I hope to convey the terrifying scope of volatility and disruption at the core of the global financial system, which for me, overshadowed any stock fluctuations.

FOLLOWING THE PATTERN

To understand my pre-COVID positioning, we have to go far back in time. In my last book, I detailed the two "perfect" trades I was able to execute in my career. The second one was the combination of long US dollar and long US Treasury bonds, which dominated my performance in the 2010s. That theme delivered an incredible performance in 2014 and was the gift that kept on giving through the end of 2019.

Along the way, however, there was a huge test for our risk management, stamina, and fortitude. In early 2018, the market entered into what I would soon recognize as a late cycle. This is what I wrote in my Investor Letter for January 2018, which, in turn, quotes TNPT.

> A more interesting exercise is to try to identify where in the business cycle we may currently be and what this could mean for both US bonds and the US dollar. Until very recently, we didn't have a strong opinion on the timing of the end of this expansion cycle, or the next serious downturn in the stock market. Digesting recent price action in several asset classes, we now have a strong conviction that the end of the business cycle is quickly approaching.

This is what we wrote in "The Next Perfect Trade" as far back as 2014 about "the inflation fear regime".

> "...So, in fact, in 2000 my logic would have dictated that betting on higher stocks was an inferior trade, but the trade that dominated it, betting on higher rates, was inferior based on the secular trend. Betting on a strong economy was no longer a good idea! Here is an important corollary of my chicken and egg logic: When, due to inflation fears, rising rates become a concurrent necessity with respect to a strong stock market performance, the growth outlook becomes dim. This statement can be generalized: If the dominant way to express a particular economic view appears to be an inferior trade, the underlying view should be reexamined."

We believe that we have shifted into this regime again. More important than the small correction in the global stock markets is the fact that they are starting to RESPOND to interest rate moves. That is, they are going down when interest rates rise and even going down on stronger economic data, as it implies further rate hikes. This signifies that a protracted sell-off in the bonds is self-limiting, as the resulting stock weakness should ultimately bring an economic slowdown and eventually the prospect for much lower rates.

Bonds and the dollar collapsed as they had done ahead of two previous recessions. Our portfolio at the time relied on those two trades to balance each other (i.e., move in the opposite direction on most days, cushioning the P/L volatility). Both trades moving against us simultaneously caused a very severe drawdown.

Many at the time claimed that the bull market in bonds was over and that bond yields were heading much higher. I thought it more likely that the cyclical bear market in bonds was almost over and a huge rally was about to begin.

In a market note from April 2018, I cite thirteen historical indicators (often counterintuitive) of the late business cycle. This may appear to be a digression, but I am inserting here a few of them as an illustration of how I approach extreme price action to discern historic associations and provide insight into how I later approached the pandemic crisis.

1. Transition from recovery skepticism to inflation fear regime.

- April 11, CNBC: Fed minutes—"All" members see higher GDP and inflation, and more rate hikes

- April 6, Powell Chicago Speech: NY times noted, "Mr. Powell, in a speech before the Economic Club of Chicago, said the economy continued to experience tailwinds. Referring to the Fed's policy-making body, he added that "the labor market has been strong, and my colleagues and I on the Federal Open Market Committee expect it to remain strong."

- The WSJ also reported that later, in a question and answer period, Powell confirmed that "As long as the economy continues broadly on its current [growth] path, further gradual increases in the federal-funds rate will best promote these goals [solid growth with contained inflation]."

- April 6, Williams Santa Rosa Speech: "To sum up: the outlook is very positive. The economy is on course to be as strong as we have seen in many decades and inflation is moving closer to our target. The challenge for monetary policy is to keep it that way." Later, in the question and answer portion, he said "I am confident that we can carry on the process of gradually moving interest rates up over the next two years while seeing solid growth and historically low rates of Unemployment."

2. Perception that the secular bull market in bonds is over.

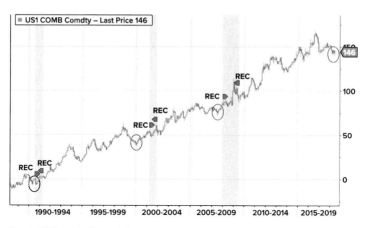

Copyright© Bloomberg Finance L.P.

Roll-Adjusted[2] US Classic Bond Future Price 1988–2019: The gray circles annotate late cycle bottoms. The red rectangles highlight economic recessions.

---

2 A "roll-adjusted" chart incorporates the economic gains/costs of rolling forward the futures position every time it approaches expiry. This type of chart most accurately represents the true profile of holding this position over its lifetime.

3. Simultaneous weakness in dollar and bonds. Bottoming in both.

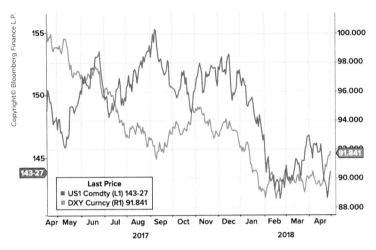

Dollar Index DXY (Blue) and US Bond Futures (Red) April 2017–April 2018: Simultaneous weakness in dollar and bonds during January 2018.

4. Oil rallying after a recent dip.

Copyright© Bloomberg Finance L.P.

Crude Oil, 1990–2019: Oil rally after a dip is another late business cycle indicator.

In addition to historical patterns, there was also a strong instance of economic gravity. US bond yields couldn't have been considered on their own. The rate differential between the United States and its developed market counterparties was too extreme. Readers unfamiliar with currency forwards may skip the technical aspects and relate to the simple idea that it is more attractive to keep cash in the currency which brings higher yield on deposits.

I wrote in the January 2018 Investor Letter:

> The important thing about being long USD against those three currencies is that due to the interest rate differentials we have a large margin of error working in our favor over long-horizons. There, the 10yr forwards on those currencies telling:

Pair	Spot	10-Year Forward	% Difference
USDCHF	0.9314	0.68	27%
USDJPY	110.17	79.9	27%
EURUSD	1.2463	1.545	24%

Sample of Foreign Exchange Spot and Forward Rates, January 2018: The USD was discounted ten years forward relative to other currencies.

While there is no inherent reason why the USD could not be at those levels in 10yrs time, we see the risks highly skewed in favor of the dollar with, for example, the euro at 1.5450 being at higher end on the long-term range and far from its average of 1.1882.

This favorable bond return would inevitably drive foreign money into the United States and eventually cause the dollar to go up, which would put deflationary pressure on the economy and force the rates to start going down.

On the flip side, I was not too concerned about the economy overheating and the inflationary pressures. The reason was the pattern I have referred to above. Low unemployment and accelerating wage growth do normally occur at the top of the economic cycle and counterintuitively, but consistently, portend lower interest rates.

That was my opinion—a very strong and well-articulated one, but just an opinion, nonetheless. There were smart market players who also had well-articulated opinions that the rates would go much higher.

My conviction was not shaken, but the portfolio was severely down on the year. I wanted to capitalize on the misprice of the forward rates expectation, but I needed to make sure that I survived long enough to do so.

TURNING TO OPTIONS

This is when I turned to an instrument I generally avoid: options. This is how I have explained my distaste for optionality in TNPT:

> Another type of trap investors have to contend with, is the seductive lure of optionality. Almost every beginning trader loves to buy options. What is there not to like? Limited downside, unlimited upside.

Expressing your directional views via buying options is a lot like trading with stops and pyramiding when the trades are going in your favor. When you keep stopping out and putting your position on again, you may get whipsawed any number of times. If you are buying an option, you are essentially paying for a certain amount of "whipsawing" upfront.

However, there are two inherent issues with options:

You are not guaranteed to make money even when the market moves in the desired direction.

Your option might expire before the move you are hoping for happens.

Why was I making an exception in 2018?

I was staring at June 2020 Eurodollar futures (EDM0), which would prove to be, to date, the most fateful futures contract in my career.

It is worth pausing to mention the Eurodollar market and interest rate bets in general. For readers who are mostly familiar only with stock market speculation, interest rate trading may at first glance appear rather tame.

On most days, futures forecasting interest rates move only a few basis points (a basis point, bp, being 0.01 percent). Let's look at a standard Eurodollar contract with $1mm (one million) notional, projecting a three-month deposit rate at some future date. A one-basis-point (1 bp) move would represent only a profit or loss of $25. Yes, $25 on $1,000,000 ($\frac{1}{4}$ of 1/100 of 1/100).

However, one must realize the tremendous volume available in the interest rate (also called fixed income) market. Some quarterly contracts may have an open interest of over one million, corresponding to one trillion notional. Over a hundred billion notional may trade on a daily basis in a specific contract.

And that is only one section of the fixed-income market. There are also several different bond futures, Fed Funds futures, interest rate swaps, and so on.

Now, suppose you want to own 40,000 Eurodollar futures—such a position is significant but attainable for a firm of our size and moderate for even bigger players. Each 1-bp (0.01%) move is worth $25 × 40,000 = $1,000,000. On a regular, slow day, you may lose or gain only $2–$3mm, but in times of high volatility, certain rates can move over 100 bps or 1% in a few weeks or even days. Keep in mind that even a 1% move is $100,000,000 P/L.

When you get to the sections incorporating the transcripts of the trade chatter, you may be surprised how little time we spend discussing the stock market. Understanding interest rates is the heart of my strategy, so it is fitting that analysis of short-term rates is where I start my book.

On February 15, 2018, the Federal Reserve target range for the overnight rate was 1.25% to 1.50%. The contract in question was trading at 97.14.

This is what I wrote in my Investor Letter for February 2018:

> While we tend to avoid using options under normal circumstances, this is one of the exceptional cases where such a

conversion is acceptable. In this specific case, the range of possibilities for the level of interest rates 2.5 years from now, projected by the June-2020 Eurodollar contract, is very wide. The current price of 97.14 implies a yield of 2.86%. And if, as some people believe, the Fed will continue relentless "normalization" to 4%-4.5% range the downside of being long the contract outright (betting on a lower yield) is very substantial. However, if the economy turns down within the next twelve months and the new easing cycle starts in 2019, the option allows time for the rates to move close to zero again by the time the contract expires! The long-term option provides better risk control to manage the possibility of larger, short-term swings in the meantime.[3]

This is when I started switching some of my risk into options.

Option pricing is based on the idea that there is a forward price defined by the market. In this case, the expiration was roughly two years in the future (remember, we are still in 2018), and the projected rate was 2.86%. Centered at that point, we construct a probability distribution curve. A blue line on the chart below shows a classic normal distribution implied by a random walk.

3 "That means that the futures market was predicting that in June 2020 the London Interbank Offer Rate (LIBOR) would be set at 2.86% (100 – 97.14 = 2.86). Note that higher contract price corresponds to lower rate. This is how bond pricing works in general: higher price means lower yield (i.e., the cheaper you buy a bond the higher interest you are earning on it)."

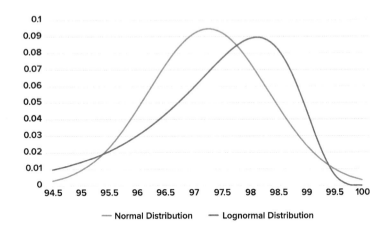

Probability Distribution Curves: Normal distribution (Blue) and lognormal distribution (Red).

In practice, market models use various modifications to that curve: using lognormal distribution, skew, kurtosis, and various adjustments implying "thicker tails"—that is, a higher probability of outlier events that can be derived from a random walk. The curve implied by those models ends up looking something like the red line.

My understanding of the situation, however, led me to visualize a very different picture, shown in the next chart.

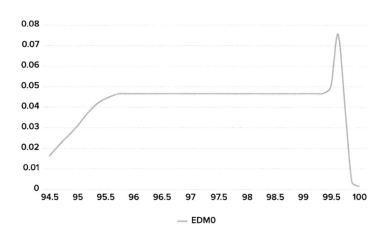

My Perception of June 2020 Eurodollar Future Probability Distribution in 2018: There was about a 4% range in which all outcomes were equally likely.

As you can see, there was about a 400-bp (4%) range in which all outcomes were roughly equally weighted. Without any bias for my personal market view, there was no preference for any of the policy paths, such as tightening further, holding rates steady, or easing. Notice, there was a probability bump when rates got close to zero and a sharp drop-off afterward; the Fed was unlikely to breach the zero lower bound, so extreme outcomes were concentrated in the same destination.

This made deep-out-of-money options mispriced. The 98.375 calls on EDM0 (the bet that would start paying out if LIBOR (London Interbank Offer Rate) set below 1.625% in June 2020) were trading around 6 bps (0.06%) premium. If LIBOR were to set around 0.25% as I anticipated (99.75 in Eurodollar contract terms), the options would expire worth 1.375% or about twenty-three-fold return on the initial premium of 0.06%.

My priority at that time was to ensure the survival of my ailing portfolio. But I also wasn't about to miss the chance to recapture the gain when the market rounded again in my favor. I wrote further in the February 2018 letter:

> This goes to say that the morale in the trenches is currently good. We have sustained losses and went on the defensive for a time, but now the barrage has abated. The enemies may be running out of ammo and we are preparing to counter-attack as confirmation of our more stable footing solidifies.

Converting some of the directional positions into options was a way to ensure I would stay in business if interest rates continued to go up, while retaining a large upside if I were proven right. The benefit was not entirely free: it left me vulnerable to the possibility that markets would turn in my favor but not move fast enough for my options to bear fruit. I could have been hit with a double whammy, the bane of so many traders: lose money on the downswing and then lose money on the way up due to option decay, despite having the right directional view.

My only remedy was to retain a smaller core position in the classic bond futures (I had named this *The One Trade*), in addition to options, and hope to navigate to positive returns, no matter what path to lower rates the market would take.

RECOVERING FROM LOSSES

In the spring and summer of 2018, I managed to recover some of the losses from earlier in the year. Bonds were still trading weakly and eventually made a cyclical low on October 9, 2018, but the dollar recovered, buoyed by the favorable interest rate differential and strong performance of the US stock market.

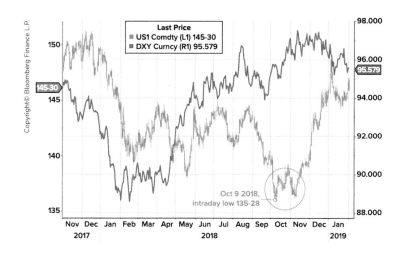

US Bond Future (Blue) and Dollar Index DXY (Red) 2018: The dollar recovered from its February bottom, while bonds made a new low in December 2018.

In the last quarter of 2018, US equities became shaky and eventually cratered, making a low on Christmas Eve. The Fed managed to get in one last hike but was then forced to acknowledge that the hiking cycle was over.

My Eurodollar option positions hadn't gotten much traction; their strikes were still nowhere close to being in the money, and the time decay was working against me. But the plain-vanilla bond position was running in my favor, and I was able to increase risk as my portfolio recovered. By the end of 2018, I was very close to flat on the year and was able to let out a big sigh of relief.

This is not a story of my struggles in 2017 and 2018, but it is worth noting that those two difficult years were a test of fortitude for me, my team, and our investors.

Being in a deep drawdown and having to cut positions, despite my conviction, was profoundly stressful (it always is). My more than two decades of experience in financial markets had taught me to see the light at the end of the tunnel. I knew that I was likely to start making money again eventually, either on the trades I had on at the time or on some other ones. All I had to do was to stay focused and disciplined.

Interestingly, staying disciplined and trading correctly was not the most difficult part of the equation. I had been in drawdowns before and I knew what to do. In TNPT, I focused on risk management procedures that should be put in place and rigorously followed during the "good times," so when the difficult times arrived, I would be one step ahead of the game. My takeaway was that even if I had to take losses reducing positions at painful levels, as the market turned there was always a chance to rebuild my portfolio for success. I wrote:

> Huge profits can be achieved by having unencumbered capital and clarity of mind during the times of challenge.

In 2018, the greater challenge was not to stay disciplined but to keep a positive attitude and convey confidence to investors. I knew I was a favorite to win the war, but the outlook was fairly grim from the trenches. And two years in the trenches is a long time, no matter your investment horizon.

The protracted strife of 2017–2018 ended up laying the foundation for our outsized returns of 2019 and 2020.

CHAPTER 2

THE PIVOT

IN EARLY 2019, THE FEDERAL RESERVE PIVOTED, ACCORDING TO traders and pundits. In December 2018, the Fed had been criticized for not paying attention to the stock market and hiking interest rates too much. Only a few months later, the Fed was conversely criticized for paying *too much* attention to the stock market and halting the tightening.

But those traders and pundits were talking nonsense. The Fed has always had a fairly consistent response system. Whether it is correct is difficult to judge because we don't all agree on what their objectives are. If you don't know the goal, how do you measure performance?

As traders, we focus on what central banks will do and how it will affect the markets, not on what they *should* do. Grant Williams likes to say, "The Fed always tightens till they break something." Indeed, for as long as the employment statistics ran hot, regardless of historical implications, the tightening continued. When markets got wobbly, the Fed would pause. When a crisis hit, they would ease to add liquidity. It's that simple. Nothing they said or did in 2018 or 2019 indicated otherwise.

The Fed's past patterns showed there was no "pivot." All the market moves simply reflected the Fed proceeding exactly as it had in the past.

Here is my tweet from February 21, 2019, which I kept pinned to my profile for a few months.

Alex Gurevich ✔ @agurevich23 · Feb 21, 2019
Every cycle end the Fed policy progresses in the same fashion:
1. We are overheating: hike!
2. Stocks aren't the economy, stay the course.
3. Stocks Are the economy. We're watching the market closely.
4. Numbers are mixed: pause and resume.
5. Just one cut.
6. Low for longer.

 💬 26   ↻ 156   ♡ 563

By then, markets had begun recovering from their December 2018 swoon. There were clearly no more hikes forthcoming, but there was no expectation of easing either. The consensus was that the Federal Reserve would make no changes in the foreseeable future. Although the level of Eurodollar futures was much higher than it had been a few months earlier, the implied volatility and, correspondingly, the price of my 98.375 calls was falling. Eventually, the calls would trade at 3 ¼ ticks (0.0325%) on March 5, 2019, not far from the lows of the fall of 2018.

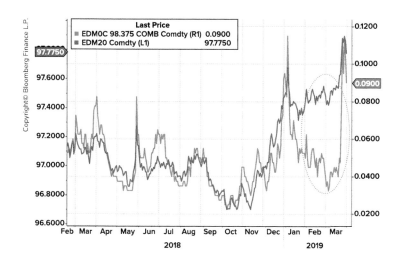

While June 2020 Eurodollar Future (Red) Stabilized in February–March 2019, a 98.375 Call Option on the Future (Blue) Declined Due to Lower Implied Volatility and Time Decay.

THE TURN OF THE CYCLE

The first week of 2019, I was vacationing in Hawaii. But portfolio managers never take an actual break from work. Wherever I go in the world, I stay connected and continue to respond to market moves. The best I can do is disconnect for a bit, with instructions on how to reach me in the event of an emergency.

I received a call from John Burbank of Passport Capital, which I took in my hotel room, while the children were at the pool. We talked about deep out-of-the-money Eurodollar options.

We both honed in on the same observation: the average time interval from the last hike in a tightening cycle to the start of the easing cycle is surprisingly short. In the moment, we tend to feel there is merely a pause in the rate hikes. Consequently, the market is slow to price the impending rate cut.

Here are some examples:

Date of Last Hike	Basis Point Increase	Rate Level	Date of the First Ease to Follow	Basis Point Decrease	Rate Level	Timing Difference (Month)
12/20/2018	25	2.25-2.5	8/1/2019	25	2-2.25	7
6/29/2006	25	5.25	9/18/2007	50	4.75	15
5/16/2000	50	6.5	1/3/2001	50	6	8
3/25/1997	25	5.5	9/29/1998	25	5.25	18
2/1/1995	50	6	7/6/1995	25	5.75	5
2/24/1989	37.5	9.75	6/5/1989	12.5	9.625	3
9/4/1987	50	7.25	10/19/1987	37.5	6.875	2
8/21/1984	75	11.75	10/2/1984	175	10	1

Time Table of First Fed Ease Following the End of a Tightening Cycle: The average time interval from the last hike to the start of the easing cycle is surprisingly short.

With this in mind, I realized the options I was holding were insanely cheap. In the subsequent weeks, I increased my exposure and held both 98.25 and 98.375 calls, as well as longer-dated rate floors.[4]

With the releases of weaker inflation data in the spring of 2019, there was a widening perception that the cycle was turning. The rally in interest rates gained momentum and carried us through the easing mini-cycle of July 2019 to October 2019, which surprised everyone except those who had bothered to study the historical data and charts.

---

4 An interest rate floor is a derivative contract in which the buyer receives payments at the end of each period in which the interest rate is below the agreed strike price. Or, in other terms, just another manner to speculate on interest rates ending below a certain level in some future period in time. The floors were simply an over-the-counter instrument.

The Hawaii discussion of Eurodollar calls was made public several months later when Real Vision TV aired my interview with John Burbank (I was acting as interviewer).[5] We reviewed the thought processes that led us to make the option trades, which were already very profitable by that time.

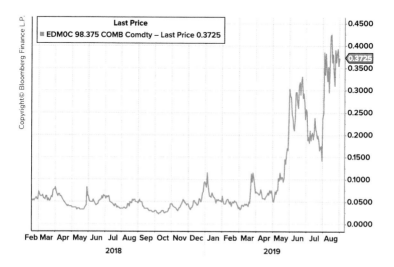

98.375 Strike Call Option on June 2020 Eurodollar Future.

We went over the logic of extreme risk-reward, and John emphasized that the trend was only beginning and the option premium could still yield multifold returns. I agreed, choosing to stick with my original investment plan. The best way I can express it is, if I bought an option because of where I thought the underlying price would be at expiration, then I hold it to the expiration.

But deep in the core of my trading soul, I had a fear that the Fed would do a few cuts, as they had in 1998, and then stop. Or even

---

5 https://www.youtube.com/watch?v=VdqiImHRmtY

resume tightening later, as they had in 1999, when they tried to brand the cuts as "a mid-cycle adjustment." Those were historically less common than full cycles, and 2019 didn't feel like 1998, but still...

There was some stock volatility in August 2019, and I scored another big gain on my interest rates position. Meanwhile, my long gold and short Australian dollar positions were gaining traction as well. Given that I was already sitting on what could be the best year of my recent trading program and that market pricing appeared to be extended in my favor, it was natural to decrease risk somewhat.

MY NIGHTMARE COMES TRUE

I headed into September with about 50 percent of my maximum risk. I had, however, kept most of my options exposure to capitalize on further rate cuts.

And then my nightmare scenario occurred, and the deep dread I experience whenever I am long options started to materialize. At the press conference following the October 2019 rate cut, Federal Reserve Chair Powell made it very clear he considered the easing mini-cycle completed:

> "We see the current stance of monetary policy as likely to remain appropriate as long as incoming information about the state of the economy remains broadly consistent with our outlook."

The June 2020 contract had rallied enormously by then and was very likely to stay above my strikes.

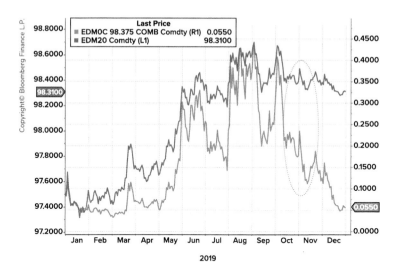

*June 2020 Eurodollar Future (Red) and 98.375 Call (Blue) in 2019: June con-
verged toward the strike 98.375. The option lost value rapidly.*

But with further action taken off the table, volatility curled
up under the table and died. How I cursed myself for not
adjusting my portfolio when I had foreseen this exact
scenario!

It was not about economic or policy forecasts; it was about the
fact that I had envisioned the exact price action—the contract
freezing just after going through my strikes. I lectured myself
mercilessly about putting my money where my mouth was
and, most importantly, on the fact that I had violated my own
warning about trading options in TNPT. What I dreaded most
had happened: I was right about the market direction, but I
was not going to make money on my options. Had I taken a
plain-vanilla directional position instead, my gains would
have been substantial.

I knew back then that my logic in using options was ex ante correct, but I was frustrated that I had missed the chance to exit my vega[6] exposure and simplify my portfolio.

Mind you, because of my prior risk reductions, my drawdown in the last four months of 2019 was very moderate and allowed me to still book an excellent year. My self-critique was about strategy and not at all about risk management.

Having suffered the damage, there was no point in selling my remaining options. They were already too cheap, and on top of this, the bid offer of getting rid of the remaining exposure to implied volatility was prohibitive.

So, after acknowledging my shortcomings and swearing up and down to never touch options again in my life, what was I to do? The answer was simple: buy more options.

I had a new approach. The market had dismissed any chance for further eases, but what if we had a confluence of two not-too-far-fetched outcomes? The first was weaker economic data, and the second was a sell-off in risk assets. In my interview with Macro-voices on October 30, 2019 (fresh after the Federal Reserve policy meeting), I mentioned that I still believed there was a 50 percent chance of further easing in the month of December.

> My point is, on the front end, you have a very clear risk/reward profile. And even if you go on a shorter horizon, if you go to just the most immediate bet on the December Fed funds meeting,

---

6   Vega measures the sensitivity of the value of the option relative to a given shift in implied volatility of the asset that underlies the option in question.

the current probability on this meeting is fairly low. It's like maybe 10% of a cut in December. While there is still enough time for them to — if we see some weak numbers or maybe some weakness in the asset markets, I think — honestly, I think the probability for the cut in December is 50/50...

It doesn't have to be the same as last year. But it could be the same as last year on the outlier. Or it could be just a more minor wave. And if this wave of negative risk senti-ment happens, then, in combination with soft economic number that we are seeing, it would be very easy to price in another cut. And, in my opinion, it's about as likely as not to happen.

The probability estimate was likely incorrect. We will touch on that a little later.

I highlighted, however, a potential misprice on a shorter-term option. On November 7, 2019, I bought a 98.50 call on the March 2020 contract (EDH0). I covered the delta on this call, making it a pure volatility bet. It took me only a few weeks to curse myself for doing this new trade as well.

THE SECOND FATEFUL CONTRACT

Meanwhile, another opportunity presented itself. This time it was a "free lunch": a trade with clear big upside and little to no downside. I wrote about those in Chapter 14 of TNPT. Once in a while, there comes an opportunity to profit hugely in the event that something widely regarded as unlikely happens, without paying any price for that option.

In this case, the event would be policy easing in early 2020. The instrument capturing this event was March 2020 Federal Funds futures (FFH0),[7] which would become the second most fateful contract of my career.

There is one fundamental asymmetry in Federal Reserve policy: they occasionally do surprise eases but never surprise hikes. The last time they tightened unexpectedly was in 1994, and the bond market crash that followed taught them not to repeat this mistake. Tightening policy is never urgent enough to risk disappointing the markets.

In recent years, I have taken multiple opportunities to buy Fed Funds futures when they priced a tiny chance of tightening, or to "fade" the tightening, in market lingo. Paradoxically, the less money that could be made, the more attractive the trade looked to me, as the probability of surprise fell disproportionately.

Let's consider a hypothetical simplified example in which the current rate is 2% and the Fed is contemplating raising it to 2.25%. If right before the meeting the futures imply 2.1%, that means a 40 percent chance of tightening is priced in. If you buy the futures and they do nothing, you make 10 bps; if they hike, you lose 15 bps. When the odds are 60/40, close to 50/50, there is no reason to expect the market to be wrong ex ante and there is no value in making the bet. However, if the futures were trading at an implied rate of 2.025%, the odds would be 90/10; you make only 2.5 bps if they keep rates unchanged and stand to lose 22.5 if there is a surprise hike. The reality of the latter situation is that the probability of them rocking the boat with nothing to gain is

---

7   Price of a Fed Funds future is equal to 100 minus expected average Fed effective rate for the contract month. The contract size is $5,000,000. The value of each price point is $4,167, representing one month interest of 1 percentage point.

less than 0.1 percent. The market risk aversion puts a meaningful premium on the unlikely outcome, where it should be almost none.

So when the market prices something like a 5 percent to 10 percent chance of tightening shortly before the meeting, the real chances are actually zero, and one can buy the corresponding futures contract with impunity.

I generally prefer trades with positive risk symmetry. Regardless of the odds, I try to choose trades that have at least as much upside as downside. For example, I only enter a carry trade if I believe there is potential for mark-to-market appreciation. This prevents me from becoming a wing seller. *Wings* in this case signify low probability outlier events and *wing selling* means collecting premium when those outcomes are avoided, while risking massive losses in the worst-case scenarios.

Think of selling insurance or lottery tickets. Such strategy is very tempting to pursue, as under normal circumstances it brings in a steady stream of revenues. Casinos, insurance companies, and lottery issuers can afford individual transactions with large downside because of their huge volume, as long as the mathematical expectation is skewed to their advantage. For a discretionary investor with only a handful of positions in their portfolio, such diversification is unattainable and a single "lottery ticket" payout can bring down their entire portfolio.

Did the Fed Funds trade violate the discipline of risk symmetry? To answer this question, one has to compare the probability of emergency easing with that of emergency tightening. *Black swans* (dire events beyond any normal expectations), such as 9/11, had in the past caused the Fed to ease unexpectedly. How often did something like 9/11 happen, you might ask?

Well, let's say between the '98 crisis, 9/11, and the global financial crisis (GFC), there were several complete surprises. Looking at my twenty-three-year career, I estimated the chance of a black swan at about 1 percent to 2 percent in any given month. With a resulting 100-bp move, it gave me at least one extra basis point (0.01%) value for purchasing a random Fed Funds future contract.

Meanwhile, even when tightening discussions are still on the table, a surprise rate hike is much less likely, since there is no upside and no urgency for the Fed to upset the markets without warning. The risk symmetry was clearly favorable.

When I initiated the trade on December 6, 2019, the March 2020 expiry contract (FFH0) was trading at 98.475 (1.525% yield), versus 1.50%–1.75% target range. It was not pricing any further easing, which in my opinion gave me a free option.

However, as can be seen from the log below, as I kept accumulating the trade through January 17, the contract did actually move against me, eventually trading as low as 98.415 (1.585% yield). As it turned out, the option was not entirely free—one had to accept some market noise related to the contract's technicalities. The Fed signaled a small increase in the interest on excess reserves, otherwise known as the IOER. The target range did not change, but because of this operational adjustment, the March funding rate was expected to average a few basis points higher.

This underscores the difficulty of avoiding market risk entirely. In such situations, I gain advantage by "accepting the noise." In other words, I am okay with a trade that combines a very good return profile with some randomness. Lose a little, or win a little, *or* win a lot.

Hence, as the adjustment progressed, I added to the position, continuously staying on the bid.

Tkt #	Trd Dt	Ticker	B/S	Size	Price	Stl Date	Trtime
14292	12/6/2019	FFH0	B	500	98.475	12/6/2019	4:53:39 PM
14293	12/6/2019	FFH0	B	200	98.475	12/6/2019	4:53:39 PM
14294	12/6/2019	FFH0	B	200	98.475	12/6/2019	4:53:40 PM
14512	12/11/2019	FFH0	B	1000	98.465	12/11/2019	1:21:18 PM
14513	12/11/2019	FFH0	B	400	98.465	12/11/2019	1:21:18 PM
14516	12/11/2019	FFH0	B	400	98.465	12/11/2019	1:21:19 PM
14635	12/12/2019	FFH0	B	1000	98.46	12/12/2019	9:36:52 AM
14636	12/12/2019	FFH0	B	400	98.46	12/12/2019	9:36:52 AM
14677	12/12/2019	FFH0	B	400	98.46	12/12/2019	1:00:40 PM
14711	12/12/2019	FFH0	B	1000	98.455	12/12/2019	2:31:28 PM
14712	12/12/2019	FFH0	B	400	98.455	12/12/2019	2:31:28 PM
14715	12/12/2019	FFH0	B	400	98.455	12/12/2019	2:31:29 PM
15284	12/18/2019	FFH0	B	6	98.44	12/18/2019	5:00:01 PM
15287	12/18/2019	FFH0	B	14	98.44	12/18/2019	5:00:02 PM
15288	12/18/2019	FFH0	B	6	98.44	12/18/2019	5:00:03 PM
15325	12/19/2019	FFH0	B	637	98.44	12/19/2019	4:56:51 PM
15326	12/19/2019	FFH0	B	254	98.44	12/19/2019	4:56:51 PM
15329	12/19/2019	FFH0	B	250	98.44	12/19/2019	4:57:04 PM
15332	12/20/2019	FFH0	B	349	98.44	12/20/2019	2:53:06 PM
15333	12/20/2019	FFH0	B	140	98.44	12/20/2019	2:53:06 PM
15336	12/20/2019	FFH0	B	144	98.44	12/20/2019	2:53:07 PM
15391	12/24/2019	FFH0	B	11	98.43	12/24/2019	1:15:01 PM
15392	12/24/2019	FFH0	B	4	98.43	12/24/2019	1:15:01 PM
15393	12/24/2019	FFH0	B	4	98.43	12/24/2019	1:15:01 PM
15651	1/3/2020	FFH0	B	1000	98.43	1/3/2020	2:15:50 PM
15652	1/3/2020	FFH0	B	400	98.43	1/3/2020	2:15:50 PM
15653	1/3/2020	FFH0	B	400	98.43	1/3/2020	2:15:50 PM
15660	1/3/2020	FFH0	B	1000	98.43	1/3/2020	2:29:33 PM
15661	1/3/2020	FFH0	B	400	98.43	1/3/2020	2:29:33 PM
15662	1/3/2020	FFH0	B	400	98.43	1/3/2020	2:29:33 PM
15781	1/13/2020	FFH0	B	500	98.425	1/13/2020	9:04:28 AM
15782	1/13/2020	FFH0	B	200	98.425	1/13/2020	9:04:28 AM
15783	1/13/2020	FFH0	B	200	98.425	1/13/2020	9:04:28 AM
15879	1/14/2020	FFH0	B	500	98.42	1/14/2020	2:29:55 PM
15880	1/14/2020	FFH0	B	200	98.42	1/14/2020	2:29:56 PM
15881	1/14/2020	FFH0	B	200	98.42	1/14/2020	2:29:56 PM
15940	1/15/2020	FFH0	B	3	98.415	1/15/2020	5:00:01 PM
15943	1/15/2020	FFH0	B	5	98.415	1/15/2020	5:00:02 PM
15944	1/15/2020	FFH0	B	2	98.415	1/15/2020	5:00:03 PM
15962	1/16/2020	FFH0	B	5	98.415	1/16/2020	5:00:02 PM
15965	1/16/2020	FFH0	B	12	98.415	1/16/2020	5:00:03 PM
15966	1/16/2020	FFH0	B	5	98.415	1/16/2020	5:00:03 PM
15974	1/17/2020	FFH0	B	3	98.415	1/17/2020	5:00:02 PM
15977	1/17/2020	FFH0	B	4	98.415	1/17/2020	5:00:03 PM
15978	1/17/2020	FFH0	B	2	98.415	1/17/2020	5:00:03 PM

March 2020 Fed Funds Future (FFH0) Transaction History December 2019–January 2020.

The table was set. The portfolio was ready for a crisis I couldn't possibly anticipate.

CHAPTER 3

FIRST JITTERS

It is not easy to reconstruct step by step how we went from business as usual to apocalyptic dread. The best way I can trace the change is by recounting several trips I took in early 2020.

On January 27 and 28, I was at an investment convention in Florida. I vividly remember attending a panel at which several economists and strategists talked of the growth projections for 2020. They were fairly cautious, but it struck me that none of them was factoring the budding epidemic in Wuhan into their projections.

By the end of January, the market still had not priced in any chance of immediate crisis.

The name of my March options was *dirt*. They traded at 2¼ bps (0.0225%), cheaper than I bought them for in November 2019.

Now, I want to be clear: at that moment, I was not really concerned about the situation evolving into a global pandemic. Back then, I held the erroneous view that the virility of the infection declined rapidly with every transmission. That seemed to be the case with the SARS epidemic of 2003, which explained why all the initial cases and deaths were concentrated in Wuhan. A different explanation—that the virus had a long incubation period—eluded me.

My thoughts at that time were colored by my being a China skeptic. I expected the shutdown of travel and trade to accelerate an economic crisis in mainland China and Hong Kong. The private debt unwind and catastrophic currency devaluation in the region would send a deflationary shock wave around the world, pushing the interest rates lower—that is, in my favor.

On a personal level, the impact was still very low. The airports looked normal except for a few people wearing masks.

PROFITING FROM PAIN

I have to confess, part of me planned for what would happen if the epidemic worsened. Of course I did not want anyone to get sick or die, but I knew I could profit from a recession. There was a contradiction in rooting for my portfolio to succeed while knowing that real people experience real pain in an economic downturn.

This is captured in the scene in *The Big Short* in which two young traders high-five after securing an effective bet on a mortgage meltdown. Another character, a reclusive ex-banker, played by Brad Pitt, admonishes them with statistics of how many people die with every extra percentage point of unemployment.

I believe that most traders are not psychopaths. If you gave them a red button and told them, "If you push this button, a stranger dies in a distant country, but you will make a billion dollars," few would push the button. I am confident that I wouldn't; I know that much about myself.

Some readers may cynically point out how all over the world some people pursue business practices and profits that harm or even potentially kill not one but thousands or even millions of people.

To distinguish such practices, let's reimagine our red button test. If you *don't* push the button (i.e., do nothing), a stranger dies in a distant land. If you push it, you can save that person, but your portfolio will suffer a catastrophic loss. In this scenario, many of us would find a way to talk ourselves into inaction. I am honestly not sure what I would do.

The second scenario reflects the complexity of a trader's perception of reality.

There are different kinds of traders. For some, making money is a vehicle to support their lifestyle and their families. For others, myself included, the market is a game.

Don't misunderstand that. I take games very seriously. I have put in many thousands of hours studying various games, including Go, chess, and poker. I don't just play—I am not a civilian. Where games are concerned, I read books, I study strategies, I get professional coaching, I think of valuation functions as I go to sleep.

My true life is conducted in what I call the strategic space. My identity is very closely wrapped into my portfolio performance, and my greatest professional fear is letting my investors down.

I have been asked on occasion, would I do what I do if I weren't paid for it? The answer is, "Absolutely yes, in some form or another." What do you think I do in my spare time? I play strategic resource management games, which are essentially the same as my day job.

So, yes, there is a large part of me that wants to minimize death and suffering in the world, but there is another part of me that views the entire world as an abstract reality, as a global economic causality flux, which I strive to transform into portfolio dominance.

THE LAST PARTY

January 2020 was one of my best months ever, thanks to the surge in the US fixed-income market.

I took profits here and there, but the great thing about being long gamma is that your positions keep growing when the market moves in your favor. In fact, in early 2020, I thought of a joke, which I considered too obnoxious to post on Twitter: "Don't you hate it when you are super long gamma and the market is moving in your favor so rapidly that you can't take profits fast enough to stay under risk limits?"

In February, we had a prospective investor visit in our office. Remember those? In-person due diligence visits? They complimented us on having performed well in January, when the risk market was choppy, but not giving ground in early February when the risk rally resumed. Still no great concerns.

The epidemic was beginning to spread in Europe, but world healthcare experts were still debating whether to call it a pandemic. US interest rates resumed their decline, but the stock market reached a new high on February 19, 2020.

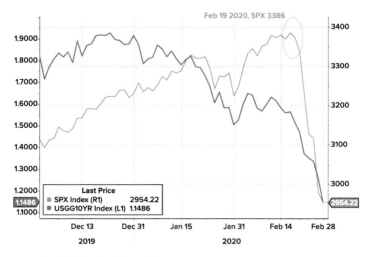

Copyright© Bloomberg Finance L.P.

S&P 500 (Blue) and US Ten-Year Note Yield (Red), December 2019–February 2020: In February 2020, ten-year yield declined, while the stock market made a new high.

Our winter 2020 Hawaii trip was during ski week: February 15–23. There was little hesitation about flying, but cautionary measures were being introduced. We did what we could with hand sanitizers on the flight. No masks, though.

Future trips involving older family members were still on the docket for March and April. The cancellations would start soon.

The stock market at last caught the virus at the end of February. The drop you see in the chart above would prove to be just the few first sniffles.

I attended a friend's birthday party on Leap Day, Saturday, February 29. It was a big date, and a few friends of ours flew in. I remember talking to a visiting friend who is also an investor. I bet him that the closure of all international travel was imminent. So I must have been taking the epidemic seriously. But was I really? Not on a personal level. At least not yet.

I went to the event, which turned out to be excellent. We were dancing; everyone was hugging and kissing hello and goodbye. All of this was done with a keen awareness of the impending global disaster but still with the sense that it was not happening to us. To this day, we refer to this event as *The Last Party*.

CHAPTER 4

WEEK 1: A VICTORY PARADE

THE MARKET MOOD SHIFTED DRAMATICALLY OVER THE WEEK-END of *The Last Party*. China printed a very weak PMI[8] report (which shouldn't have surprised anyone, given the shutdown), and NYC had its first COVID case. There was alarming news from Italy.

The timelines for price action and shifts in sentiment accelerated as if warped by the gravity of a black hole. Our normally consistent portfolio and low turnover strategy started to operate in the time-space metric of March 2020.

This is where I open up our Slack chat to your scrutiny.[9]

---

8 PMI (Purchasing Managers' Index) report consists of two components: Manufacturing PMI and Services PMI. They are diffusion indices that track sentiment among purchasing managers at manufacturing, construction, and/or services firms. An overall sentiment index is generally calculated from the results of queries on production, order, inventories, employment, prices, etc.

9 All Slack screenshots are in PST time zone.

We will start on March 1, Sunday afternoon in California. The action started as the Asian markets opened. With the gap up in all interest rate futures, our positions increased due to options gamma, and we were taking profits. This was a part of my "struggle" to keep within the risk limits.

I did not have a strong view on COVID, and if anything, I was too optimistic. As you look through our trading transcript, you may note how little discussion of pandemic parameters entered our process.

I had confidence in my core bet on falling interest rates, because the historical pattern had taught me that the market invariably underpriced the scope of the central bank's response. This was all I needed to know, and so, protected by the *Shield against Uncertainty*, I stuck to my strategic plan.

MARCH 1: SUNDAY AFTERNOON

March 1st, 2020 ⌄

2:50 PM QZ There was only 1 lot done on FFH0 sale on Friday.
Just wondering if you still have the interest to sell

2:55 PM Alex Gurevich Yes I am trying to figure if it's trading now.

2:56 PM QZ In 5 minutes

2:57 PM Alex Gurevich I put in .665

2:57 PM QZ Seeing pre open indication 98.665

2:57 PM Alex Gurevich To see what happens

2:57 PM QZ Ok

3:04 PM CK 71.5/73 super small market looks like on mobile

07/7.5 EDM0 small market

3:09 PM QZ 3600 total sold

3:27 PM CK Nice. China all time low data print and Jerome ad hoc
Friday comments feels pretty close to panic.

On the actual execution side, I proved to be a bit impatient. I put in an order where we thought the Fed Funds futures would open. The 98.665 (1.335%) yield implied 0.25% of easing for the entire month of March, which implied either an intermeeting easing or a more than 0.50% cut at the scheduled meeting on March 18. But the market immediately surged further, swallowing my initial orders. We continued to sell.

When rapid changes in the market occur, macro traders look for nascent dislocation. A simple approach: discover which assets are trading as if everything were going great and which are priced for Armageddon. Sell the former, and buy the latter.

I have learned to pay attention to differences in the interest rates of developed market countries. As I mentioned, it is unsustainable for those differences to be extreme for too long, so traders often have the chance to play mean reversion.

Over the tightening cycle of 2016 to 2018, the US rates rose significantly, and Treasury bonds became among the highest yielding sovereign securities in the developed world. When the "pivot," described in Chapter 2, occurred, the tide reversed to an extent.

By the end of 2019, the interest spread between the US and Canadian ten-year notes had narrowed dramatically compared to the high of 2018 (i.e., the US rate was only about 0.2% higher versus 0.8% a year prior).

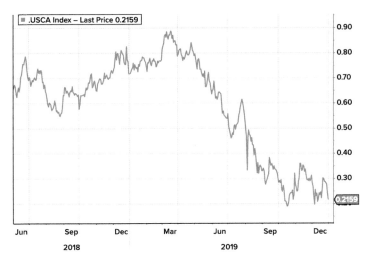

US Ten-Year Minus Canadian Ten-Year Bond Yield, July 2018–December 2019: The yield spread contracted.

When the COVID crisis started to brew, US treasuries once again charged ahead. And it was beginning to look like Canada was temporarily left behind, with the rate relationship actually inverting (UST rates became lower). This was the case when Canadian securities were pricing a lesser case of the pandemic crisis than US ones.

I went on a prowl to increase my Canadian bond futures positions, but they don't trade in the Asian time zone. Here is the chat:

Friday comm   March 1st, 2020 ∨   ie to panic.

3:29 PM Alex Gurevich I am considering. Buying Canada bonds on the back of selling more US. No way their rates stay at 1.5% as US goes to 0?

Is Canada trading yet? Shout we receive on swaps to reduce our margins?

I don't think MAv is updating is our FFH0 position

3:35 PM QZ Can not trade CAD rates electronically

let me see if there is any coverage people around

3:36 PM **CK** CNM0 is 11:30 PST if I recall

3:36 PM Alex Gurevich So no swaps overnight? We could just do
CNA for now

Ok we'll wait.

3:36 PM QZ allocation issue with one FFH0 trade, will fix

3:37 PM **CK** It's been trading tightly to Us last I checked so I doubt
there is a ton of juice once the market opens. But yes if
it widens relative to Us at any point we should
absolutely receive cuz no way their rates can stay up if
Us and oil are slowing down.

3:39 PM QZ CAD swap market does not look active right now

image.png ▼

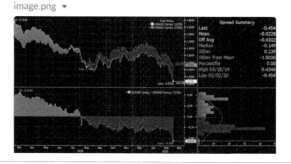

3:41 PM Alex Gurevich Cad rates seems like a buy

3:42 PM QZ Receiving 10yr?

3:43 PM Alex Gurevich Or buying CNM0

3:44 PM QZ Waiting for reply on CAD swap coverage overnight

3:45 PM **Christopher Lutton** Thinking along those NAFTA lines,
MX TIle at 7.30% stands out

3:46 PM QZ Likely have to trade CNM0. Initial reply is to wait till
NY open. Still checking

Throughout the evening, we kept trying to take advantage of the big move, align positions, and take profits.

3:44 PM QZ Waiting f(March 1st, 2020 ∨) coverage overnight

3:45 PM **Christopher Lutton** Thinking along those NAFTA lines, MX TIle at 7.30% stands out

3:46 PM QZ Likely have to trade CNM0. Initial reply is to wait till NY open. Still checking

4:00 PM QZ FFH0 position should be good now

4:28 PM Alex Gurevich Is my last order filled?

Also Aussie is down now again? I want to normalize distribution by using oasis as benchmark and taking down the rest.

4:33 PM **CK** Checking EMSX sec

Aud back at 65, low all day and Friday was basically 6460

4:44 PM QZ not filled

4:44 PM **CK** 341/1200 FFH0 done

859x working still

5:04 PM QZ FFH0 is filled

All day sold 3600 FFH0, 120 EDH0

1200 EDH0, sorry

5:10 PM Alex Gurevich Was I selling EDH0?

5:11 PM QZ Yes I see one trade EDH0 1200 sold at 98.7475

5:11 PM Alex Gurevich Ok

5:13 PM QZ Remaining FFH0 position: ▇/1618, ▇▇/1457, ▇/4440

▇ has slightly more due to new allocation

The exchange in the last two screenshots may appear a little embarrassing. It seems that in the commotion, I forgot that along with selling March Fed Funds (FFH0), I'd done a trade taking profits on EDH0 (March Eurodollars), where my position was increasing due to the optionality. In fact, such reconciliations and double-checks are fairly normal during high-volume transaction flows.

Generally, I have a very good recall of my recent trades, but as I mentioned earlier, my memory has limits. That's why we have operational checks and balances, which go beyond the Slack chat.

Next, we discussed the US thirty-year swap rates and swap spreads, the positions that would become central to our narrative a few days later. Our exchange demonstrates how awkward it was to transact those products in Asian time. Still, we tried to do what we could whenever we saw an opportunity. "Money never sleeps."

█ has slight' March 1st, 2020 ⌄ allocation

5:28 PM **Christopher Lutton** I just got this from Alex

Please confirm with him if this is right...
Alex Gurevich [5:26 PM]
Can we pay 30 yrs swap / sell ERIS futures here. I would do 30K outright and 30K on asset swap here. Could be against WN if it's still cheap - repo already adjusted.

5:29 PM QZ ERIS future is not active right now unfortunately

5:31 PM **Christopher Lutton** He's just looking for █ portion if that's all he can do

5:31 PM QZ You want to pay 14k 30yr swap for █?

5:32 PM Alex Gurevich Yes 7K outright 7K vs WN or cash

5:33 PM QZ Market very wide on electroninc screen, asking desk right now

5:33 PM Alex Gurevich Do the asset swap part first - outright backed up

Asset swap maybe not where I think. But anything under -38 is good.

5:35 PM QZ I am checking iwth desk right now

That's about 3m 30yr spread

The best shot is headline 30y spread

5:38 PM Alex Gurevich Ok actually do $5mm if the price is good.

Yes headline spread is good.

5:40 PM QZ complication here is that headline has to go on SEF

But SEF is too wide to trade

asking the desk if they can quote match maturity

5:51 PM **Christopher Lutton** Nice job Qin!

"pleasantly persistent" pays off

5:52 PM **CK** 30y $5mm is done Alex

-38.625

any level in 30y o/r you want us to work? bouncing all over. 1.25 > 1.23 post China PMI just now...currently 1.24....low 1.20, low offer probably 1.21 ish including the wider market in actuality today

5:54 PM Alex Gurevich Good!

Probably around 1.22 is good. Can do $5mm there.

5:57 PM QZ You want to leave ▮▮▮ an order there?

We just traded the spread with ▮▮▮ in Australia

5:58 PM Alex Gurevich Only if it's close - not too much gap risk.

5:58 PM QZ right mid 1.235

5:58 PM **CK** anywhere < 1.25 I'll think we should work it...its an 'at best' kind of night wherever possible

6:01 PM QZ we are about 2 bp away, we can work it now until it moves away, we are watching the screen. let us know

6:03 PM Alex Gurevich Ok let's give them an order at 1.23

6:03 PM CK k

6:03 PM QZ ok

7:14 PM QZ Will do repo tomorrow morning.

if you want to use cash, please let me know

No luck on 30yr rate

can't leave order because this is SEF mandate.

7:15 PM Tony Peng Trend model execution for Monday 3/1/2020: Despite the market rout, Trend model remains calm with no signal change. Leverage that the model used to hit the target vol(10%) is reduced from 6.12 -> 5.78 amid the spike in vol. Equity and FX contracts roll from March to June as well. Will confirm with CK.

image.png ▼

FX futures	Contract Value	CRNCY	xccy	Score	Signal	Theoretical Positions	Theoretical Exposure	Trade Position Positions	Existing	New	Exposure	Tracking Error
JY1 Curncy	116,025	USD	1	1	3	15.27	1,771,257	16	16	0	$1,858,400	5%
CD1 Curncy	74,613	USD	1	0	2	0.00	0	0	0	0	$0	0%
NV1 Curncy	62,560	USD	1	3	1	-84.94	(5,313,770)	-84	-84	0	($5,255,040)	-1%
AD1 Curncy	65,340	USD	1	3	1	-81.45	(5,313,770)	-82	-82	0	($5,349,680)	1%
SF1 Curncy	129,588	USD	1	0	2	0.00	0	0	0	0	$0	0%
EC1 Curncy	137,994	USD	1	0	2	0.00	0	0	0	0	$0	0%
BP1 Curncy	79,988	USD	1	3	1	-66.43	(5,313,770)	-66	-66	0	($5,279,175)	1%
Total				10				248	248	0	$17,740,295	
Bond futures												
TY1 Comdty	134,844	USD	1	2	1	-45.01	(6,068,711)	-46	-48	2	($6,202,813)	2%
JB1 Comdty	154,070,000	JPY	0.00925	1	1	-2.13	(3,034,365)	-2	-2	0	($2,850,295)	-6%
XM1 Comdty	149,696	AUD	0.6515	1	1	-31.11	(3,034,365)	-32	-32	0	($3,120,867)	3%
CN1 Comdty	144,000	CAD	0.7487	1	1	-28.22	(3,034,365)	-28	-30	2	($3,010,694)	-1%
RX1 Comdty	177,460	EUR	1.1026	2	1	-31.02	(6,068,711)	-32	-34	2	($6,281,357)	3%
Total				7				140	146	6	$21,446,025	
Equity futures												
ES1 Index	147,550	USD	1	2	1	-11.76	(1,735,260)	-12	-12	0	($1,770,600)	2%
DFW1 Index	59,095	EUR	1.1026	2	2	26.63	1,735,260	26	26	0	$1,694,112	-2%
NH1 Index	10,507,500	JPY	0.00925	2	2	17.85	1,735,260	18	18	0	$1,749,499	1%
Z 1 Index	65,285	GBP	1.2823	2	2	20.73	1,735,260	20	20	0	$1,674,299	-4%
Total				8				76	76	0	$6,888,510	
Total Trades								464	470	6	$46,074,830	

7:16 PM QZ Can do RFQ through SEF if market is close, Asian cover will quote .2 from mid if the RFQ request is sent through BSEF

Right now seeing mid at 1.27

7:19 PM Tony Peng fwiw, the last time when the model's signal on TY1 Comdty changed from bullish from bearish occurred on 7/4/2019, while 10-yr yield bottomed around 9/4/2019.

9:58 PM Alex Gurevich Asset swaps moved more...

9:59 PM CK Yea been floating around -39.5/40 ticker, can get a live quote if of interest?

10:00 PM Alex Gurevich Yes see if you can do another $5mm of same for ███ and then we'll try to catch tomorrow on allocations

-39.5 or better

10:01 PM **CK** Sounds good, I'll let you know what comes back in a sec

K mom

10:11 PM **CK** -39.4 offer

just slightly outside, shall i go ahead?

10:17 PM Alex Gurevich Yes

10:22 PM **CK** We are done there, $5 @ -39.4

10:30 PM **CK** So $10 done all day in the 30y spread.

10:32 PM Alex Gurevich Great. Thx.

10:33 PM **CK** About to drop off online but before I do in other news: AUD relatively unch'ed since we last spoke, low was 6460, currently 6530.....it's a buy of 212x ADH0 Curncy (144 ███ / 68 ███) if you choose to reduce overnight keeping ███ constant.

10:34 PM Alex Gurevich Can check in the morning... I also canceled EDM1 balance...

10:35 PM **CK** K great

CNM0 opens in 30min or so if you want to transact at the open. We have 1943x on currently (1131/452/360) or $158k USD DV01

Nothing working in 30yr o/r overnight. Low since we spoke was 1.24. Qin and I will pick it up tomorrow. Just let us know if you want us to repo the TSY tomorrow AM on the two ASW we did tonight.

10:40 PM Alex Gurevich I'll check on CN before bed... I assume repo treasuries - unless futures are so cheap you want to do basis...

10:40 PM **CK** K

11:44 PM   Alex Gurevich Trying to buy 250 CNM0 150
           ████/100██cto bring allocation roughly into balance

11:54 PM   Alex Gurevich And then added 300 classic

           In the morning let's have a new interest rate risk file
           with all possible adjustments.

This concludes the Sunday evening session, which as you can see from the chat above lasted for at least nine hours. Several team members put in a full day's worth of work before Monday even started.

MARCH 2: MONDAY MORNING

Qin worked in the New York time zone, so she was the first one to pick things up in the morning. A little later, Joann, our head of operations, jumped in to help book everything that was done overnight.

March 2nd, 2020 ⌄

4:29 AM   QZ all overnight trades allocated and processed. Sorting
          out risk now

          CNM0, DEDZ4, EDM0, M1 all done

          👍 1   😊⁺

4:46 AM   QZ Also, doing repo.

7:01 AM   Joann Shie-Chen please let me know how/if I can assist

          with bookings etc

7:33 AM   CK alex -- 30yr o/r slipping back towards 1.23 -- would
          you like us to start working that interest again?

7:54 AM Alex Gurevich Seems turned again I feel less urgency as I sold some more overnight and bought DEDZ. But definitely worth watching.

Also consider add into asset swaps in other portfolios if there is ERIS a liquidity. But don't need to chase.

7:54 AM QZ Copy. If 30yr spread goes to -38.5 or better, adding asset swap for ███████ and ██?

8:08 AM Alex Gurevich Yes.

Is there a new IrBD file in mail or on box?

8:12 AM QZ Sending you now. There is an issue on CNM0 bucketing in order to capture intraday risk. Waiting for Bloomberg resolution but not optimistic. Total number is right, but what should have been in 7-10y bucket got spread out to 5y and in.

8:13 AM Alex Gurevich Ok

8:14 AM QZ Sent

After the flurry of overnight activity, we slowed down. FFH0 continued to rally, making me regret my earlier selling, but I continued to take profits.

8:14 AM QZ Sent   **March 2nd, 2020** ⌄

8:18 AM **CK** done on the FFH0 @ 76.25

8:18 AM Alex Gurevich Yes keep taking profits.

8:18 AM **CK** great

8:46 AM **CK** Trend trades done this AM (o/r @ 7AM, rolls from 7-9AM depending on liquidity) -- trend model is fully rolled out of March and into June contracts:

image.png ▾

EXECUTION					
Security	Action	Qty	LH	OA	Fill
TYM0 Comdty	Buy	2	1	1	135.2344
CNM0 Comdty	Buy	2	1	1	143.1
RXM0 Comdty	Buy	2	1	1	175.16
FX ROLLS					
JYH0JYM0 Curncy	Buy	16	8	8	0.38
NVH0NVM0 Curncy	Sell	-84	-42	-42	0.035
ADH0ADM0 Curncy	Sell	-82	-41	-41	0.098
BPH0BPM0 Curncy	Sell	-66	-33	-33	0.235
EQ ROLLS					
ESH0ESM0 Index	Sell	-12	-6	-6	-6.45
DFWH0M0 Index	Sell	-26	-13	-13	-14
NHH0NHM0 Index	Buy	18	9	9	-195
Z-H0Z-M0 Index	Sell	-20	-10	-10	84.5

👍 1   😊

10:32 AM QZ Intraday risk is refreshed. CNM0 problem fixed. File sent in email. Please let m know if you have question.

MARCH 3: TUESDAY MORNING

At 7:00 a.m. PST (my time zone) on Tuesday, March 3, the Fed made an intermeeting rate cut of 0.50%, bringing their target range down to 1% to 1.25%.

Unlike in my days as a market maker, I don't spend my entire workday glued to the screen. I like to say that my main job is to think. Certainly, I check markets first thing in the morning, and I rarely resist the temptation to monitor them if I happen to wake up in the middle of a weeknight. But during the daytime, I can do a variety of things. I can sit at a computer and go through a chart and try to grasp the price action. I can also sit on a couch reading printed research pieces. I can stroll on a beach while listening to a financial podcast. Or I can completely unplug, contemplating the capital account balance while in a sauna. All of this is work.

My coworkers checked to see if I was present at the screen.

My "Yes!!" referred to how much the Fed policy action benefited our portfolio. Not only did June Eurodollar options continue to be a fountain of cash, but the March options exploded in my favor mere days from expiration. March Fed Funds futures were a jackpot with immediate payout.

However, the main thing I remember from the day of that first emergency rate cut is not whether I was watching the market at the moment or the magnitude of our gains but a terrible misstep I made in the confusion.

When I started reconstructing the events of March 3, I thought that this mistake was due to me not seeing the rate cut soon enough, which cost me a chance to immediately orient myself to the situation.

Now, delaying action can be advantageous. In fact, I rarely respond immediately to a big market event. My theory is that my edge comes from carefully contemplated strategies and not from hunches or gut reactions. My first impulse is just as likely to be stupid as to be useful.

I, however, had been harsh on myself in my 2016 annual letter, despite a highly successful year, for not taking proper advantage of the price action surrounding Brexit and the US election.

> Mostly, we gained our edge by reducing exposure into the post-Brexit rally and then our subsequent re-building of positions gradually as the late year sell-off extended. Once again, while the direction of our thinking was correct, we wish we were more decisive at the same two critical junctures.

> In July, post-Brexit, the bond rally was clearly overextended, and an even deeper position cut was called for. What undermined our thinking was observing the parabolic rally in JGBs and wondering if treasuries could follow suit.

> The night of the US election was a clearer opportunity: Trump victory was distinctly negative for USTs, but the initial reaction was an unusually large equity sell-off and a moderate bond rally. This was an excellent "get out of jail free card" for bond bulls, but we had sold only a tiny amount as the situation was confusing and the fear of an unraveling stock market and dollar led to keeping bonds as a hedge. Once again, our thinking was reasonable, but more decisive action may have been called for.

There are times when post-factum it is easy to see that there was enough information to make the right trade. If one failed to do so, it means one either didn't think quickly enough or didn't have the courage to act. What is impossible to measure is the extent to which those junctures are offset by the times when this spur-of-the-moment, ex ante certainty turns out to be wrong.

Whatever the overall track record of instant actions is, there is no doubt in my mind that in the immediate aftermath of the ease, the market itself made a huge mistake in pricing the next monthly contract, April Fed Funds futures. And I did recognize it, though possibly not as fast as I should have, leaving me only minutes, if not seconds, to act. Let's look at the time stamps of the chat below.

7:00 AM **Christopher I** March 3rd, 2020 ⌄

7:01 AM Alex Gurevich Yes!!!

Increase short AUD in ▮▮▮ to bring it in line with ▮▮ and ▮▮

7:05 AM **CK** k

7:07 AM Alex Gurevich Watch for other dislocations. I think they'll cut again at the meeting at least 25.

Asset swaps. Looks like their backing up - time to catch up in other ports. Also look to do more In ▮▮ if there is margin space. Today's Libor is good!

7:08 AM QZ yes

7:10 AM **CK** Kk! Aud done

7:11 AM QZ no room for ▮▮

as of now. can ask for more

on spreads

7:11 AM Alex Gurevich April funds way too cheap.

Climbing now...

7:13 AM **Christopher Lutton** Qin, can i help go get you some space
on credit? i'm free to call

7:13 AM QZ Sure

7:13 AM Alex Gurevich Not priority now

7:13 AM **Christopher Lutton** copy

7:14 AM QZ ERIS is .5bp wide. Trying but may be hard

0.5 point wide, not bp

7:14 AM Alex Gurevich But 1200 April funds at .02 classic

Missed it :(was hesitating - but we have plenty on as we
are keeping match funds

Too Slow

You can see that we are trying to take advantage of currency
moves and continue to pursue asset swaps, which included
checking specific margin limits on the fly. The most important
thing going on, though, is the observation I make at 7:07:48 a.m.,
about eight minutes after the event.

There was a Federal Reserve policy meeting scheduled on
March 18, 2020, and none for the month of April. Right before
the intermeeting cut, April Fed Funds were trading at 98.89
(1.11% yield) which priced 47 bps (0.47%) of easing compared
to February. That was a blend of probabilities between a potential cut at the March meeting, some potential for intermeeting
action, and some chance for added liquidity ahead of an official
policy change (as happened in September 2001 and August
2007).

In response to the emergency action, the contract jumped incrementally to 99.05 and in the subsequent two minutes dipped to 98.95, taking almost all the weight of the anticipated easing out of the scheduled meeting. Within minutes, it had recovered somewhat but was still too cheap if you thought the rate cuts would continue.

Such price action was contrary to all logic and precedent. Indeed, if the situation were so dire that the central bank felt the need to surprise the market with extra liquidity, why would it risk surprising the market by not providing more liquidity only two weeks later?

The several prior instances of intermeeting cuts during my career, starting with one during the Russian debt/LTCM crisis of 1998, were all followed by additional easing at the next scheduled meeting.

FOMC Inter Meeting	Event	Action	Rate After Cut	Next FOMC	Followup Action	Rate After Cut
10/8/2008	Lehman Collapse	−50	1.50%	10/29/2008	−50	1%
1/22/2008	Weakening Economy	−75	3.50%	1/30/2008	−50	3%
9/17/2001	Terrorist Attack	−50	3%	10/2/2001	−50	2.50%
4/18/2001	Economic Slump	−50	4.5%	5/15/2001	−50	4%
1/3/2001	Tech Bubble	−50	6.0%	1/31/2001	−50	5.50%
10/15/1998	LTCM/Russian Crisis	−25	5.0%	11/17/1998	−25	4.75%

Historical FOMC Actions: In recent Fed history, every intermeeting cut is followed by easing at the next meeting.

I knew at that moment there was virtually no downside in buying the April contract and a huge upside if rates were driven to zero by the persisting crisis.

The sheer magnitude of moves and P/L swings could have given me pause, but I am not one to be easily perturbed. I am given to occasional waffling, though.

It took me another four minutes to zoom in on the April Fed Funds. From the chat, it appears that they bounced and then sold off again. I put in a moderate-size order another three-and-a-half minutes later, almost fifteen minutes after the event. Too slow. The price slipped away, and I didn't want to chase it.

It is psychologically difficult to buy a contract that was seconds ago a few ticks lower. But it is critical in times of extreme price action to forget the past. When things really blow up, it doesn't matter what trades you were doing or planning to do yesterday. It doesn't matter whether you are up or down money on the day, on the month, on the year, or over your lifetime. It doesn't matter where assets traded ten minutes ago. The only things that matter are the price that is in front of you this very second and whether transacting at this price will allow you to make money in the future.

Minute-by-Minute Price Action of April 2020 Fed Funds Future (FFJ20): From 9:55 a.m. to 10:45 a.m. on March 3, 2020.[10]

_____

10   All intraday charts and tables are in EST time zone.

To be fair, I had passed that test on other occasions. During the catastrophic appreciation of the Swiss franc, due to its depegging from the euro in January 2015, I missed the best price point. I was likely asleep in California, where it was 1:30 a.m., while the events were unfolding in Europe. I was also caught with the wrong position, a small Swiss franc short. I didn't let either of those things deter me, and I rapidly increased my short position tenfold, recognizing that this extreme appreciation was not sustainable.

But this time, in early March 2020, I faltered. I didn't grab any of the Aprils fast enough and didn't chase them hard enough when they started running away. Recall, I spoke earlier of this failure to execute as a terrible misstep. A trader's career is a continuous aggregation of profits and losses, and missing a trade that would make money is no better than entering a losing position.

I made light of it on the chat, correctly pointing out that we already had a significant position in the right direction. But I knew I had made a mistake. There would never be a second chance with that contract.

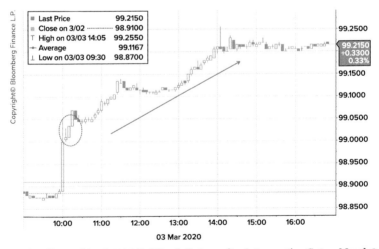

Intraday Chart of April 2020 Fed Funds Future after Intermeeting Cut on March 3, 2020.

I remember thinking at the time that volatility was so extreme, even a relatively small position decision could within seconds have significant profit implications.

Having My Cake and Eating It Too

0.5 point wid

March 3rd, 2020 ⌄

7:14 AM Alex Gurevich But 1200 April funds at .02 classic

Missed it :(was hesitating - but we have plenty on as we are keeping match funds

7:17 AM **CK** Not working anything other than the ASW, lmk if you want me to insert the FFJ0

7:18 AM Alex Gurevich Reduce Canada dollar by 60 standard allocation

7:18 AM **CK** K

7:19 AM QZ We added 25k to ■■, To match we need 82k dv01 (53.5/28.5), will try to do 1/2 at a time due to LIEH20 liquidity

7:21 AM Alex Gurevich Just add to ■■■■ to bring more in line.

7:23 AM **CK** CAD just raced away (currently at 95), sitting at 90 unless you want to chase it

7:24 AM Alex Gurevich Don't chase.

7:25 AM **CK** Cool, sitting on it

7:27 AM QZ realistically need headline spread to go down to -39.25 to get something close to -38.5 done using ERIS. Slipping away right now, will keep watching

7:31 AM **CK** Done on the CAD

Unsurprisingly very choppy so going to work patiently throughout the day moving forward unless we have a particular level/desire to aggress.

7:46 AM Alex Gurevich Reduce ■■ and ■■ JPY positons to bring them in line with ■■■■.

7:47 AM **CK** K

7:51 AM Alex Gurevich Will receiving on Canadian swaps free up
margins?   _____

7:51 AM **CK** Done JPY

7:54 AM Alex Gurevich Reduce CHF position in ▮ and and ▮ to
align with ▮▮.

(not EURCHF)

7:54 AM **CK** K

Just doing SFH0

7:55 AM Alex Gurevich Yes

7:55 AM QZ Will not increase. May not decrease

7:55 AM Alex Gurevich K

7:59 AM **CK** Partially done SF

Done

With the Federal Reserve having made an aggressive policy response, I was beginning to question my long dollar positions. Indeed, the main logic driving this position against other developed market currencies was the historically favorable interest differential. Now the Fed was rapidly taking away this differential.

This is when I started to recognize that I had managed to have my cake and eat it too. I was gaining a lot on my interest rate positions but not giving much ground on the dollar. It was time to start taking profits, before the market caught on. I reduced my shorts in the Canadian dollar (CAD), the yen (JPY), and the Swiss franc (CHF).

Over an hour had passed after the event, before I had time to even inquire about the technical details of the rate cut, such as the change in the interest on excess reserves (IOER).

Done

March 3rd, 2020 ⌄

8:13 AM Alex Gurevich Missed what he about OIER? Is it 1.10? Are there other tweaks?

8:14 AM QZ 1.1

8:15 AM **CK** yea

here is the implementation note:
https://www.federalreserve.gov/newsevents/pressrelea
ses/monetary20200303a1.htm

Board of Governors of the Federal Reserve System
Implementation Note issued March 3, 2020
Board of Governors of The Federal Reserve System

8:20 AM Alex Gurevich Did we do anything on asset swaps in ▇▇▇ - no rush/pressure there...

8:21 AM QZ not yet. ERIS liquidity is poor

the best level we could get was worse than -38,

We need headline around -39.25 to get something close to -38.5, which is level we target for

8:27 AM Alex Gurevich Ok

8:34 AM QZ I saw receiving 10m 10y cad reducing margin 200k. But it is iffy stuff. Emailed ▇▇▇ for confirmation

8:38 AM Alex Gurevich Got it. How much margin is $5mm 30yr?

8:39 AM QZ USD?

521k

8:40 AM Alex Gurevich 10%?

8:41 AM   QZ yes, I think they may have increased in the last couple days

This is LCH. On CME 405k

8:42 AM   Alex Gurevich K can you adjust for today's trades in risk files?

8:43 AM   QZ CME/LCH basis is converging to 0.8bp as rates lower

8:43 AM   Alex Gurevich If hard don't worry...

8:43 AM   QZ will try to get them in

risk file

8:43 AM   CK CME margins def increased overnight (link on general chat yesterday around 9AM or so)

8:54 AM   Alex Gurevich Ok let's not push anybody on margins too much - we don't want to get in trouble.

10:05 AM   QZ Sent in email. also on box: https://honteadvisors.box.com/s/kh4zyvrkiwtt5micpcd mclq86gdspg1j

1:37 PM   QZ ▇▇ says $2.74 for early exercise and pairing off shorts

1:44 PM   Alex Gurevich Reasonable??

I dont know if that includes clearing costs, but seems like a thing to do...

1:49 PM   QZ Was told everything included. But will double check each fee item before pulling trigger tomorrow

▇▇ will give us number too

1:50 PM   Alex Gurevich It's ok close enough...

As you can see in this chat, I moved from adjusting currency positions to working on long-dated US interest rates and swap spreads.

There are a few related things going on here.

The One Trade

First of all, as I discussed earlier, for several years preceding March 2020, I had maintained a position in the long end of the US Treasury curve (by the long end I mean the bonds with long-term maturity—not to be confused with a long position on the bonds, which means betting on the bonds to go up. In this case, I was long long bonds).

That position was the focus of TNPT, wherein I described it as one of the best single-asset trades in the history of markets. The US Classic Bond Future Chart is the chart I used. I called being long bonds The One Trade and, later, even wrote a poem about it.

And by the way, if you don't get the reference in the poem, please close this book—I don't accept you as my reader. Okay, kidding. But seriously...

After 2014, when my first book was written, The One Trade had lots of ups and downs (more ups than downs), testing the thesis outlined in TNPT against multiple headwinds (stronger than expected employment growth, strong stock markets, 2016 US elections and the subsequent fiscal expansion).

Three ancient and exhausted majors
Losing their fiscal might,
Seven members of G-7
Against deflation waging fight,
Nine big emerging markets,
Debt burden, their plight.

One Trade to rule them all,
One Chart to find it,
One Trend to bring it far
    Into the land of printed money
Where yields no longer are.

Copyright© Bloomberg Finance L.P.

US Classic Bond Future Chart 1991–2021: Performance after my first book came out is circled.

After the surge up to early March, I recognized that the trade had moved to the upper end of the channel on the chart above and that it was time to take some profits, as I had done post-Brexit in the summer of 2016.

Furthermore, history suggested that in the environment of rapid rate cuts, the yield curve tended to steepen—that is, short-term rates fall faster than long-term rates.

This gave me additional incentive to reduce risk in the long end and focus on the short end, where I stood to benefit most from my options.

Inverted Swap Spreads

There was another perspective from which the US long bonds remained extremely cheap: swap spreads. In the Slack screenshots, the thirty-year spread mentioned was at levels between -38 and -39. That means the yield on the thirty-year bond was 38 bps (0.38%) higher than on the corresponding thirty-year interest swap. The swap reflects the market projection of quarterly settings of LIBOR.

I have been writing about the curious phenomenon of inverted (negative) swap spreads for quite a few years now. This is from a market note I wrote in November 2015:

Inverted Swap Spreads — "Not an Apples-to-Apples Comparison"

Today's market participants are thoroughly puzzled by the recently renewed inversion of swap spreads. In other words, the fact that the yield on the long-dated US Treasury notes and bonds is higher than the corresponding interbank swap rate for the same maturities.

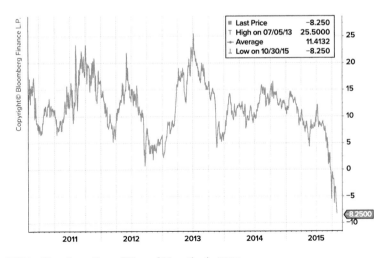

US Ten-Year Swap Spread Turned Negative in 2015.

Several portfolio managers, financial journalists and market spectators are joining a louder chorus calling this inversion completely illogical, and even mathematically impossible.

Indeed, at a big-picture level, it seems to make little sense that the swap curve which is based on LIBOR (London Interbank Offered Rate) would reflect a lower lending rate than the full faith and credit of the US Government.

From a market perspective, those who follow me know that I am big fan of US bonds and that I think they are currently cheap on both an absolute basis as well as relative to swaps. But in the interest of intellectual honesty, I must concede that the inversion of swap spreads is NOT mathematically meaningless.

Allow me to share an observation I made in my very early days after entering the swap market in 1997. The popular "swap spread" is not a spread between apples and apples.

In fact, the spread compares two completely different types of financial instruments.

A bond, which is an asset, is a security which represents term lending of cash to the government and includes all associated risks.

A swap, which is a derivative as opposed to an asset, represents a bet on a string of three- month interbank lending rates which includes no principal risk.

In other words, the swap spread does not compare 'term lending to the government' with 'term inter-bank lending'. If you doubt it, see where a bank can borrow money for ten years - I can assure you the rate would be higher than that of a ten year US Treasury.

So, we are comparing term lending to the government with a projection of a rolling short-term interbank lending rate. And if the interbank market breaks down, the payers of Libor will be nailed for a period of days, quarters, etc., but will not risk the whole principal investment like the bond holders.

Importantly, the way to think of the inversion of the swap spreads is not a mathematical break-down, but rather a spike in the term premium.

That said, we can still perform a "carry" or "terminal value" analysis of the trade of being long bonds vs. paying interest rate swaps, similar to the examples I discussed in Chapters Two and Three in my book The Next Perfect Trade.

Mathematically, we are comparing three month LIBOR with the rolling funding rate for Treasuries; the rate at which you can borrow money if you offer your bonds as collateral. Note: in the unlikely event of imminent default, the funding rate will go to virtually infinity.

While most of us are not actually afraid of a US default, we cannot secure the funding rate that would allow us to secure arbitrage profits. Banks can likely secure the funding, but they are limited in their ability to take additional market risk or expand their balance sheets.

In summary, the swap spread inversion is not mathematically impossible and does not indicate a collapse of the financial system. And betting on its normalization is a good, but not riskless trade.

In November 2017, I addressed the cheapness of bonds when viewed on the asset swap basis.

Don't Equate Treasury Yields with Borrowing Rates

When we say, "we are long USTs," it often elicits an assumption that we expect interest rates to go down. However, while our secular disinflation bias indeed leads us to lean slightly toward a lower yields view, we have no conviction as to the immediate direction of interest rates.

By way of an example, let's go back to the post-Brexit yield lows. On July 8, 2016, 30-year bonds hit a generational low yield of 2.099%. We, however, argued that is when they were the CHEAPEST in observable history. Amazingly during the same time, the 30-year swap spread (difference in yield between the 30-year swap rate and the bond of the same maturity) traded in the mid -40s to -50s basis points. Yes, negative; which means that the interbank swap yield was lower than the Treasury yield by more than 40-55 bps, putting swaps at 1.6761% on July 8, 2016. Now that is low! (In the aforementioned post we have discussed why it was peculiar, but not mathematically impossible).

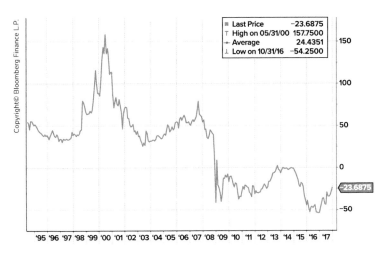

Thirty-Year Swap Spread 1995–2017: Near Brexit in 2016, the thirty-year swap rate was over 50 bps lower than the thirty-year Treasury yield.

Back then there was already some talk of the yield curve being too flat. However, historically the yield spread between the 2-year and 30-year bond was not that narrow.

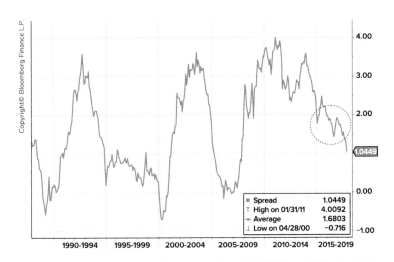

Thirty-Year versus Two-Year US Government Bond Yield Differential 1987–2017: Middle of the range in 2017.

Meanwhile, because the 2-year spread was positive, the difference between 2-year and 30-year swap was much lower.

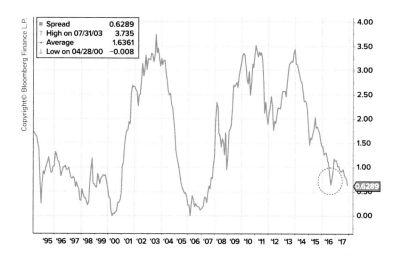

Thirty-Year versus Two-Year Swap Rate Differential 1995–2017: At the bottom quartile.

The 30-year yield trading 0.9% above its guaranteed funding rate indicates those 90 basis points represent the credit risk priced by the market, as the interest rate risk is hedged via the swap. Is this a lot? Remember when other debt trades at a spread, the spread represents not only the default risk but also the funding risk. In this case this risk is purely default.

If the bond were to be priced at a zero chance of default, it would rally 90 bps from the price of 100 to roughly 122, or a 22% price increase. Conversely, one can say that in 2016, 30-year bonds traded about 82 cents on a dollar in a state of deep "workout".

The reasons for such cheapness probably had to do with foreign central bank selling and balance sheet constraints, not with people thinking that the chance of default being that high.

Thus, one can be a bond bull even after allowing for a moderate rise in interest rates.

This is how swap spreads played out in 2020:

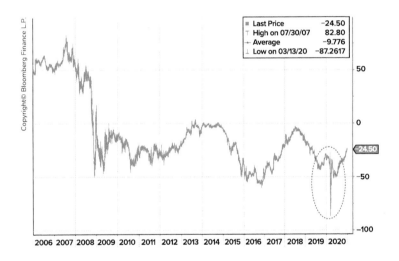

Thirty-Year USD Swap Spread 2006–2020: A dramatic collapse of the spread in March 2020.

Swap spreads have typically been positive in the past—that is, the yield on the government bonds has been lower than on the swaps. This relationship has been inverted over the past few years in the long end of the curve, giving the impression that the US government now has worse credit quality than banks. I have written on several occasions about this relationship, discussing why the spread is not exactly "apples to apples" and why, nonetheless, the inversion presented a great trading opportunity.

At this stage in early March, I wanted to take advantage of the spreads moving further into negative territory by increasing my positions. But I also saw this as an opportunity to decrease my interest risk. Instead of selling all of my bond futures, I could "pay" on interest swaps, which means entering a position that succeeds when the rates go up.

This would be a switch from being outright long bonds to being long bonds on the spread basis—that is, betting on the spread to go higher (less negative in this case). In other words, by doing a single swap, I could accomplish two goals: reduce interest rate risk and increase spread risk.

Trading such asset swap spreads is technically more complex than simple directional positions. Different portfolios that we ran required different instruments. The managed futures portfolios, by definition, allow us to trade only in futures form, but swap futures are a little tricky to execute in long maturities (you saw the reference to ERIS futures). In the institutional fund portfolio, we access trading actual swaps, but the margins on those derivative transactions had to be watched carefully. You saw (and will see) us spending quite a lot of energy managing operational issues surrounding the spread bets. Spoiler alert: the energy was well spent.

We take it up on the next day.

MARCH 4, WEDNESDAY MORNING

6:29 AM QZ
March 4th, 2020 ˅
image.png ▼

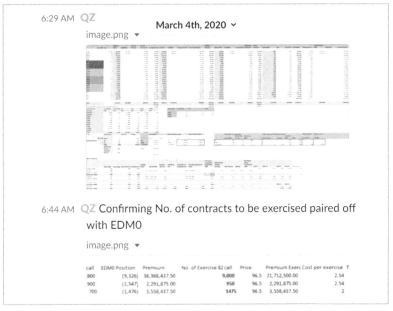

6:44 AM QZ Confirming No. of contracts to be exercised paired off
with EDM0

image.png ▼

call	EDM0 Position	Premium	No. of Exercise 82 call	Price	Premium Exerc	Cost per exercise	T
800	(9,326)	36,368,437.50	9,000	96.5	21,712,500.00		2.54
900	(1,547)	2,291,875.00	950	96.5	2,291,875.00		2.54
700	(1,476)	3,558,437.50	1475	96.5	3,558,437.50		2

Continue to work 30yr spread for ███? (28.5k DV01)

7:16 AM Alex Gurevich Yes on spread.

7:17 AM QZ copy

7:19 AM Alex Gurevich RFH0 let's using ██ as Benchmark
increase in ██████ and ██ (promise to CK just a small
increase)

7:19 AM CK hah sounds good

RFH0 is the futures contract on EuroSwiss currency cross
(EURCHF). In the chat, I apologized to CK for increasing our
position, because he had pointed out earlier that our firm had a
significant portion of open interest on this contract, which made
us vulnerable to a loss of exchange liquidity.

This trade, however, was a great success for us despite the fact that it was not going anywhere. What do I mean by this? When I construct a portfolio, I try to balance it between "risk-on" and "risk-off" trades. Risk-on trades (often referred to as positive-beta trades) tend to benefit from times of normalcy and strong performance of stock markets and the overall economy. Risk-off trades tend to be profitable in times of crisis. If I succeed in my design, I have something working for me in every scenario, cushioning me from potential losses.

Being long the ratio of euro to Swiss franc via RFH0 implies betting against the Swiss franc (CHF), which is traditionally a safe-haven currency. Thus, my position would be unequivocally considered a risk-on trade. However, as the pandemic crisis rolled in, the trade proved to be very resilient, losing almost no money. Once again, I was having my cake and eating it too. But in this case, instead of taking profits, I was reaching for even more cake.

In the middle of the meaningful position adjustments, we did take some profits to clean up our portfolio. Some of our Eurodollar options were very deep in the money and had already been fully offset by futures. We worked to exercise those options and close offsetting positions to free up the maximum amount of cash for future opportunities.

7:19 AM **CK** hah sounc   March 4th, 2020 ⌄

7:27 AM Alex Gurevich The priority is to exercise 98.25 calls. In ■ macro they are exactly matched against EDM0 hedge. In ■ there are many more calls but we can exercise those which are matched against hedge. 9,236. In ■ we should exercise at least the 950 calls against hedge. We could later exercise a few hundred more from ■ .375.

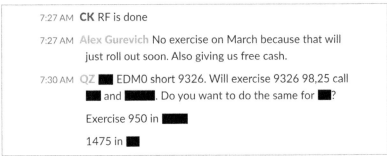

7:27 AM **CK** RF is done

7:27 AM Alex Gurevich No exercise on March because that will just roll out soon. Also giving us free cash.

7:30 AM QZ ▪ EDM0 short 9326. Will exercise 9326 98,25 call ▪ and ▪▪. Do you want to do the same for ▪?

Exercise 950 in ▪▪

1475 in ▪

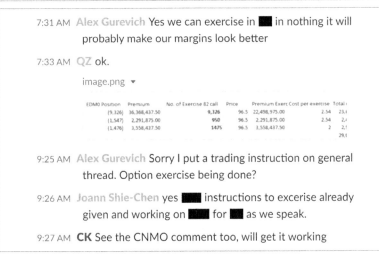

7:31 AM Alex Gurevich Yes we can exercise in ▪ in nothing it will probably make our margins look better

7:33 AM QZ ok.

image.png ▾

EDM0 Position	Premium	No. of Exercise	82 call	Price	Premium Exerc	Cost per exercise	Total
(9,326)	36,368,437.50		9,326	96.5	22,498,975.00	2.54	23,(
(1,547)	2,291,875.00		950	96.5	2,291,875.00	2.54	2,(
(1,476)	3,558,437.50		1475	96.5	3,558,437.50	2	2,!
							29,(

9:25 AM Alex Gurevich Sorry I put a trading instruction on general thread. Option exercise being done?

9:26 AM Joann Shie-Chen yes ▪▪ instructions to excerise already given and working on ▪▪ for ▪ as we speak.

9:27 AM **CK** See the CNMO comment too, will get it working

9:42 AM **CK** done

▪ swap and ▪/▪ futts

9:57 AM QZ ERIS spread trade for ▪▪ is done

9:57 AM Alex Gurevich Good.

At this point, I was raking in cash. After two excellent months in 2020, the first three trading days of March were hugely positive, with March 3 (the day of the emergency rate cut) being one of my best trading days ever.

This, however, didn't preclude me from looking for every possible way to optimize my performance. Success invigorates me and makes me excited to search for new ideas.

In this case, I observed that the Canadian rates gave me an opening for a strategy exactly the opposite of the one I had for the US rates.

Earlier that morning, the BOC (Bank of Canada) followed the example set by the Federal Reserve and cut rates by 0.50%. The longer maturities in Canada still looked cheap to me in relation to the falling rates in the front end.

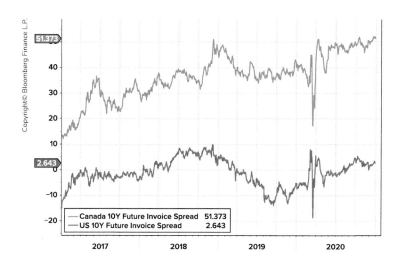

Canadian Ten-Year Invoice Spread[11] (Blue) Recovered to the High End of the Range, while US Ten-Year Invoice Spread (Red) Hovered below Zero during the Highlighted Period of March 2020.

---

11 Invoice spread is the difference between the yield of a forward starting interest rate swap with a maturity equal to the maturity of the cheapest-to-deliver issue of a futures contract and the forward yield of the futures contract. An invoice spread position is expressed through liquid futures instead of cash bonds and is highly correlated to the swap spread.

First, I was looking to increase my duration (bonds) exposure in Canada while decreasing it in the United States. Second, whereas the spreads in the United States were too narrow (low), in Canada they were too wide (high).

Hence, I started thinking of receiving in Canadian swaps instead of buying Canadian bond futures. This would increase my rates risk and allow me to bet on the narrowing of the spread. As an additional benefit, it would offset my exposure to US swap spreads.

9:57 AM	QZ ERIS spre March 4th, 2020 ⌄ done	
9:57 AM	Alex Gurevich Good.	

10:49 AM Alex Gurevich Can we analyze the level of swap/invoice spreads in Canada. Recent performance/curry. If levels and carry are favorable. It maybe worthwhile to convert all CNM in ██ into swaps. Further reducing margins - and putting us in a better carry position with no further toll costs.

10:49 AM QZ copy

10:55 AM QZ -0.2 for 10y receiver

overr 3m

10:57 AM Alex Gurevich Are talking about outright trade carry or asset swap carry?

Only asset I.e relative carry matters

10:57 AM QZ just outright on 10y receiver swap. looking at asset swap now

10:58 AM Alex Gurevich The question is what gives better carry receiving swaps or owning futures. And also where are the swap spreads on MTM basis relative to range.

10:58 AM QZ copy

11:19 AM QZ On selling future and receiving swap as a package, carry and roll down is approx 0.2bp positive, invoice spread at 34 is on the cheap side, 1y range is about 32-43

11:20 AM Alex Gurevich CAN you send me a chart of invoice spread

11:21 AM QZ

image.png ▾

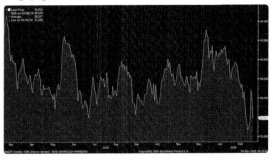

11:22 AM Alex Gurevich Hmmm big move maybe wait for levels to convert... 36/38/40 each time 1/3?

11:23 AM QZ looks like it

Will watch those levels

11:25 AM Alex Gurevich Also probably don't want to pay today's BAC?

11:26 AM QZ yes, 1.685, nasty

11:26 AM Alex Gurevich Worth 1bp on 10yr

Later that afternoon, the Governor of California declared a state of emergency. I was unperturbed.

The next day was Thursday. We took it up with Canadian swaps but also looked to continue reducing risk in the US bond futures, which continued to rally.

MARCH 5: THURSDAY MORNING

6:50 AM QZ

March 5th, 2020 ⌄

image.png ▾

7:00 AM Alex Gurevich Confirming we are full on swap margins?

How are Canadian swap spreads doing?

How do I looks them up?

7:02 AM QZ

image.png ▾

Yesterday's comments:
14:39:11 Desk likes wideners here:

CAD swap spreads have compressed on the back of heavier receiving flows in this move lower in yields / cross-mkt cheapening. These flows are perhaps still not over, but we are scaling into belly spread wideners at these levels. Not only will some of these sizable received flows have to be unwound at some point, we also look ahead to what could be a very active spring season of Canadian mortgage origination/renewal – though this seasonality trade failed last year, we are at attractive entry levels and think there will likely be more demand for fixed rate mortgages at these levels in rates.

7:15 AM Alex Gurevich Thx

9:27 AM Alex Gurevich Put on min to sell some classic bond futures. Allocated in a such a way that remainder should 60 in standard allocation.

9:30 AM CK ok, see it working

The next moment marked a shift in my thinking. I still expected the actual COVID spread in the United States to be mild, but I was confident that the economic damage and fear would continue driving the short-term interest rates lower. However, I started to think that the long rates had moved decidedly too far. When the disease blew over, the bonds would be due for a vicious snapback.

So in the following chat, I began to investigate buying options. This time, it was payer swaptions: options betting on long-dated swap rates going higher!

Buying an option required evaluating more parameters than needed for executing a "vanilla" trade. One couldn't rush into such a transaction. Observe a long discussion of pricing as well as margin requirements and related operational issues.

9:30 AM **CK** ok, see it   March 5th, 2020 ⌄

10:34 AM Alex Gurevich Ok to hell with swap margins. Let's price some payer swaptions. 1year into 30yr 25bps out. Should be around 40 delta. $25-50mm. Let's gear it up and on the next run up we can execute...

😄 1   ☺⁺

10:47 AM QZ 25bp out? Ck and I are looking at it right now.

10:48 AM Alex Gurevich Feels about right 1.40% strike. Targeting 2% on pull back.

10:48 AM QZ ok. somehow not seeing 40% delta. checking

32.7%

checking with desk as well

11:02 AM Alex Gurevich 32.7 is fine I was just guessing

11:11 AM QZ Getting some indication shortly

BBG shows 4.67% or 1.164 mm on 25 mm, ATM 1.17

1.4% strike

11:16 AM Alex Gurevich Ok. How's the vol looking has it gone up a lot?

11:16 AM QZ 70bp

11:17 AM Alex Gurevich So it's 23 out?

11:17 AM QZ did go up

11:18 AM Alex Gurevich What was the low on vol?

11:18 AM QZ one sec

image.png ▼

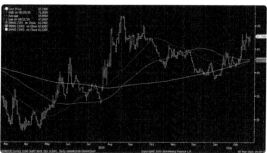

11:22 AM Alex Gurevich Normal no so high, lognormal....

CAN we give them an all-in order?

11:24 AM QZ They just came back, 1y30y atmf+25 Payer (CME),
they offer 4.75% seeing mid 4.6%, works for up to
50mm

that is at expiry, settle into CME swap

cash settle seems to be messy these day, most people
do physical settle according to ███

there will be an IA(margin) posted for the trade,

11:26 AM Christopher Lutton Qin, sorry just trying to follow along

what's the breakeven on 4.76% in bp terms?

11:27 AM QZ 4.76% of notional

sorry 4.75% of notional

11:27 AM Christopher Lutton i don't think that way.

i see 1.60% break even

11:44 AM QZ IA amount is 1.12% of notional

11:46 AM Alex Gurevich Would it affect our swap margins?

11:47 AM QZ It should not

it is OTC bilateral

unless we exercise into the swap

11:48 AM Alex Gurevich Btw can we trade any other swap futures besides ERIS to circumvent margin issues?

11:49 AM QZ There is CME swap future, but not familiar

about liquidity or other strings attached

can look into that

11:51 AM Alex Gurevich Worth looking so we could balance positions.

11:51 AM QZ We will need to check with future execution brokers whether or not we are set up to trade those

11:52 AM Alex Gurevich We should check to make sure we have every option and understand the mechanics

11:53 AM QZ Looking into them now, but not very optimistic in 30yr sector

To be clear on the swaption, you want leave an order with a reference 30yr rate level ?

11:56 AM Alex Gurevich Yes I may do that. Still thinking about it.

11:57 AM QZ ok

I was wobbling about paying up for the option. As I discussed earlier, I rarely resort to that strategy.

11:57 AM QZ ok   March 5th, 2020 ⌄

11:58 AM Alex Gurevich Mixt feelings. You know how I feel about options. Yet experience suggests that we are close to the juncture when 30yr swap will blow out 50-100bps back.

11:58 AM QZ This is not a cheap option

11:58 AM CK haha yes exactly re 'cheap'

do we think there is any chance of vol calming before rates rip back higher? working a vol apathetic level order and/or just doing the trade here are both high conviction terminal value/level trades

just level setting

12:00 PM Alex Gurevich Nah vol won't clam down at this levels. Not til the fed settled. And the first blow-out is probably before that.

12:00 PM QZ Why don't ask for increase in swap margin?

12:01 PM CK or in other terms, is this the preferred expression of your view in a world where we have more swap margin?

12:01 PM Alex Gurevich They already did - I don't want to push them.

Till we can document increased AUM.

12:02 PM CK diplomacy reigns, sounds good

12:02 PM Alex Gurevich As for whether it's preferred / close call.

12:03 PM CK level wise then, what do you have in mind? and do you have a max vol where that level doesn't hold?

12:03 PM Alex Gurevich I think their increased swap margin was off $68mm AUM at the year end (10%). Otherwise how did they come up with that number?

12:03 PM QZ It was based on 68mmm

12:06 PM Alex Gurevich We can ask to increase based on Feb AUM - which is not officially reported though. Or make it once a quarter process. And ask for $10mm on April 1st (though probably won't be confirmed till mid-April)

12:07 PM QZ That's fair

Will try to get Feb out asap. Then we decide if we ask for increase. Let us know your decision on the swaption if you prefer to do it

12:10 PM **CK** quarterly process seems most manageable, agreed

12:11 PM Alex Gurevich No rush with swaption as it came off a bit. We got bond futures out. Will wait for next level - around 1.14% on 30yr.

The day ended with more money made and more operational cleanup. After a short break, we jumped into the Asian session, and rates gapped down further.

MARCH 5: THURSDAY AFTERNOON

12:11 PM QZ Coppy   March 5th, 2020 ∨

1:33 PM QZ On cash, there is 46.6 mm available for withdraw in ■■'s USD segregated account, additional 10 mm in non-USD account, total equity 55.9 mm as of 3/4 EOD Could exercise another 597 98.375 in ■■■■.

Joann confirmed this with ■■■.

5:03 PM QZ Wow, 1.105 30 yr rate

5:03 PM **Christopher Lutton** Jeezus

2y 0.57%
5y 0.646%
10yr 0.877%
30yr 1.50%

AUD 10yr -7.3bp to 0.70%
AUD .6608

5:46 PM Alex Gurevich Are Kaplan remarks flattening the curve?

5:46 PM **Christopher Lutton** seems it

5:46 PM Alex Gurevich I don't suppose we can buy payers in Asian time?

5:48 PM **Christopher Lutton** yes, you looking for same thing we looked at earlier?

Qin/CK can get quote

5:48 PM **CK** I'll check and see

5:48 PM **Christopher Lutton** CK, ███ said "yep, what do you need"

ck getting quote

5:49 PM Alex Gurevich Can we buy this payer with reference rate 1.08 spot?

5:50 PM **CK** We'll see what they say

5:51 PM QZ BBG showing 4.68%

71.6 vol

30y ref 1.8075

5:53 PM Alex Gurevich Lower now. See If they can 1.33 strike at 4.75% on 25mm

5:55 PM QZ No offfer? strange

5:55 PM **Christopher Lutton** Not seen that before

5:55 PM **CK** That's a new one

Liquidity was tricky, as chaos was beginning to rein in the markets.

Besides turning my position around at the long end of the yield curve, I was beginning to bottom-fish. What does that mean? For years preceding the pandemic crisis, my portfolio was slightly negatively correlated to the stock market and other risk-on assets.

I wasn't actually short stocks, nor did I always lose money on the days when equities went up. Rather, my P/L was consistently driven by my exposure to bonds, which tended to be negatively correlated to stocks (e.g., when the stock market went down, investors expected the Fed to cut rates, and bonds rallied).

This bias allowed me to buy anything that looked cheap at any point. I never had to worry about owning equity indices, oil, or emerging market currencies. When those assets collapsed, I was almost certain to make money on my huge interest rate positions.

Going into March, my exposure to risk assets was very moderate. When I saw panic spreading, I went shopping. In such situations, I generally try to buy what I think will end up higher five years later and not worry about the immediate price action.

This evening, I started to grow my exposure to Mexican peso (the future ticker is PE in the next chat), which was getting very cheap. Meanwhile, I was still hunting for swaptions.

5:55 PM **CK** That's a n   March 5th, 2020 ∨

5:56 PM Alex Gurevich What no offer?

5:56 PM QZ crisp answer, says "Nope"

5:57 PM **Christopher Lutton** ■ time

5:57 PM QZ showed 451 c bid ref 1.088, no offer

says could try and work but unlikely due to Asian hour

CK, shall we contact ■?

6:00 PM **CK** Let's see sec

6:00 PM QZ Not sure if chat is active

6:02 PM **CK** Limited Asia coverage, see if I can grab someone but will take a moment

6:02 PM **Christopher Lutton** 1.056% again. whoa

6:08 PM Alex Gurevich Don't kill yourself over it - just seems like a good chance to short long-dated rates, but we don't have any WNs to sell. The only thing I have left to sell. Is my last 60 USAs.

6:08 PM **CK** Yup I got it, I'm getting someone. Deep into the Rolodex!

6:29 PM Alex Gurevich Add 60 go PE futures standard. MXN is at 20.

6:29 PM **CK** K

6:30 PM Alex Gurevich Actually make 120

6:30 PM **CK** K

6:33 PM **Christopher Lutton** Whoa! Nice catch

Think market really starting to feel like Banxico has more than 100bp of cutting to do

6:38 PM **CK** PE is done

7:11 PM Alex Gurevich Put of couple of sell orders in. Trickling out duration.

> **7:13 PM CK** great
>
> here is what I have tentatively: 19:05:50 spot premium 482c (for live) on 1y30y atm+25bps, bilat, physical settle
>
> that was a 1.30 strike...will adj to your request from above in a sec
>
> sorting through few other things associated with our first trade w them and then will refresh

> **7:15 PM Alex Gurevich** That is reasonable assuming vol is slightly up on this move.
>
> ?
>
> 4.8 at 1.30 would nice and clean (but don't need to squeeze them on the first one)
>
> **7:16 PM Christopher Lutton** US done
>
> **7:19 PM CK** yea █
>
> **7:19 PM Alex Gurevich** I'll do the levels they showed if they can
>
> But rates better now
>
> **7:19 PM CK** yup, sec, will refresh in a mom
>
> **7:19 PM Alex Gurevich** Under 1.04
>
> Maybe they can do 1.29%?

> **7:20 PM CK** i'll refresh +25bps when i have all the info i need
>
> waiting on IA
>
> **7:22 PM Alex Gurevich** IA probably won't change our minds.
>
> **7:23 PM Christopher Lutton** Get ready to scratch head when they give us something other than "premium" amount
>
> **7:24 PM Alex Gurevich** Should be less or equal to premium
>
> **7:30 PM CK** yea premium

It is important to observe that the fixed-income market on March 6 was rallying in a very dramatic "flattening" fashion. A flatter curve means a lower differential between short-term and long-term interest rates. This meant that long-dated rates were falling much more than the rest of the curve.

This was unusual relative to the historical pattern. Typically, at the beginning of the crisis when the Fed cuts rates, the curve steepens, irrationally pricing that rates will go back up again soon (they never do). This is how much the difference between two-year and thirty-year rates widened in 2001, for example:

Thirty-Year (Blue) versus Two-Year (Red) US Government Bond Yields: In the 2000 easing cycle, the two-year rate dropped a lot more than the thirty-year rate, resulting in a much steeper yield curve.

My position, influenced by this old pattern, had a steepening bias and was no longer capitalizing on The One Trade.

7:30 PM **CK** yea premi·

March 5th, 2020 ⌄

7:30 PM Alex Gurevich First time we are not making money on bond rally...

7:31 PM **Christopher Lutton** ITS WEIRD FEELING! I told Qin tonight' sthe night you can really feel the twist

my first response was "MAV BROKEN"

7:31 PM Alex Gurevich Because Canada bonds are closed?

✔ 1   ☺⁺

7:33 PM **CK** refresh coming

ATM+25 and 1.30%

7:38 PM Alex Gurevich Is this live?

If so let's do it.

Should be getting a little better again

I am going to put kids to bed. Feel free to execute. With a little wiggle room.

7:42 PM **CK** unless the level has gotten materially worse, i will be executing in $25mm

(notional)....circa $1mm premium

7:46 PM Alex Gurevich Correct

1.205mm

7:49 PM **CK** 19:49:33 104.6ref

484c sp offer for 1.3%
and 487.5c sp offer for a+25

going to be done at 484 1.3%

7:50 PM Alex Gurevich Ok

7:52 PM **CK** done live

hopping off to dinner, if you need me give me a ring at ███████████!

7:52 PM Alex Gurevich K first trade with ██ bilateral!

7:52 PM **CK** thanks for your patience, huge battle to do Asia time zone and first trade in ▉

yes exactly

lets cheer when it makes money

haha

but yes, mini win

7:53 PM Alex Gurevich K thx for working round-o-clock this days

7:53 PM **Christopher Lutton** nice job you two.

7:54 PM **CK** no problem, its worth it in this market

After much wrangling, we purchased the swaption payer. At the 7:53 p.m. marker, I noticed the long hours that my coworkers were putting in and thanked them for working "round the clock." Spoiler: it wasn't going to get less intense in the following weeks.

MARCH 6: FRIDAY MORNING

Friday morning was "unemployment" day. The monthly nonfarm payroll numbers are usually released on the first Friday of the following month. The report for February 2020 came out stronger than projected.

Nobody cared. It was pretty clear by then that any statistics reflecting the economic activity in early 2020 would be irrelevant going forward.

I like to say, "History is not an experimental science." There is no way to convincingly play out a "what if" alternate-universe scenario. Still, looking at such reports was the closest I could get to gauging what would have happened if someone hadn't eaten the wrong bat.

Earlier, I quoted my Macrovoices interview in which I gave a high probability to a continuation of the easing cycle in the winter and spring of 2020. When someone says there is a 50-50 chance of something, there is no real way to prove them wrong. But if I am to be intellectually honest, I was wrong. The objective probability of the Fed continuing to cut rates, despite having stated that they were done, was likely much less than 50 percent.

The robust economic numbers, which continued to roll out throughout the first quarter of 2020, proved that the economy had stabilized in late 2019. It was thus likely that barring a "black swan," the central bank would have sat on the sidelines for a few months.

Although my forecast was wrong, my positioning wasn't. I might have felt some pain from further option deterioration had nothing happened in the first half of 2020. But my losses were controlled, and I was prepared to stick to my course. The rate differential wasn't closed, and the dollar was bound to continue grinding up, putting deflationary pressure on the US economy. Sooner or later, something would happen—a crisis or a run-of-the-mill recession.

In either case, the market would fall into a financial black hole and the rates would have no path to follow except toward the central singularity, which is the zero interest rate policy (ZIRP).

On that Friday morning, I was trading under the assumption that the long bonds had completed the bulk of their upward journey, while the short-end rates would inevitably compress further.

6:36 AM QZ

image.png ▾   March 6th, 2020 ⌄

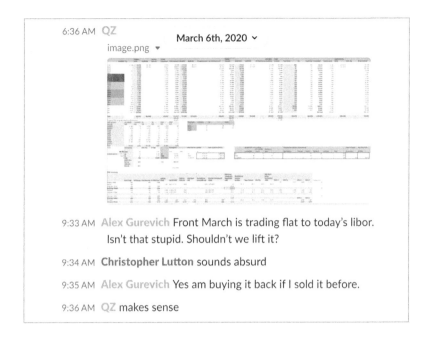

9:33 AM Alex Gurevich Front March is trading flat to today's libor. Isn't that stupid. Shouldn't we lift it?

9:34 AM **Christopher Lutton** sounds absurd

9:35 AM Alex Gurevich Yes am buying it back if I sold it before.

9:36 AM QZ makes sense

Term LIBOR and Overnight Funding

I promised to discuss LIBOR more. Here it comes.

The Federal Reserve directly controls the Fed Funds rate at which banks lend to each other overnight. There are occasional spikes and dislocations, but the Fed has ways to get the Fed Funds rate under control very quickly. LIBOR, however, is a highly subjective rate based on the largest banks submitting their *opinion* on where they could borrow money for three months.

Normally, there is a moderate "term premium" in LIBOR. That is, you pay about 20 bps (0.2%) for the privilege of having your funding assured for three months compared to the projected cost of rolling your borrowing every night. Notice that extra premium or "LIBOR OIS spread" (OIS stands for overnight index swap) is calculated not against the current setting of overnight Federal Funds rate but against the projected forward rates, which can be calculated using the levels of Federal Funds futures.

However, "normally" didn't apply to March 2020. The funds rate was projected to keep dropping down, but the market started to project LIBOR to stay at the same level, thus pushing the LIBOR OIS spread wider.

By that point, I had already reversed my position in the long bonds, but my options in the front were still a significant position. All I had been doing there up to this point was taking profits. In particular, I was selling some EDH0, the front March contract.

My trading in early 2020 consisted almost exclusively of taking profits. On occasion, it seemed that I had given away fortunes untold solely through "risk management."

Trades	1/31/2020	3/6/2020	Profit in BPs
FFH0	98.44	99.1225	68.25
EDM0	98.495	99.38	88.5
EDM0 98.375 call	0.175	1.015	84
EDH0	98.36	99.065	70.5
EDH0 98.5 call	0.0225	0.575	55.25
7Y Treasury	1.4199	0.711	70.89

Gains in Basis Points of the Front-End Positions Held by March 6, 2020.

This is how much the front-end market rallied over the few weeks from the end of January. Notice in particular that the calls on EDH0 had appreciated twenty-five times!

After the rate cut of March 3, I felt I had a license to kill. There was no longer a need to hedge or take profits. Surely, LIBOR had no path but to go down, as the Fed was pumping liquidity.

So I started to reverse my hedges and once again buy March Eurodollar contracts higher than I had sold them only days ago. This turnaround was not a mistake in itself. As I have discussed before, one shouldn't get hung up on where one sold or bought something recently. One should always try to do the best forward-looking trades based on the current environment and current available information. So pressing risk when the tide rises in your favor is not only valid but often necessary.

The danger in this approach in betting on March lay in the extremely short-term nature of the trade. I knew that no matter the scope of the crisis, sooner or later the Fed would get a handle on the funding. But how long would it take?

The LIBOR OIS spread had widened in previous times of uncertainty, such as the 1998 crisis, Y2K, or 9/11. It really exploded in August 2007 during the first financial markets freeze-up.

I felt confident, though, that the banks were in good shape and the GFC-like funding crisis was not about to happen, so I charged forward.

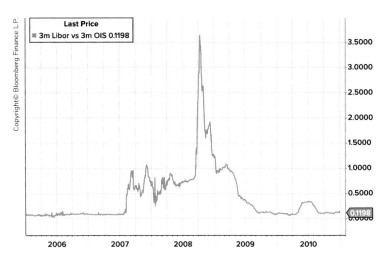

The Spread between Three-Month LIBOR and Three-Month Overnight Index Swap (OIS) Spiked during the Global Financial Crisis (GFC).

9:36 AM QZ makes ser **March 6th, 2020** ⌄

h0 fra/ois around 44

9:39 AM **CK** 2500 limit on the ▇▇ thats why you were rejected

i'm having them up to 3k, one se

*sec

9:40 AM QZ we do short edh0

9:41 AM **CK** ok you can reload the EDH0

limit is 3,000x now

9:41 AM QZ short 2964

across all port

9:42 AM **Christopher Lutton** that was fast

9:43 AM **CK** i'm sure you saw but the 1500x EDH0 is done at 99.10\

remaining 1500 done at 99.0875

9:44 AM Alex Gurevich Yes funky!

9:45 AM **Christopher Lutton** did you pull and re-insert

9:45 AM **CK** we can thank ███'s limits for the extra 2 ticks we saved

9:45 AM **Christopher Lutton** or staggered it?

haha

9:45 AM Alex Gurevich I staggered

9:46 AM **Christopher Lutton** sneaky. love it

9:46 AM **CK** Alex, fwiw, if you get stuck on limits ██ Futures chat can rectify pretty quickly but as you are clearly adept at dealing w these issues, cutting the order in 25% or 50% will resolve it just the same

9:46 AM Alex Gurevich About to start driving v

At this point, I was taking off for the weekend. I still had no hesitation about attending FogCon in Walnut Creek, my favorite local science-fiction convention and an annual event to which I very much looked forward.

Of course, taking advantage of Tesla autopilot, I stayed connected to the trade chat and continued to think about the markets.

March 6th, 2020 ⌄

9:46 AM Alex Gurevich About to start driving v

9:46 AM **CK** less human interaction, same result

k

anything you want us to work / keep an eye on?

9:47 AM **Christopher Lutton** PLEASE NO ONE TEXTING GUY WITH QUASI - AI BATTERY CAR

Alex, Eyes on road please!! No prep work for FogCon

10:01 AM	Alex Gurevich It another 3,000 March at 7 or better. Standard.
	Buy
10:02 AM	CK buying another 3k EDH0 at 99.07 or better
	loading
	working at 7

10:22 AM	CK thats done
11:28 AM	Alex Gurevich Did it bounce?
11:31 AM	CK nope
	03/03.5 now
11:34 AM	Alex Gurevich Let's buy more then... another 3000.
	Even if libor jumps on Monday it will have time to come down again.

March continued to drift down as I bought it, while LIBOR was now projected to go *up,* reflecting fears about availability of borrowing. Such dislocations represented a liquidity squeeze. Every crisis starts with fear and ends with necessity. In the beginning, people start selling their stocks and other risk assets and hoarding cash, as they recognize mounting problems such as the pandemic. The subsequent cash drain, the difficulty of obtaining credit, and the margin calls create a snowball effect whereby market players have no choice but to retrench regardless of their market view.

I spoke about the effect of involuntary market flows in my last book. The efficient-markets theory and behavioral finance operate on the assumption that market participants transact (or do not transact) as they *choose* to, rationally or irrationally. The assumption breaks down in a fashion similar to the Newtonian mechanics. The theory describes the financial system well when the market moves on a "normal" scale and at a "normal" velocity. But if the events suddenly accelerate to a "relativistic" speed or the volume of "forced" transactions distorts the financial continuum, a very different, Einsteinian mechanics arises.

I saw this distorted continuum as an opportunity and increased my bet further.

---

down again.   March 6th, 2020 ⌄

11:35 AM **CK** k

i'm 03 bid

11:45 AM Alex Gurevich K

11:56 AM Alex Gurevich .035 is fine use your judgement

11:56 AM **CK** yup

just sitting <4

1:01 PM **CK** ntg done on the last bit of EDH0, bounced to 07 into the close....also ntg done on DEDZ4

stocks went from 4% down to 1.5% down in the last hour of the day btw

whacky liquidity so we might get lucky on the EDH0 into 2pm but point is that it has calmed a bit since we spoke

---

1:05 PM Alex Gurevich Ok

1:10 PM QZ CAD spread blew out as well. But market choppy, let us know if you still have interest in moving some CNM0 to swaps for ■

1:15 PM Alex Gurevich How far did it go? I assume for this afternoon trading is done?

1:16 PM QZ 4.5-5bp, probably drying up now, can take it up on
Monday morning

1:18 PM Alex Gurevich Probably worth doing the switch. At for
1/2 of what we have in ███. But don't need to push
against absence of liquidity.

1:18 PM **CK** cool

seems worth it at these levels

liquidity wise we def wait until Monday but if we are
here or better we'll do 50% in ███

1:21 PM Alex Gurevich Ok

1:21 PM **CK** futs close in 10min and OTC is wide at this time even
in an ordinary day/week

The day closed with a discussion of Canadian rates and swaps and
dividend futures (DEDZ), which would come to the fore later.

In the first week of March, it felt like all my efforts of the past
few years had come to fruition. I had been proven right about the
interest rates without giving ground on my other positions.

If I were to stop the year right there, it would have been one of
my best years of trading. But, of course, stopping was nowhere in
the same galaxy as my thinking. Crisis, recession, recovery...This
is where the greatest dislocations and greatest opportunities are
to be found. I was dealt a strong hand. I fully intended to pyramid
my gains.

CHAPTER 5

WEEK 2: THE LOSS OF INNOCENCE

THE SCI-FI CONVENTION WAS A GREAT WAY TO PUT ASIDE THE market stress and related concerns for a few days. But unlike at *The Last Party*, I was not willing to hug old acquaintances or even shake hands. My name tag labeled with "minimizing hugs" made its way onto Facebook. Out-of-towners were surprised at how cautious Bay Area residents were. It turned out we were ahead of the curve.

Speaking of the curve and speaking of science fiction, I used an analogy earlier about how the black hole of the pandemic was curving financial spacetime in early March. That Sunday afternoon, we got so close to the event horizon that the tidal gravity tore apart the coherent structure of the markets.

Over the weekend, the reality of the imminent global shutdown and the blow to global travel and commerce had settled in. From the time stamps, it appears I started working before even returning from the convention.

MARCH 8: SUNDAY EVENING

The session from the evening of March 8 through daytime March 9 proved remarkable. That trading day was the last one belonging to an age now long gone: the era of COVID innocence.

The oil prices gapped down on the open, eventually losing almost 19 percent on the day. The currencies of oil-producing countries, such as Mexico, Canada, and Russia, started to fall like dominos. I was taking profits on my short Canadian dollar position and buying more of the Mexican peso. Overall, I was getting less long the US dollar based on the idea that the central bank liquidity would overcome the dollar shortage.

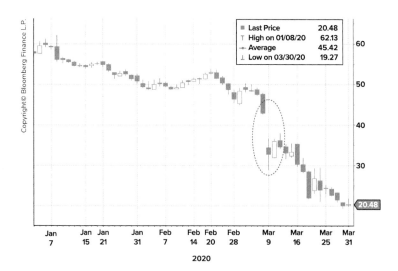

The Front WTI[12] Crude Oil Contract Price January 1, 2020–March 31, 2020: The red circle shows the down gap on March 8.

---

12 West Texas Intermediate (WTI) is a light, sweet crude oil that acts as the benchmark for US produced oil.

March 8th, 2020 ⌄

1:04 PM **Christopher Lutton** Mexico, changing my thoughts
around mexico, thinking much higher USDMXN and
much steeper curve
Word doc can be found here
https://honteadvisors.app.box.com/file/630298881245
PDF can be found here
https://honteadvisors.app.box.com/file/630298624816

Also in your email

PDF ▾

 _Cautious_Mexico.pdf
499 kB PDF

HonTe ██████████
Author: C Lutton
Trade Highlight #001: March 8, 2020

If US moves into recession, USDMXN could move much higher, curve steeper

- Economics: As one of the most open economies in the region, Mexico is the most exposed to a slowdown in the US. Mexico's economic slowdown was apparent prior to the Coronavirus.
- EMFX: While MXN has traded ~9% cheaper since early January, the peso depreciated by >20% in summer '98 & by >55% from mid-'08 to March '09. Past corrections from large dislocations happened when S&P turned up.
- RATES: MX rate curve is at the flat end of its ranges as Banxico historically waits too long before it cuts more aggressively.

Summary

Assuming US rates are accurately projecting the US & global growth slowdown, countries on weaker economic footing or with important bilateral linkages to the US will be increasingly vulnerable. As one of the most open economies in the region, Mexico's economy is exposed to a slowdown in global trade, and more specifically, to a downturn in US economic activity.

3:07 PM Alex Gurevich Add 60 PE standard

3:08 PM **CK** Nice note thanks for writing that up. All good points.
The oil point is tricky as you note: Mex is both a net
energy importer and has a huge annual oil hedge that
protects their budget BUT the market doesn't
necessarily consider these things when in full panic
mode and tends to revert to prior historical precedent
(when MX still was a net exporter). Certainly think there
is space for this to keep running weaker, which can
provide better entry, but I think we need to decide how
substantive we think this will be. Def a leveraged play to

US and risk and global trade. Will revert back further tomorrow on the more specific points

K

(On the PE)

3:09 PM Alex Gurevich Reduce 60 CD at equivalent of 1.36

3:12 PM **CK** K I'm on mobile right now, bear w me one sec. 1.3595 last high I saw

3:19 PM **CK** PE is done at 70 MX equiv. CD is still working at 1.36 equiv

👍 1   ☺⁺

3:54 PM **CK** Mx just gapped to 21.30 FYI

CD is done

4:03 PM **Christopher Lutton** is MAV about right?

4:05 PM **QZ** Checking

4:06 PM **Christopher Lutton** Thx, i guess CAN bonds wouldn't be included

showing +28m

4:08 PM **QZ** I don't think it is right

Not sure about the swap curve

Don't think it's updating properly

way off, only US bond futures are updated

4:12 PM **Christopher Lutton** copy. seemed wrong

To my chagrin, given that I had already reversed my position in the long end, the bonds managed to leave their previous massive rally in the dust.

Our P/L began to look funky with the offsetting swap position not properly updated in the Asian time zone. Such kinks are not that unusual; this time, they were exacerbated by the size of the move but still easily resolvable. We could estimate our gains fairly easily and see the screen had given us a wrong number.

At this point, Qin made a very sensible suggestion. With the market now pricing at 75 bps (0.75%) cut on March 18, the Eurodollar contract (EDH0) we had loaded up on Friday bounced, despite the LIBOR setting staying high. The market was beginning to price my thinking that the Fed would drive short-term funding rate down very quickly. Qin's thinking, soon to be proven correct, was that the risk now lay with LIBOR getting "sticky" and disappointing my hopes.

My focus, however, was on bottom-fishing, and I was not too concerned about LIBOR.

4:12 PM **Christopher I** March 8th, 2020 ˅ wrong

4:13 PM QZ EDH0 trading 99.17. Shall we take some profit in case credit blows out and libor does not set down aggressively?

4:23 PM **CK** Mx back to within reason

5:50 PM Alex Gurevich Not so worried about libor here but thinking

Let out on Nikkei 30 large or 60 small standard

Also open to adding PE we are doing very small increments

5:54 PM **CK** To be clear on Nikkei you want to buy $6mm equiv around here?

5:54 PM Alex Gurevich Correct

We were looking for sub 20,000 forever.

6:00 PM **CK** Yup on the same page

6:07 PM **CK** NK done

Down to revisit at 21.10 equiv on PE, the 21.30 print earlier was a little ahead of itself

6:51 PM **Christopher Lutton** CK i'm on this thread

7:17 PM **CK** 21.87 equiv avg on the last 240x Mex we added....20.70 for the 60x we added first thing today

---

7:27 PM **CK** 10pm PST RUB OTC opens i believe though the daylight savings is really inconveniently timed for being certain....RUH0 Curncy is the future, which is open and seems to imply 73ish $RUB...ie 7% bounce from 68.50 close OTC market

its trading 1x1 (30 contracts is $1mio it appears) 0.5% wide so if we want to do anything it will have to be level specific until OTC mkt opens

7:39 PM **CK** NKH0 19500 otherwise things are nervously stable for the moment since we last spoke....i'm stepping away from screens for 30min for dinner but have my mobile so call me direct if need

👍 1   😊⁺

9:13 PM Alex Gurevich Thinking July WTI under $30? Or do you prefer Brent?

9:15 PM **CK** I'm indifferent there. The US shale guys may get fully washed out if this keeps up so may be further downside.

FYI computer just kicked me out so flying a bit blind again

9:16 PM Alex Gurevich I'll do it

9:16 PM **CK** K ty

9:30 PM **Christopher Lutton** ▮ did say on their conference call
that base case now for them was $30, and thought it
there was enough of a spat around supply could see
$20. There was a lot of talk that politically bad (from
russian perspective) for US shale companies to go
bankrupt. Instead, they would prefer zombie companies
(so something around $40 better).

9:36 PM Alex Gurevich Adding to silver (a little)

9:39 PM **CK** K great

10:10 PM **Tony Peng** Trend portfolio positions for Monday
3/8/2020: CD1 Curncy has turned from neutral to
positive (Bearish USDCAD). BP1 Curncy has got weaker
bullish signal from the model. Overall model leverage
went down to 5.63 from 5.72. Everything else has
remained the same.

image.png ▾

10:18 PM **CK** Well recvd

I have discussed earlier how I was not afraid to buy risk assets
because of a broader risk negative slant to my portfolio.
However, there is another theme here, having to do with position accumulation.

I have noticed that the majority of managers in my space try to invest in an asset when they see a catalyst for favorable price action, saying things like, "I know the XYZ will be higher in five years and I am planning to buy it, but currently the flows are adverse, so I will wait for more of a pullback before entering the position."

This approach is not a priori wrong, but in my opinion, it causes a lot of investors to miss big trades, which they have correctly identified. This is what I wrote in TNPT:

> But opportunities to capture a massive move of a developed market currency are very rare. You will only have a few of those in your career.
>
> So if you have a profitable short-term technical strategy - by all means, trade it on its own value. But overlaying a rare and valuable long-horizon macro call with tight stops and technical entry points will only "muddy-up" your risk profile and create a potential for missing your move.

I didn't know how the pandemic would play out, how far down the risk assets could fall, or how long it would take them to recover. It was sufficient to know that they *would* recover because policymakers were giving them no choice. All I needed to do was to size my positions to survive the interim volatility, and the *Shield against Uncertainty* was deployed.

This is how I defined my approach to position sizing in TNPT:

> Thus, I introduce the concept of *psychologically neutral positioning.*

Your "core" position - the size of the trade you should gravitate towards over the long horizon should be psychologically neutral. When you are exactly at your core position, on a given day you don't worry about the price action:

If the market doesn't do much, no problem. Your capital is not completely tied up and you can afford to wait.

If the market moves in your favor, great. You make money quickly and can sooner move on to the next trade.

If the market goes against you, even better. You might get a great entry point to increase your position and make even more money.

The core position should be considerably smaller than your "maximum" position. I define the maximum position as the most you can hold without fear of being stopped out by a violent correction. There is no precise formula what the maximum position should be either - you will have to use your judgement.

If you have the maximum on, there is no space to add, so you will certainly be hoping for the market to go in your favor.

At the time, I believed my exposure to risk assets was well below "core" and I welcomed a further rout to keep accumulating. My scope of assets to acquire kept expanding; besides EM currencies, it now included equity index futures (Nikkei), European dividend futures (DEDZ), and precious metals.

MARCH 9: MONDAY MORNING

(so somethir   March 8th, 2020 ⌄   .

9:36 PM Alex Gurevich Adding to silver (a little)

9:39 PM **CK** K great

2:16 AM Alex Gurevich Put on DEDZ2, added DEDZ4. Got 300 more to route below 87 on DEDZ4. If ruble is 74 or worse let's put on $6mm standard. Use futures if you can. (if only forwards can $1.5mm for ██, but I think futures are décent.

Also double (another $6mm) Nikkei if it dips below 19,000 again

2:37 AM Alex Gurevich And also let's look at Canadian swap spreads in the morning...

3:52 AM Alex Gurevich Nikkei is routed. One batch of DEDZ4 still outstanding.

Nikkei filled.

5:47 AM **CK** K taking a look at RUB. BRL 4.75 open fwiw

5:59 AM Alex Gurevich There were decent futures last time. Also I started to be denied on DEDZ4, do we have an overall risk limit there? I can go into other maturities...

6:00 AM **CK** I upped that limit earlier today to 1500x

Was at 1000 I think, I can further up from that if need be

6:00 AM Alex Gurevich When ruble is executed check oil and consider taking profits.

Order limit or positon limit?

6:01 AM **CK** It was a daily limit

6:02 AM Alex Gurevich Ah yes up that further of possible. And route the last DEDZ badge if can do 97 or better...

6:11 AM **CK** RUB is done

DEDZ4 I am buying 300x at better than 87 to be clear?

6:20 AM **CK** covering CLN0 as we speak

will do last batch of DEDZ4 in a moment (more static market)

6:22 AM QZ Fed increased repo operation 100 bln or more overnight, 20 billion or more for two-week term
3m Libor set lower by 12 bp

image.png ▼

image.png ▼

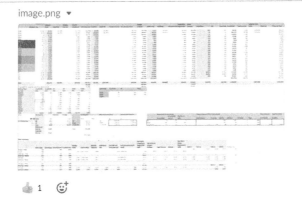

👍 1 😃⁺

Cad Spread market is sketchy at the moment. 10y marked at 48 (+3.5bp), no trading. Will check later

6:24 AM **CK** CLN0 (WTI July) is fully covered, sold 120x @ 33.85

$500k banked on that trade

😶 1 😃⁺

6:37 AM **CK** 1/3rd of the DEDZ4 bought at 85.20

2/3rd bought

wait to see equity moves at S&P open before doing the last 1/3rd

*S&P re-open

Notice the time stamps in this chat: all of us worked through the night. My memory is that after executing a few trades, I went back to bed. I wasn't setting an alarm clock. The adrenaline in my system was causing me to pop up every hour.

Once upon a time, back in high school, I wrote a line of poetry, which roughly translates to "nerves being stretched by success." (Yes, I wrote poetry in high school as well.) At this point, my nerves were definitely being stretched as the exhilaration of my portfolio performance wired me up to an almost unhealthy degree.

Fortunately, my childhood training in academic competitions and strategic gaming (which inspired the aforementioned line) came in handy. I continued to function with clarity. The constant chatter and sanity checks with my team members helped me stay grounded.

I've written before about how an instant response to events will only deliver an inconsistent advantage. Furthermore, in the beginning of the process of taking profits or accumulating positions, almost by definition, it appears that you are only doing damage and that you would be better off staying asleep. That could be the case in a normal market but not inside the accretion disk of a pandemic black hole.

When I formulate my strategy pertaining to a given asset, I decide in advance at which levels I will look to add to my position or to take profits. Usually, months pass between such adjustments, and it takes years for a specific theme to play out.

The Time Warp

In the time warp of March 2020, years turned into hours and months into minutes. New levels were being constantly achieved.

Thus, to implement my plans faithfully, I *had* to trade through the night. And although, in the short run, I may regret certain position adjustments, in the long run, I rarely regret adhering to my strategy rigorously.

The oil "day trade" is an example. I had bought oil earlier in the night, not because I was targeting a short-term price swing, but because it had reached a level that I considered cheap on a long horizon. And within hours, it was no longer so cheap.

---

*S&P re-ope   March 9th, 2020 ⌄

6:50 AM **CK** low @ 2715 (20% down level)...holding there for now

70x DEDZ4 still working

6:53 AM Alex Gurevich Get the next 300 batch working

6:53 AM **CK** k

ill be 85 bid unless you care otherwise

6:54 AM Alex Gurevich Yes sounds good

6:59 AM **CK** to summarize what has happened this AM: 1) bought RUB, $6mio worth in RUH0 @ 1.3421 (~74.40 equiv USDRUB spot, which is not open today due to holiday)......2) sold 120x CLN0 @ 33.85, we are flat crude currently....3) we have bought 230x DEDZ4 @ 85.2, currently on bid for 70x @ 85.20 & another 300x @ 85.00.....4) CAD invoice in our favor but nobody showing any prices

---

7:15 AM Alex Gurevich Where is invoice?

Theoretically...

Are there no prices on electronic swap trading?

7:15 AM QZ No

46

sorry one sec

7:16 AM Alex Gurevich Hmmm

FFH0 cane off a little bit was pricing 100% of 100bps cut?

Or à other inter meeting now?

7:17 AM QZ invoice is around 50

theoretically

7:18 AM Alex Gurevich But not tradable?

7:18 AM QZ let me check again

Might be easier to trade CNM0 vs CAD 10y swap rate

7:22 AM Alex Gurevich That's what I thought…

What about FFH0 - it seems just wrong

7:23 AM CK softer FFH0 in last 1hr imho is just trading tick for tick w the bounce in S&P (4% from the lows)

see you in the FFH0, nice

7:25 AM QZ Bloomberg marks CAD 10yr much higher seeing 0.991

While jumping between asset classes, I started to become aware of how much more easing was priced into the March Fed Funds (FFH0). The market was beginning to expect another intermeeting easing, which seemed excessive to me at the moment. My idea was to take profits and maybe even reverse the position on March Fed Funds, while keeping, or even increasing, the bet on March Eurodollars (EDH0).

In addition, I was accumulating dividend futures as they kept falling. My attention also stayed on Canadian invoice spread (the difference between Canadian swap rates and bond futures).

8:10 AM Alex Gurevich Try to buy 300 2023 at 88. The odd year curve is priced in

Missed the FFH0 mis price

8:11 AM CK yea handful of things completely out of whack shortly before/after equity close

we'll get the next one

working 300x bid @ 88.00 in DEDZ3

8:12 AM Alex Gurevich They probably won't do another inter meeting. So current pricing is virtually impossible.

8:12 AM CK agree, we should be fading that

8:12 AM QZ it was pricing in inter meeting this week

8:13 AM CK we are one week from next FOMC

8:13 AM Alex Gurevich My base case is now 75 at the meeting.

8:14 AM Christopher Lutton Is that because you think they want to get to QE as quickly as possible?

Is that 75 plus some QE ?

8:17 AM Alex Gurevich Yes could be 100bps at meeting but that's fairly radical

 1

8:21 AM QZ Trying to piece together CNM0 vs cad 10y, at least 1.5 bp from mid

let us know if you would to do it

roughly 48 on invoice, but choppy

8:25 AM Christopher Lutton Thx color Alex

8:30 AM QZ my CNM0 is delayed,

8:35 AM QZ mid invoice spread right now is 46.5, 10y spread marked at 51

8:59 AM **CK** alex, let us know if you want us to trade any of the invoice...its wide but good level, maybe we just do half today?

which is 265x (30k CAD DV01)

we will likely leg it on our own if we do, which would be tighter than dealer prices

9:34 AM **CK** DEDZ3 @ 88 is done

9:37 AM Alex Gurevich Good.

Let's try to add 300 to DEDZ4 at 84 or better before it closes.

9:41 AM **CK** roger that

9:42 AM Alex Gurevich Canada bonds came off 4 points from highs...

9:43 AM **CK** yea nuts

done on the DEDZ4

83.70

9:44 AM Alex Gurevich Another 300 83 bid.

9:45 AM **CK** roger

half done

the ole smash equities into the EU close routine

10:04 AM Alex Gurevich Spreads snapped back hard in US I assume same in Canada?

10:05 AM QZ 49.25 for 10s

vs 51 earlier

10:05 AM Alex Gurevich TIPS are u derapeforming with B/E below 1%. Will be a hard hit on the front to inflation from energy

51 was not really exécutable? Have things come down maybe we can do something at 49? Since US is moving in the other direction...

10:08 AM QZ We can piece it together buy receiving 10s vs selling CN. They showed us roughly 1.5 from mid from 10y rate the last time we asked

Bid/offer still wide. Can give it another try

10:09 AM Alex Gurevich They don't offer package - we could leave them an order if package...

10:10 AM QZ copy. do full size or half

530 CNM0 is full size

10:18 AM Alex Gurevich Half soze

10:18 AM **CK** k

10:29 AM **CK** Trend Model executed @ 7:45AM PST:

image.png ▾

EXECUTION					
Security	Action	Qty	LH	OA	Fill
CDM0 Curncy	Buy	26	13	13	73.7735
NVM0 Curncy	Sell	-8	-4	-4	63.91
ADM0 Curncy	Sell	-6	-3	-3	66.41
BPM0 Curncy	Buy	42	21	21	131.286
TYM0 Comdty	Buy	4	2	2	139-16
XMM0 Comdty	Buy	4	2	2	99.39375
CNM0 Comdty	Buy	2	1	1	149.61
RXM0 Comdty	Buy	2	1	1	178.87

The global stock market continued to slide, with the circuit breakers causing temporary trading halts. While earlier on Sunday I was rejoicing in buying Nikkei below 20,000, now the price target of 18,000 (10 percent lower!) was coming into focus.

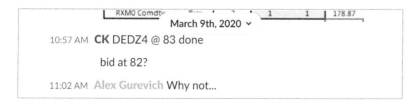

| RXM0 Comdty | | | 1 | 1 | 178.87 |

March 9th, 2020 ▾

10:57 AM **CK** DEDZ4 @ 83 done

bid at 82?

11:02 AM Alex Gurevich Why not...

11:07 AM **CK** its working, we'll see what happen

stocks falling off a cliff again

11:38 AM QZ Equity and EM about 50% of risk limit

12:23 PM Alex Gurevich Ok.

3:17 PM **CK** ok on Nikkei, will keep an eye on 18,000

(in other chat)

3:18 PM QZ Sorting out excess cash. Cash is low as far as I see. A lot excess equity is in repo treasuries while cleared OTC is taking up a lot of cash. Just something to be aware in case of option buying interest

---

3:19 PM Alex Gurevich Low???

Well when March options roll out we should h ave an influx...

3:21 PM QZ I am only talking about ██████,

Yes. Till 16th

5:05 PM Alex Gurevich The back end flattening is very strong. 30yr swap almost on top of 10yr. Given rates at 0. Seems a very reasonable carry trade to put a DV01 neutral steepener. There is convexity risk in this trade though...

5:13 PM **Christopher Lutton** more academic question, so not something for today but curious what the convexity risk is

---

5:18 PM **Christopher Lutton** ah, i think i just visualized it. If entire 10s 30s shifted down to 2s (another 20bp), the 30 year paid position would start to get big bigger than the 10yr so you'd have to reduce the paid position (or increase the 10s receiver along the way)

6:00 PM Alex Gurevich Some Equity futures such as NKH0 are delayed on my bbg - can we splurge on real time data?

> 6:01 PM **CK** 19.5k market now....which equity futures do you need beyond the NKH0?
>
> 6:02 PM **Christopher Lutton** He should have all of WEIF but Joann can you permission if you tell her ticker/exchange. That Nikkei he has real-time for is not what you're trading
>
> 6:05 PM Alex Gurevich I know where they are now because Nikkei is open. Those are my high priority since we trade them to have when Japanese market is closed.

The movements of various parts of the portfolio were so rapid and disconnected (remember tidal gravity!) that despite making boatloads of money, we were actually finding ourselves short on cash in some of the accounts.

A Crazy Day

The session on March 9 ended here. The S&P 500 was down 7.6 percent on the day—the worst drop since December 2008. The bond price action, however, was even more astonishing. The demand to park money in the safest asset in the world became insensitive to the economic yield.

The thirty-year bond yield fell 29 bps (0.29%), one of the largest rallies ever, but even this number belies the violence of what happened overnight.

Swaps followed bonds, and given the persistently negative long-term swap spread, at some point the thirty-year swap rate touched 0.40%. The three-month LIBOR reference rate for the swap was still 0.768%.

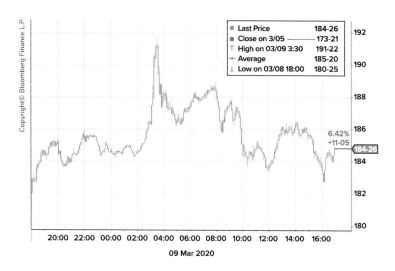

March 8, 2020 Overnight Price Action: At one point during the overnight session, measured from March 8, 2020 18:00 to March 9, 2020, US Treasury Classic Bond Future rallied almost eleven big figures (6 percent).

Characteristic of the market disconnect on that day, the option we bought on the long-dated rates going higher was not suffering at all. Despite the underlying making a huge move against me, the implied volatility spiked so much that it made up for the loss.

My first experience of a crisis was the summer of 1998. Then, the price action was entirely different: the bonds were surging while swaps were moving in the opposite direction, causing the swap spreads to explode upward.

There was a logic to that credit widening. Prior to the 1998 crisis, a common position for investors was to be long "spread products," such as corporate or EM bonds and short treasuries against it. The asinine idea was to hedge the interest rate risk and pocket the spread.

The Russian debt default introduced the coordinated sell-off of risk assets—price action hitherto unfamiliar to market participants. The investors, such as the infamous LTCM,[13] experienced a double whammy as the bonds they were short rallied and the assets they held sold off. Their "hedge" only made things worse.

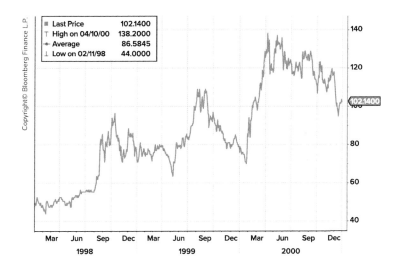

USD Ten-Year Swap Spread 1998–2000: The spread widened during the 1998 crisis and continued to trade higher afterward.

Notice the original swap spread explosion in 1998 did not fade; instead, the swap spreads continued to march higher, peaking in March 2000.

---

13 Long Term Capital Management (LTCM) was a hedge fund founded in 1993 by John Meriwether. The fund's initial strategy was engaging in fixed-income arbitrage by taking advantage of discrepancies between bond prices but eventually expanded to other asset classes. The Russian debt crisis in 1998 led to a huge rise in swap spreads (a measure of risk premium) and caused massive losses within LTCM's portfolio. The Fed had to step in to stave off potential global financial contagion. A loan fund, composed of a consortium of Wall Street banks, was created to bail out LTCM in September 1998.

The spread dynamics were very different during the GFC. Despite a huge widening of the LIBOR OIS spread (on a much greater scale than anything in the last few decades, including 2020), the spike in the thirty-year spread was relatively mild and had reversed even before the 2008 crisis fully arrived.

As I discussed earlier, this new market paradigm involving negative long-term spreads still persists, despite making little economic sense.

Economic sense, though, gave way to involuntary flows, such as mortgage convexity hedging.

In retrospect, paying the thirty-year swap rate 0.40% or anywhere in the neighborhood (no matter how hard it would have been to do that in the Asian session) would have been a no-brainer. But I blame myself less for missing the chance to add to the trade at that specific point than for the April Fed Funds debacle.

The swap trade was less clear cut. By accumulating positions, I would expose myself to an unlimited downside if the swap rates (not to be confused with swap spreads) were pushed into negative territory.

Overall, I did what I could to take advantage of the market disruptions. It was not possible to catch every single opportunity.

The Full Trade Log

Here is the log of all trades performed by HonTe Advisors during the March 9 trading session. Normally, our turnover is very low, and any of the transactions below would occasion days of discussion prior to execution. These were not "normal" times.

Tkt #	Trd Dt	Exchange Code	Ticker	Short Note 6	Amount (G)	Price	Security Type	Stl Date	Trtime
18610	3/9/2020	NYM	CLN0	B	60	29.549667	Physical commodity future.	3/9/2020	12:22:15 AM
18611	3/9/2020	NYM	CLN0	B	32	29.549667	Physical commodity future.	3/9/2020	12:22:15 AM
18612	3/9/2020	NYM	CLN0	B	28	29.549667	Physical commodity future.	3/9/2020	12:22:16 AM
18619	3/9/2020	CMX	SIK0	B	30	16.809333	Physical commodity future.	3/9/2020	12:37:01 AM
18620	3/9/2020	CMX	SIK0	B	16	16.809333	Physical commodity future.	3/9/2020	12:37:01 AM
18621	3/9/2020	CMX	SIK0	B	14	16.809333	Physical commodity future.	3/9/2020	12:37:01 AM
18634	3/9/2020	EUX	DEDZ2	B	7	97.9	Physical index future.	3/9/2020	4:57:02 AM
18635	3/9/2020	EUX	DEDZ2	B	4	97.9	Physical index future.	3/9/2020	4:57:02 AM
18636	3/9/2020	EUX	DEDZ2	B	4	97.9	Physical index future.	3/9/2020	4:57:02 AM
18639	3/9/2020	EUX	DEDZ2	B	143	98.2	Physical index future.	3/9/2020	5:08:58 AM
18640	3/9/2020	EUX	DEDZ2	B	76	98.2	Physical index future.	3/9/2020	5:08:58 AM
18641	3/9/2020	EUX	DEDZ2	B	66	98.2	Physical index future.	3/9/2020	5:08:58 AM
18644	3/9/2020	EUX	DEDZ4	B	150	87.6	Physical index future.	3/9/2020	6:15:43 AM
18645	3/9/2020	EUX	DEDZ4	B	80	87.6	Physical index future.	3/9/2020	6:15:43 AM
18646	3/9/2020	EUX	DEDZ4	B	70	87.6	Physical index future.	3/9/2020	6:15:43 AM
18653	3/9/2020	OSE	NKH0	B	15	18980	Physical index future.	3/10/2020	6:53:12 AM
18654	3/9/2020	OSE	NKH0	B	8	18980	Physical index future.	3/10/2020	6:53:13 AM
18655	3/9/2020	OSE	NKH0	B	7	18980	Physical index future.	3/10/2020	6:53:13 AM
18658	3/9/2020	EUX	DEDZ2	B	150	98	Physical index future.	3/9/2020	8:24:23 AM

Tkt #	Trd Dt	Exchange Code	Ticker	Short Note 6	Amount (G)	Price	Security Type	Stl Date	Trtime
18659	3/9/2020	EUX	DEDZ2	B	80	98	Physical index future.	3/9/2020	8:24:24 AM
18660	3/9/2020	EUX	DEDZ2	B	70	98	Physical index future.	3/9/2020	8:24:24 AM
18672	3/9/2020	CME	RUH0	B	42	1.342103	Currency future.	3/9/2020	9:11:31 AM
18673	3/9/2020	CME	RUH0	B	90	1.342103	Currency future.	3/9/2020	9:11:31 AM
18674	3/9/2020	CME	RUH0	B	48	1.342103	Currency future.	3/9/2020	9:11:31 AM
18681	3/9/2020	NYM	CLN0	S	13	33.9	Physical commodity future.	3/9/2020	9:22:53 AM
18682	3/9/2020	NYM	CLN0	S	27	33.9	Physical commodity future.	3/9/2020	9:22:53 AM
18683	3/9/2020	NYM	CLN0	S	15	33.9	Physical commodity future.	3/9/2020	9:22:53 AM
18686	3/9/2020	NYM	CLN0	S	15	33.8	Physical commodity future.	3/9/2020	9:23:57 AM
18687	3/9/2020	NYM	CLN0	S	33	33.8	Physical commodity future.	3/9/2020	9:23:57 AM
18688	3/9/2020	NYM	CLN0	S	17	33.8	Physical commodity future.	3/9/2020	9:23:57 AM
18695	3/9/2020	EUX	DEDZ4	B	5	85.3	Physical index future.	3/9/2020	9:34:00 AM
18696	3/9/2020	EUX	DEDZ4	B	10	85.3	Physical index future.	3/9/2020	9:34:01 AM
18697	3/9/2020	EUX	DEDZ4	B	5	85.3	Physical index future.	3/9/2020	9:34:01 AM
18700	3/9/2020	EUX	DEDZ4	B	19	85.2	Physical index future.	3/9/2020	9:36:38 AM
18701	3/9/2020	EUX	DEDZ4	B	40	85.2	Physical index future.	3/9/2020	9:36:38 AM
18702	3/9/2020	EUX	DEDZ4	B	21	85.2	Physical index future.	3/9/2020	9:36:38 AM
18705	3/9/2020	EUX	DEDZ4	B	23	85.2	Physical index future.	3/9/2020	9:37:12 AM
18706	3/9/2020	EUX	DEDZ4	B	50	85.2	Physical index future.	3/9/2020	9:37:12 AM
18707	3/9/2020	EUX	DEDZ4	B	27	85.2	Physical index future.	3/9/2020	9:37:12 AM

Tkt #	Trd Dt	Exchange Code	Ticker	Short Note 6	Amount (G)	Price	Security Type	Stl Date	Trtime
18768	3/9/2020	EUX	DEDZ4	B	23	85.2	Physical index future.	3/9/2020	10:45:21 AM
18769	3/9/2020	EUX	DEDZ4	B	50	85.2	Physical index future.	3/9/2020	10:45:21 AM
18770	3/9/2020	EUX	DEDZ4	B	27	85.2	Physical index future.	3/9/2020	10:45:21 AM
18797	3/9/2020	EUX	DEDZ4	B	70	85	Physical index future.	3/9/2020	11:04:36 AM
18798	3/9/2020	EUX	DEDZ4	B	150	85	Physical index future.	3/9/2020	11:04:36 AM
18799	3/9/2020	EUX	DEDZ4	B	80	85	Physical index future.	3/9/2020	11:04:36 AM
18806	3/9/2020	EUX	DEDZ3	B	70	88	Physical index future.	3/9/2020	12:24:34 PM
18807	3/9/2020	EUX	DEDZ3	B	150	88	Physical index future.	3/9/2020	12:24:34 PM

Tkt #	Trd Dt	Exchange Code	Ticker	Short Note 6	Amount (G)	Price	Security Type	Stl Date	Trtime
18808	3/9/2020	EUX	DEDZ3	B	80	88	Physical index future.	3/9/2020	12:24:35 PM
18825	3/9/2020	CBT	FFH0	S	11	99.3025	Financial commodity future.	3/9/2020	12:38:58 PM
18826	3/9/2020	CBT	FFH0	S	6	99.3025	Financial commodity future.	3/9/2020	12:38:59 PM
18827	3/9/2020	CBT	FFH0	S	5	99.3025	Financial commodity future.	3/9/2020	12:38:59 PM
18843	3/9/2020	EUX	DEDZ4	B	70	83.7	Physical index future.	3/9/2020	12:44:09 PM
18844	3/9/2020	EUX	DEDZ4	B	150	83.7	Physical index future.	3/9/2020	12:44:09 PM
18845	3/9/2020	EUX	DEDZ4	B	80	83.7	Physical index future.	3/9/2020	12:44:09 PM
18858	3/9/2020	EUX	DEDZ4	B	70	83	Physical index future.	3/9/2020	1:41:48 PM
18859	3/9/2020	EUX	DEDZ4	B	150	83	Physical index future.	3/9/2020	1:41:48 PM

Tkt #	Trd Dt	Exchange Code	Ticker	Short Note 6	Amount (G)	Price	Security Type	Stl Date	Trtime
18860	3/9/2020	EUX	DEDZ4	B	80	83	Physical index future.	3/9/2020	1:41:48 PM
18568	3/9/2020		/IRS	B	25000	4.84	Swaption	3/10/2020	2:43:11 PM
18867	3/9/2020	CBT	FFH0	S	5	99.27	Financial commodity future.	3/9/2020	5:00:05 PM
18868	3/9/2020	CBT	FFH0	S	3	99.27	Financial commodity future.	3/9/2020	5:00:05 PM
18869	3/9/2020	CBT	FFH0	S	3	99.27	Financial commodity future.	3/9/2020	5:00:06 PM
18575	3/9/2020	OSE	NKH0	B	7	19860	Physical index future.	3/9/2020	9:07:13 PM
18576	3/9/2020	OSE	NKH0	B	15	19860	Physical index future.	3/9/2020	9:07:13 PM
18577	3/9/2020	OSE	NKH0	B	8	19860	Physical index future.	3/9/2020	9:07:13 PM
18579	3/9/2020	CME	PEH0	B	30	4.833	Currency future.	3/9/2020	9:53:26 PM
18580	3/9/2020	CME	PEH0	B	16	4.833	Currency future.	3/9/2020	9:53:26 PM
18581	3/9/2020	CME	PEH0	B	14	4.833	Currency future.	3/9/2020	9:53:27 PM
18588	3/9/2020	CME	PEH0	B	28	4.563192	Currency future.	3/8/2020	9:54:14 PM
18589	3/9/2020	CME	PEH0	B	60	4.563192	Currency future.	3/8/2020	9:54:14 PM
18590	3/9/2020	CME	PEH0	B	32	4.563192	Currency future.	3/8/2020	9:54:14 PM
18601	3/9/2020	CME	PEH0	B	28	4.579967	Currency future.	3/8/2020	9:56:47 PM
18602	3/9/2020	CME	PEH0	B	60	4.579967	Currency future.	3/8/2020	9:56:47 PM
18603	3/9/2020	CME	PEH0	B	32	4.579967	Currency future.	3/8/2020	9:56:48 PM

Our Full Trading Record on March 9, 2020.

The portfolio was way up. If paused on that day, March would have been a record month for our portfolio and, in itself, would have been considered a good performance for an entire year. But, as I mentioned before, pausing was not on my agenda.

Overnight, market sentiment reversed, causing US equity futures to halt trading limit-up in the middle of the night. Even with my transcripts, it is difficult for me to determine whether there was any particular reason for this change. Most likely, there wasn't.

Even when the direction of a river's current is clear, it forms eddies, spots where counterflows form. The faster the current, the more intense the turbulence and the more challenging to parse and analyze the counterflows.

The world, however, continued its inexorable spiral into the black hole; the indications were there.

Yes. Till 16th **March 9th, 2020** ⌄

5:05 PM Alex Gurevich The back end flattening is very strong. 30yr swap almost on top of 10yr. Given rates at 0. Seems a very reasonable carry trade to put a DV01 neutral steepener. There is convexity risk in this trade though...

5:13 PM **Christopher Lutton** more academic question, so not something for today but curious what the convexity risk is

5:18 PM **Christopher Lutton** ah, i think i just visualized it. If entire 10s 30s shifted down to 2s (another 20bp), the 30 year paid position would start to get big bigger than the 10yr so you'd have to reduce the paid position (or increase the 10s receiver along the way)

6:00 PM Alex Gurevich Some Equity futures such as NKH0 are delayed on my bbg - can we splurge on real time data?

6:01 PM **CK** 19.5k market now....which equity futures do you need beyond the NKH0?

6:02 PM **Christopher Lutton** He should have all of WEIF but Joann can you permission if you tell her ticker/exchange. That Nikkei he has real-time for is not what you're trading

6:05 PM Alex Gurevich I know where they are now because Nikkei is open. Those are my high priority since we trade them to have when Japanese market is closed.

The bonds sold off alongside the positive risk sentiment, but the swap rates didn't follow, causing the swap spreads to plunge even further into negative territory. In a testament to the market fracture, the LIBOR OIS spread widened, with LIBOR actually setting *higher*. Until this point, March contract levels had appeared to be disconnected from the fact that the daily LIBOR fixings were rapidly coming down.

MARCH 10: TUESDAY

The market gave me a clear warning that the funding pressures were rising. But to my detriment (spoiler!), I ignored that warning and kept betting that the liquidity would normalize. I continued fishing for EDH0.

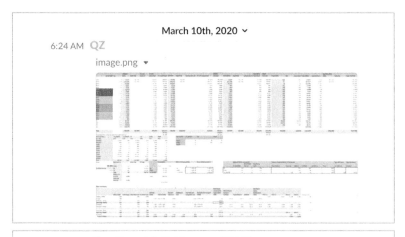

7:07 AM Alex Gurevich Put in more EDH0

7:08 AM QZ See the order to buy 3k

8:25 AM Joann Shie-Chen Hi Alex - I enabled your OSE (NKH0) data feed just now

if you can please log out and log into BBG again whenever you have a moment

8:48 AM Alex Gurevich Ok thx!

8:59 AM **CK** AUD squeeze below 65

basically back at Feb 28 / Mar 2 levels

9:14 AM Alex Gurevich We missed working DEDZ4. Try 82 again for 300.

9:15 AM **CK** roger

9:15 AM Alex Gurevich Also keep monitoring Canada invoice... I would like to free up some swap margins as we may have a chance to add to swap spread trades.

9:16 AM **CK** yea, watching, has moved a bit against us this AM

9:16 AM QZ will do

9:16 AM Alex Gurevich But it traded below 82 briefly. Let's stay on it.

9:17 AM **CK** got it re DEDZ4....meant invoice had moved against us

9:24 AM Alex Gurevich Cover 120 AUD futures around here. Standard allocation.

9:24 AM **CK** k

done

9:33 AM **CK** DEDZ4 is done

shall i presume 300 every 1.00 lower in DEDZ4 for now?

if so ill get the 300x working at 81.00

I started to take tiny profits on my Australian dollar short.

The price action in currency markets would prove extraordinary later in the month, but for now, it made complete sense.

The United States appeared less affected than other countries. The dollar rallied against the euro, reaching a high on February 20. When it became clear that the domestic economy wasn't "immune" to the virus and that the Fed was going to add liquidity, the dollar sold off, bottoming out on March 9. On the chart of euro, a higher number means higher euro/weaker dollar, while on the chart of yen, a higher number means weaker yen/stronger dollar; such are historical quoting conventions for the currencies.

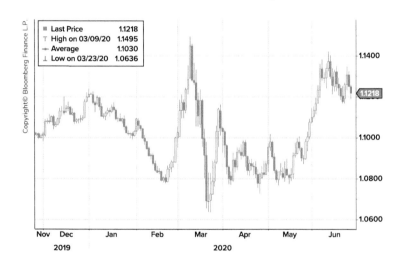

EURUSD December 2019–June 2020: The euro bottomed out on February 20, 2020, and reached a local high on March 9, 2020, and fell again in mid-March.

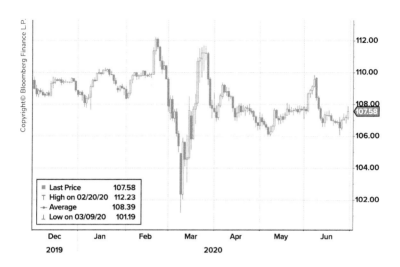

Spot USDJPY Candle Chart December 2019–June 2020: US dollar weakened against yen as COVID struck and quickly rebounded afterward.

It made sense that on March 10, when sentiments improved, the dollar rebounded as well (i.e., the euro in the EURUSD chart moved lower).

The relationship between the USD and EUR is not directly tied to the overall market sentiment. There are times when the United States is more of a safe haven, and there are times when Europe is.

There are currencies, however, that tend to be reliable risk barometers. During times of panic, investor cash tends to flood into Switzerland (CHF) and Japan (JPY), while MXN and other EM currencies perform better during good times.

This is how the current crisis was playing out. USDJPY plunged almost all the way down to 100 (lower number means stronger yen), marking a dollar low on March 9. A weak dollar was not good for our portfolio, since we were long against a variety of currencies including the yen and Swiss franc. But that was fine at the start of March because the gains from our interest rate positions had overwhelmed any currency setbacks.

A Secret Weapon

Thus far, I have focused on rate gains as the major driver of portfolio performance, with everything else being an afterthought. I had, however, another secret weapon: Australian dollar (AUD or Aussie).

Australia (somewhat like Canada and New Zealand) has a very distinct risk profile. On the one hand, it is a developed country with a reliable financial system and risk-free sovereign debt. On the other hand, it has an economy heavily reliant on commodity exports and world trade in general. The latter makes it a "high-beta currency"—that is, its performance is strongly correlated to the performance of global equity markets and other risk assets.

Over the years preceding the COVID crisis, Australia experienced a slowdown in its overheated housing market. This led to idiosyncratic recession concerns and a dramatic fall in interest rates. Notice how, in the following chart, Australia started with rates significantly higher than those in the United States (negative differential) and then moved to relatively much lower rates (positive differential).

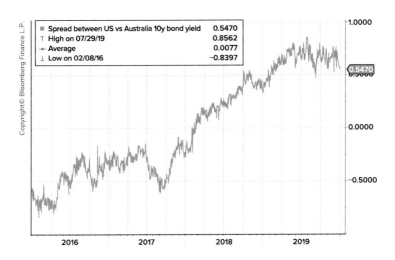

US versus Australian Ten-Year Government Bond Yield Differential 2016–2019: Australian ten-year yield was over 50 bps above US ten-year yield at the beginning of 2016. However, Australian bonds outperformed in the following years and by the end of 2019 were yielding 50 bps less than the United States.

I failed to capitalize on that interest rate move. That was one of the significant misses in my career. I didn't take a position on Australian bonds back then because I had concluded that such a position would be inferior to a more dominant trade of being short AUD.

Indeed, should global growth falter, Australian rates were bound to go lower, but so would the Aussie dollar. On the other hand, should global growth and inflation pressure have proved stronger than anticipated, I expected broad US dollar strength, driven by historically favorable rate differentials and capital account surplus. Remember my reasoning in 2018, as US rates were projected to keep rising and I bet against that: I was convinced that the dollar would continue rallying if the rates did not come down.

There was a possible flaw in my logic, though. It had an embedded assumption that in a bond bear market, Australian bonds would outperform US treasuries (i.e., Australian rates would not rise as much). This was a sound assumption given the above-mentioned headwinds to the Australian economy.

However, if that is the base assumption, then Australian bonds were dominant with respect to the US bonds and should have replaced them in the portfolio.

Anyway, having missed the Aussie bond trade of 2018, I piled into the Aussie dollar trade of 2019. The rate shift had already occurred and now the dominance of the AUD trade was correctly established. In particular, it helped me move past my earlier mistake of betting heavily on Chinese yuan (RMB) devaluation.

Discussing the China trade in detail is beyond the scope of this book, but I will mention that it was integral to my trading success in 2015–2016 and to the major setbacks I suffered in 2017–2018. In my quest to score a major "big short" win, I strayed from the rigorous application on my own strategy. Short AUD was strictly dominant with respect to short RMB, because Australian exports were so dependent on China that AUD would go down in *every* scenario wherein RMB devalued (concurrent necessity), but there were also possibilities of AUD going down idiosyncratically.

In early March 2020, the dominance of the AUD as a way to express the USD (US dollar) long started to play out. Even as the USD was weakening up to March 9 on a broad basis, the AUD still went lower in USD terms, but on March 10 when risk sentiment and the dollar direction reversed, AUD went lower anyway. Hence, I took a first clip of profits.

10:12 AM **CK** k   March 10th, 2020 ⌄

11:34 AM **CK** alex you are done on the EDH0 @ 99.2150

11:36 AM Alex Gurevich Good

12:04 PM Alex Gurevich Small edition to asset swaps in ███ and
██████ 20 and 10K respectively -40 or better.

keep an eye on canada psreads

12:04 PM **CK** see you

we see the headline screen below that level but trying
to maneuver the fact ERIS has no market at this exact
moment

we are working 50% of the CNM0 x 10y CAD swap as
we speak and yes keeping an eye alongside

12:17 PM Alex Gurevich Working another 3,000 March

12:17 PM **CK** k see you

for ERIS swaps they have been incredibly wide the past
few days so that will inhibit our ability to trade when
headline spreads appear to be at -40

so some version of market calm (tighter bid/offer) or
wider (say -41 or worse) is what we'll need

partially done on your EDH0 btw

12:19 PM Alex Gurevich Ok

12:26 PM **CK** fully done on the EDH0

1:17 PM **CK** 50% CNM0 x CAD 10y swap done

1:19 PM Alex Gurevich Great. Thx!

1:23 PM **CK** picking up ASW 30y tomorrow....screen is showing its
there but its mega wide so essentially untradeable at
our level....hopefully get a bit tighter in the morning

DEDZ4 will continue to pick back up in the AMs at 81
(unless gap lower o/n) unless hear otherwise

In the remainder of the "low-volume session," I continued to accumulate dividend futures and EDH0, the March Eurodollars. The P/L was negative on the day due to the pullback in rates but nothing to make me worried.

MARCH 11: WEDNESDAY

It was probably the next session that began the pivot toward the loss of my pre-COVID innocence. On March 11, travel from Europe to the United States was shut down. The stock market reversed the previous day's gains.

I am flailing to come up with more black hole analogies. We were already "sucked into the accretion disk," and the coherence of the markets was already "ripped apart by the tidal gravity." Now what? On March 11, we were not yet through the event horizon— though, mind you, it is theoretically possible to fall into a super-massive black hole without noticing when you cross the event horizon.

The best I can do is imagine that the already frayed texture of the market continuum started to form wormholes, which defy the regular causal sequence of price action. The stock market reversed its previous day's rebound entirely, and pricing moved in the direction of even more aggressive easing. However, the response from the Treasury bond market and the currency market was the opposite of what we had observed up to that point.

Bonds continued to severely underperform swaps on the way up, even though on the previous day they had underperformed on the way down. This was a turning point when the treasuries lost their luster as a risk hedge. Historical causality broke down in the currency market as well. Up until March 11, the logic was, good economic news means higher US rates and stronger dollar, whereas bad news means lower rates and weaker dollar.

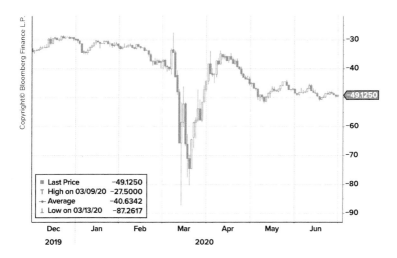

USD Thirty-Year Swap Spread Chart December 2019–June 2020: The bonds underperformed swaps in March 2020 as the Treasury market liquidity seized up.

However, as global trade and travel seized up in the second week of March, the dollar funding that lubricated the global economy started to dry and a universal shortage of dollars arose.

Dollar Shortage

The dollar refused to weaken as the interest rates resumed their decline, not because of any sense that the dollar or the United States in general was a safe bet; there was simply a shortage of dollars in the global economy. Some of you might have heard that later in 2020, there was a shortage of coins. Indeed, during the shutdown, people weren't spending their change and didn't want to touch change handled by others. As such, the coins just left circulation.

Think of the coin shortage as a proxy for the global financial system. For a dozen days or so in March, dollars left circulation. So, uncharacteristically, the USD started to catch a bid, not only against risky currencies but against the safe-haven currencies as well.

My initial focus was on the relative cheapness of cash treasuries, and despite the overnight's rebound, I bought as much Treasury collateral as I could. Much of the morning effort went into navigating US and Canadian swap spreads, trying to take advantage of the dislocations between sovereign bond, bond futures, and swaps.

March 11th, 2020 ⌄

4:56 AM QZ Sent 8mm treasury purchase approval request for ▇▇▇▇ this morning. But market came back this morning. Please let me know if you want to hold off.

6:16 AM QZ Without any front end exclusion, ▇▇▇▇ is slightly over dv01 risk limit. Maybe taking some profit on EDH0 at 99.27?

•• 1   ☺⁺

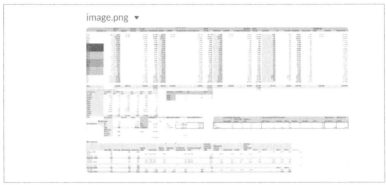

image.png ▼

I sent the purchase request. If we don't like the level here, can sell ED futures.

I mean treasury purchase

6:39 AM QZ currently no market on ERIS 30y. though 30 yr swap spread is marked around 45. Will update

7:09 AM Alex Gurevich Can go ahead with treasury purchase. Are 7 yr spreads correct? Can sell futures then...

I think a little more to rally in front anyway...

We didn't do anything on 30yr spreads yesterday? Seems like a good place to pay?
In Canada did we sell futures or actual bonds against swaps yesterday? The confirm came as a swap spread trade...

7:15 AM **CK** sounds good re TSY purchase, still waiting on confirmation there from the team before we go ahead and do the futures

30y US haven't done anything, no price in ERIS this AM still

agree good place to pay, trying to source liquidity

in CAD, we sold half the futures we had on (265x/530x) and replaced w DV01 equiv recvr in the 10y CAD swap

7:22 AM QZ May ask for block quote on ERIS, need to do total of 35k for block, is this ok?

7:22 AM Alex Gurevich Canadian swap spread seem to be going to the right while US to the left...
If so we should replace Rhe rest of Canada in ■■ since we can...
and increase US using ED futures in front end

30K 10/20 ■■■/■■

7:24 AM QZ ok, so buy TY vs ED future

Copy on CAD spread, will get it going

7:26 AM Alex Gurevich We can buy cash in ▇ too.

Depending on what you think of basis...

7:26 AM QZ copy

7:28 AM Alex Gurevich Hard to tell where intermediate swap spreads are without actually looking at the urge.

7:28 AM QZ we may do the basis, TY looks a bit expensive

7:28 AM Alex Gurevich When do ▇▇ buys usually price?

Regarding EDH0 I think it's mostly a one-way train for next 3 trading days with very little downside.

CK are you in the process of rolling any FX forwards in EM? This maybe time of evaluating our positions there. Same applies to RMB futures. Most likely I will roll but worth contemplating.

The LIBOR rate came down just a little bit, and EDH0 (March 2020) was near the highs while still not pricing in the aggressive easing by the Fed as fully as I would expect. I ignored Qin's sensible suggestion to take profits on the contract, as I was convinced it had much further to run. In hindsight, the "very little downside" comment was cavalier, but the decision to run a winning position was not ex ante wrong. Often, there is a lot of value to be gained in sticking around for those last few ticks.

7:28 AM QZ we may c   **March 11th, 2020 ⌄**   ι bit expensive

7:28 AM Alex Gurevich When do ▇▇ buys usually price?

Regarding EDH0 I think it's mostly a one-way train for next 3 trading days with very little downside.

CK are you in the process of rolling any FX forwards in EM? This maybe time of evaluating our positions there. Same applies to RMB futures. Most likely I will roll but worth contemplating.

7:35 AM **CK** usually by now, though they seem to be slow today, sounds like in next hour today

here are the "upcoming" expiries that I'm rolling by the end of this week:

image.png ▾

Rates	XMH0 Comdty	3/16/2020
Rates	EDH0 Comdty	3/16/2020
Rates	EDH0C 98.5	3/16/2020
FX	XUCH0 Curncy	3/16/2020
FX	SFH0 Curncy	3/16/2020
FX	RFH0 Curncy	3/16/2020
FX	PEH0 Curncy	3/16/2020
FX	NVH0 Curncy	3/16/2020
FX	JYH0 Curncy	3/16/2020
FX	CDH0 Curncy	3/17/2020
FX	ADH0 Curncy	3/16/2020
FX OTC	USDHKD Curncy	3/18/2020
FX OTC	USDCNH Curncy	3/18/2020

RUH0 & NKH0 new positions as well

7:42 AM **CK** so in FX OTC land its just $10 USDCNH (out of $10 total) & $5 USDHKD (out of $50 total)....on the CNH futs its $34 equivalent that I'm currently planning on rolling

CNH (futs & fwds) has regularly been 1.1% carry ann. when I've rolled the last few months....as for the underlying trade being short Asia FX I do think we should be sensitive to the fact the picture in Asia is already somewhat on the upswing and you have relatively more willing authoritarian governments ensuring that remains the case

7:44 AM   QZ Off the run 7y is around libor +3 to libor +5

CAD spread is odne

done

7:52 AM   Alex Gurevich Negative spread to be clear in in 7yr?

March was the month when quarterly currency futures contracts had to be rolled into June; that was routine portfolio maintenance made extra difficult by the market disruption. The focus of my attention continued to be the bond market. We have already discussed the pressure on the LIBOR setting, and the strange price action in the US swap spreads (which was not mirrored in Canadian spreads).

There were relative prices falling into wormholes. One was a cash/futures basis. Basically, some Treasury issues started to trade very cheaply relative to the contract for their future delivery. So in order to make money, all you had to do was buy the bonds today and lock a better price for them later via selling a futures contract.

The catch was that today you needed to borrow the money to buy those bonds. And if the ability to borrow vanished, you'd be in trouble. This dislocation was related to the one happening with swap spreads. Another dislocation, related to both swap spreads and futures basis, was the price difference between on-the-run and off-the-run treasuries.

I realize I am risking some eyes glazing over here. Trust me, on March 11 the subject was quite exciting. In only a few days, it was going to get truly wild.

Notice, in the Slack chat I am incredulous that the asset swap spreads became negative even for the medium-term treasuries (seven-year sector). On-the-runs are the most recent issues, while off-the-runs are the ones currently trading less actively. This week, a price gap started to open between those categories, as people flocked to the more liquid securities.

---

ensuring th/ **March 11th, 2020** ˅

7:44 AM QZ Off the run 7y is around libor +3 to libor +5

CAD spread is odne

done

7:52 AM Alex Gurevich Negative spread to be clear in in 7yr?

7:55 AM QZ The off-the-runs cheapened up on thin liquidity, currently trading Libor + 3, so negative spread

Headline 7y spread jumps around at Libor + 1, also negative spread

8:45 AM Alex Gurevich Let's replace the Canada spread position - with cash vs. bundles this is a good moment - treasuries under pressure in 10yr sector

---

8:46 AM QZ we are doing it right now

CAD is done

working on bundle vs TY, then do basis

8:47 AM Alex Gurevich When complete. Will consider adding to all portfolios more spreads...

8:47 AM QZ 1/3 is done on TY vs 5y bundle

Currently working on 30k dv01 for ██/██████

Those will be in TY and bundles.

10k dv01 for █████?

8:49 AM Alex Gurevich ██/████ you are working in 30 yr? Yes when replace cad can add another 10K in 7yr sector for ██

8:50 AM QZ ██/██, we are also working on 7y, NOT 30yr

30yr ERIS is too wide to work on

Is this agreeable? 30yr ERIS is 3bp wide, if you want to do 30yr, let us know. We will give it a try.

8:53 AM Alex Gurevich Can work 7yr for now. I am concerned about building too much ERIS... seems no exit there...

8:54 AM QZ ok. We are on course

As I built my exposure to cheaper treasuries, I had to think about the liquidity of the instruments I was using. Some of my portfolios could only use swap futures to execute long-dated swap spread trades (ERIS exchange); in the chat above, I expressed my concern about securing a quick exit from those futures if the need arose. Fortunately, as the value proposition rolled to the middle of the curve, I had a broader range of instruments available.

8:54 AM QZ ok. We a' **March 11th, 2020** ˅

9:00 AM Alex Gurevich Next target on DEDZ should be not 81 on 2024 but 85 on 2023

9:00 AM QZ We are done on TY vs 5y bundle on 30k, for ██/██

9:01 AM **CK** roger on the DED

9:01 AM Alex Gurevich And replacement for ██?

9:01 AM **CK** will work the 85 DEDZ3 ongoing

working on the ██

9:11 AM Alex Gurevich Spread seems very negative in 2-3 year sector probably because of tax postponement- flooding the market with t-bills. But they probably will QEd. Should we look at front end TED trade?

Meanwhile confirming: ███ and ██ added to spreads thorough bundles vs. futures

██ covered Canada sold futures vs. swap. ██ didn't do anything yes to replace swap spreads, correct?

9:14 AM QZ Confirming: ████ and ██ spreads through bundles vs. future is done, total 30k dv01

CNM0 vs Swap in ██████ is done. Nothing yet on TY vs ED (10k) for ██████, working

For TED, are you thinking about TU? Cash may have repo restriction

9:15 AM Alex Gurevich I want not only 10K for ██ but replace the whole Canada position from yesterday and today. Seems like 70K total?

Any futures not expensive? So we don't have to put it all in cash for ██? (though ████ might not care now).

9:16 AM QZ In dollar terms, 60k

9:17 AM Alex Gurevich Ok...

Still almost $100mm is 7yr sector.

9:20 AM QZ Both TY and FV look expensive. But we can try to see if ███ can quote cash 7y off the run vs 5y bundles

9:21 AM Alex Gurevich Or there cheaper shorter issues vs. corresponding bundles. It feels like repo is not the flavor of worry for today?

9:26 AM QZ Looking at shorter issues 3 yr sector

Crazy market. Cheapened a ton in 3y sector, but what the heck..

10k dv01 for ██████ through TY is done

9:32 AM Alex Gurevich Ok

Let's look at basis and shorter end - huge spread move today - let's take aDVANTAGE.

Try to stay below $500mm cash so they don't flag us. We are slightl over $300mm now?

9:34 AM QZ getting repo clearance right now

9:36 AM Alex Gurevich 10yr muni swap showing at 95% on the screen...

9:45 AM QZ Did the basis on 10k for ███ , sold TY buy T 1.625 10/26

repo is a bit high today 1.28

Can do additional up to 150m repo

can't go above 500m

9:49 AM Alex Gurevich Yes should expect repo panics - good opportunity relief will come...

As mentioned above, taking advantage of dislocation in cash treasuries necessitated the ability to buy those physical treasuries, which in turn would expand the balance sheet. Fortunately, at the onset of the pandemic crisis, the size of our balance sheet was very modest, so we had ample opportunity to put new positions on. However, we had to be careful not to exceed our notional limits.

Repo Panic!

Notice my final comment in the last Slack screenshot: it has two very important components.

First, I was prepared for a repo panic. *Repo* is a repurchase agreement for bonds; it allows traders to achieve *leverage* by buying bonds in excess of cash they have in hand. Immediately after buying a bond, they enter a repo agreement, borrowing the money needed for the transaction and using the freshly purchased bonds as collateral in the repo transaction.

Repo funding typically is very easy and cheap because treasuries make very good collateral, but this funding lasts for only one night and has to be rolled on a daily basis. Should cash become scarce one day, there is no theoretical limit on how much interest it will cost to fund your bonds overnight.

One such repo panic had occurred in September 2019, when the borrowing cost spiked from 2.25% to 6%. This embarrassed the Fed, who were supposed to control the overnight rate, but had no meaningful economic impact.

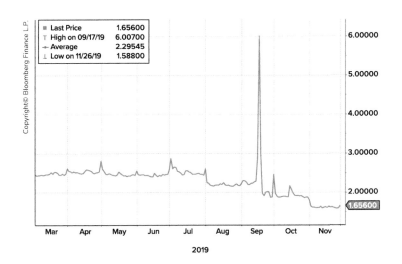

The Depository and Trust Clearing Corporation (DTCC) General Collateral Finance (GCF) Repo Index March 2019–November 2019: Repo rates soared from 2.25% to 6% in September 2019.

Second, I expressed my confidence that "relief would come" and any such problem would be very short-lived. There was an element of an "I know that you know that I know" game going on there. Given their previous repo debacle, the policymakers had no choice but to provide a flood of liquidity.

A much broader economic crisis was developing, but for the purposes of my asset swap trades, I believed that funding issues would be addressed immediately and vigorously. This may lead to a perception of "moral hazard"—that is, that I, along with other speculators, was taking unreasonable risk while relying on the Fed to bail me out.

I believe that regardless of what ethical stand a reader may take, there was nuance that separated me from that controversy. I was not an asset manager, overleveraged during the calmer times to chase returns, who was caught in trouble and needed a government rescue. In fact, as I have written earlier, my portfolio was performing very strong up to and during the early days of March. I could easily find liquidity to take profits and sit out the volatility. I didn't *need* to be bailed out. Rather, assessing that other people *would* need to be bailed out, I chose to ride on the coattails of that process. I prepared to take some pain on funding and then make it to the light on the other side of the tunnel (I didn't know we were falling into a black hole). I may have been wrong in my assessment of the *gravity* (okay, I'm sorry, but I had to) of the situation, but I am unapologetic about trying to take advantage of major market forces and flows. That is what my investors hire me to do.

opportunity   March 11th, 2020 ⌄

9:50 AM   Joann Shie-Chen 8mm treasuries bought for ████ - done
at
Purchased 912828M56 vs $8,767,358.9
Price 108.868772 Yield .656284

9:51 AM Alex Gurevich What issue was that?

Yes let's do another close 150mm in various issues. To replace most of Canada spread loss

9:52 AM Joann Shie-Chen T 2 1/4 11/15/25

10:21 AM QZ Shall we do 75m today on 3y just in case if spreads move even further?

also leaving room for other sectors? 150mm is max,

10:27 AM Alex Gurevich Where is 3yr?

It's pretty crazy with spreads now. If something like -7 we should do 150mm today... can always put more on later via futures

10:31 AM QZ L+16 or 17, all over the place

10:35 AM Alex Gurevich +16? Definitely do all you can ....

Meanwhile, the swap spread insanity was deepening. Both Qin and I used to make markets on asset swaps. Normally, we would know where every bond issue was within at least 1/4 of a basis point. Now I couldn't tell within 10 bps; it normally takes a year for swap spreads to move that much! As I mentioned earlier, the discrepancy between the liquid, on-the-run and off-the-run bonds was widening, creating a deeply negative level of asset swaps on short-dated bonds. This was happening, despite the carry on owning bonds improving due to the high LIBOR setting. "Carry on interest rate trades" is the running difference between all the interest you are paying and receiving—a new yield of the transaction, if you wish. A swap spread carry consists of four components: you receive the bond yield and the LIBOR rate, and you pay the repo (funding) rate and the swap yield.

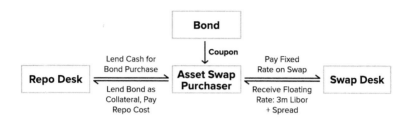

Asset Swap Flow Chart.

The price of assets was totally ripped away from actual cash flows on those assets. Remember: black holes, wormholes, tidal gravity.

Inflation-Protected Bonds

10:35 AM Alex Gurevic'   ll you can ....
                          March 11th, 2020 ∨

10:41 AM QZ headline at -6.5

          but for CK and I, our bond price is wrong

          from BBG

          off by 5 bp

10:43 AM Alex Gurevich Just see what you can do - this is time...

10:43 AM QZ no worries. we know headline spared. Just hard to
          figure out relative value on off the runs

10:57 AM QZ Probably missed it,

11:02 AM QZ spread jumped wider, now headline -3,25, trying to
          get half done unless we hear from you

11:06 AM Alex Gurevich Do half

11:16 AM CK 42% of the half done

12:00 PM Alex Gurevich Told you fed would come to rescue. Let's do the rest.

If short end moved too far can do longer but as long as we are in the negative zone in front …

12:04 PM **CK** yup, you nailed it

we've done 50% (so the first half)…working on the last half

12:07 PM Alex Gurevich Where are we getting done?

12:08 PM **Christopher Lutton** On my way.

In the commotion, we did what we could, chasing prices that were trying to slip away. My attention went to Treasury Inflation-Protected Securities (TIPS). Each coupon payout on those bonds is calculated as the sum of a fixed yield and inflation over the coupon period. The difference in yield between regular nominal bonds and inflation-indexed should theoretically be the market inflation expectation for the duration of those bonds. In fact, it *is* the market-projected inflation by definition, since this is how the inflation expectation is calculated.

The nuance here is that the two kinds of government bonds (nominals and TIPS) are driven by buyers and sellers, not by some theoretical computations or economic projections. Furthermore, those yields are calculated based on the market prices, and then projected inflation can be derived. But none of this says that the inflation number you come up with has to make sense. And in the warped reality of 2020, it didn't.

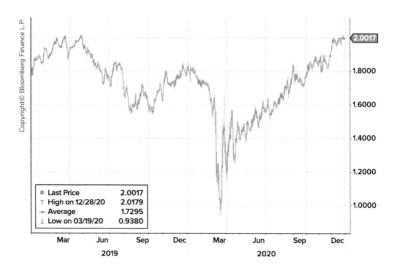

US Thirty-Year Inflation Breakeven Rate 2019–2020: Implied inflation rate collapsed from near 1.8% pre-COVID to 1% in March 2020.

No matter how severe the pandemic was, how was it supposed to reduce the inflation over the next thirty years from 2% to 1%? The pricing had nothing to do with economic reality; it was a function of a crashing price of TIPS. In fact, I realized that, if anything, the stimulus and liquidity triggered by the crisis would have long-term inflationary consequences. The chart above jumps ahead, showing that I was right on this count.

Another way to look at TIPS is from the simple price perspective. It also illustrates the incredible price swing in March.

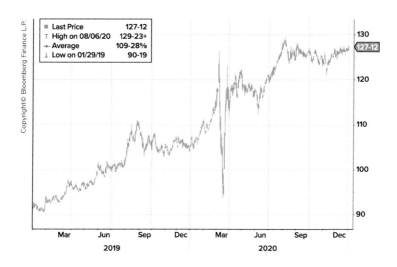

■ Last Price	127-12
T High on 08/06/20	129-23+
◆ Average	109-28⅜
⊥ Low on 01/29/19	90-19

Price Chart for TII ¾ 02/15/42 Inflation-Protected Security (TIPS): Extreme swings in March 2020.

I am a very patient trader, but when I identify a new trade, I have very little patience about initiating the position. I don't think this sense of urgency is a flaw; being decisive and timely about your trade execution is paramount.

Having said that, the following Slack chatter may portray me as a bit neurotic, as I tried to chase the jumping prices and overwhelmed banks struggling to provide liquidity.

12:08 PM **Christopher** ′ March 11th, 2020 ⌄

12:28 PM Alex Gurevich We should look at tips. We could switch our bullet bonds into TIPS when breaks end are low enough. The CPI dip will probably from oil for a while. But then will probably go back to higher levels with all the stimulus.

30yr tips are positive yield!!! What kind of joke is that!

10yr tips -14 still super cheap. What are the chances of inflation below 1% for 10yrs? For 30yrs?

👍 1   😊⁺

12:32 PM QZ A lot of legs, no worse than libor +7

12:32 PM Alex Gurevich 3yr?

12:32 PM QZ yes

12:33 PM Alex Gurevich Good level!

12:33 PM QZ did basis, so we are long T 1.5 1/15/23

12:33 PM Alex Gurevich Ok

12:33 PM QZ Will work on the other half, but a bit tough, may try FV

12:34 PM CK DEDZ3 @ 85 got done during all that madness when stocks were collapsing too btw...

12:34 PM Alex Gurevich Good!

Next level 84.

12:34 PM CK k

if you need us urgently just call my cell ▮▮▮▮▮▮
▮▮▮▮...just know we are pushing as hard as possible on the remainder of the front end in the meantime

---

12:36 PM Alex Gurevich Let's try to do the front end it might be not there to stay. And next look at switching long-dates bonds into TIPs

12:36 PM CK roger that, on the same page

12:37 PM Alex Gurevich When you have a chance let's go over what we have on the longer end in cash that can be switched if worth it.

Cash 30yrs is not cheap against futures we were think of switching into them - May as well do TIPs

12:49 PM   **Christopher Lutton** Would anyone be interested in a 15-minute catch-up after the close via conference call? Can be informal but curious if it would be worth going over Alex's wish list for tonight/tomorrow in things to be doing/watching/etc. No pressure, i realize everyone very busy

12:50 PM   Alex Gurevich Let's execute first. Still trying to get done on spreads and then turn to TIPS.

 1   ☺⁺

30yr tips are pretty much outright buy here. .18 yield flat month on month

.20 outright buy and hold here.

Don't even have to switch. Can switch our existing 10mm into futures. If balance sheet is a concern.

Buy $10mm TII 0 1/4 2/15/50. Unless there is a much h rapper issue. .19 yield or better.

Or close...

Actually 0.75 2/15/42 highest yield.

But $10mm on that one!

(has a little worse optionality but worth the risk...)

Hearing me?

1:01 PM   **CK** seeing you

working this in the chats

1:02 PM   Alex Gurevich .34 offered now 2/15/42

1:03 PM   QZ Sorry, not able to get an offer from ███ right now

says "trader jammed"

1:05 PM   Alex Gurevich What about ███████? Can we trade those electobically?

1:06 PM   QZ Not yet with ███████

1:08 PM   Alex Gurevich   I just tried to put order in to see how it works

Maybe can do it electronically with ████?

Missed 3bps now have to have a way to execute...

1:11 PM   **CK** working all the angles, still nothing on the TIPs

1:11 PM   Alex Gurevich   But relative to long bonds similar level...

1:11 PM   **CK** spread is 100% done now

1:12 PM   Alex Gurevich   Ok.

Now that levels snapped - can do a switch...

TIPS ARE INSANE. We could replace all our positions with TIPS at this level and probably have a better portfolio. Don't even need hedges. Own bonds at inflation + , when they are taking rates to 0 and introducing fiscal stimulus!

1:15 PM   **Christopher Lutton** I'm having a hard time understanding how you're not right. It seems nuts

Other parts of the portfolio stayed in motion, with dividend futures (DEDZ) still being accumulated and short-end nominal bonds swaps being painstakingly executed. But TIPS were at the forefront of my mind. The last exchange illustrates the level of conviction I was developing.

how you're   March 11th, 2020 ⌄   ˢ

1:15 PM   Alex Gurevich   Tips just rebounded 1/2 point without bonds moving

TIPs are rallying now! As bonds are selling off - that was the moment! I am mad they didn't trade...

1:17 PM   QZ That was why ████ could not show offer!

1:17 PM Alex Gurevich We did 150mm spreads?

1:18 PM QZ we did the other half in 10/23 about L+13.5

1:18 PM Alex Gurevich Crazy

1:56 PM Alex Gurevich Is the trading done for the day? Never go any prices in tips: on the screen see 2/15/42 still at 32 now.

Worse price now given that bonds came off but still very good level.

1:57 PM QZ looking

1:57 PM CK yes i'm looking at it and trying to do it electronically as we speak....saw it slip away

1:58 PM Alex Gurevich It's now 109 offered maybe can do something?

2:12 PM Alex Gurevich Anything at all?

2:13 PM CK no

■ refused to show...couldn't get the e to work (even though it did show 0.34 again into the close) though worth noting the e is priced by the voice trader who didn't want to show via voice anyways

■ showed a 110-16 indicative offer when BBG was showing 109 offer indicatively

2:17 PM Alex Gurevich Lol

3:45 PM CK re the earlier point, def think a touch base via conference call would be good, though maybe tomorrow AM if OK? in the meantime....

currently watching:
1. 300x DEDZ3 @ 84 (adjust if gaps) classic alloc
2. $10mm TIPS 0.75 2/15/42 ~0.34 level -- potentially switch out with our $10mm 2/15/50 bonds in ■ -- hopefully ■ shows tomorrow either via voice or on e

3. 30y spreads once ERIS liquidity returns for ██/██
4. munis
5. NK @ 18,000 add or ~24,000 exit

today's voice trades in summary:
1. CNM0 switched into 10y CAD swap (██)

2. 30k DV01 5y bundle vs TY done (██:██ 2:1) + 10k DV01 5y bundle vs cash TSY (10/26) (██)
3. legged 3y bundles vs cash TSYs (1/23 & 10/23) (██)
4. in aggregate, spreads ~$150, all the cash TSY done on repo -- balance @ ██ is ~$450-$500 so very limited space now
5. $8mm cash TSY purchase in ██

worth noting:
1. BBG screens have been super unreliable the last 48hrs and dealers equally unreliable so liquidity and flat out price discovery is going to be a challenge until things calm down
2. equity & FX futures approaching expiry so unless we are reducing in next 24hrs, pls push all trades into the 'M' contract here on out

The day's work was moving toward the close; in the last three screenshots, CK summarized what we were in the process of executing.

into the   March 11th, 2020 ∨   out

obviously lmk if we are missing anything important in advance of the touch base

3:48 PM Alex Gurevich Looks good.,open to buying TIPs outright they keep trading down. And if no liquidity on off-runs can buy on the run 30yr.

3:54 PM Alex Gurevich ECB overnight?

3:54 PM **CK** oh yea, that too haah

5:45 our time I think

5:23 PM Alex Gurevich Goody watch 5 on USDBRL but start with only $1mm for ■■. I don't know if there are futures for other accounts can do in proportion.
Also give me heads-up if any Asian currencies are up for roll. I may want to review.

Shifting Focus Away from China

It appears that after a super-busy session, none of us took much of a break and we slid right into the opening of Asian markets. I was continuing to accumulate depreciating EM currencies, now looking at Brazil.

roll. I may w **March 11th, 2020** ⌄

5:25 PM **CK** $5mm USDHKD & $10mm USDCNH are FX fwds up for roll....340x XUCH0 ($34mm USDCNH) is FX fut up for roll

all are being completed imminently (i was about to do the CNH Fut roll)

i will wait until i hear from you on those before completing (we can handle tomorrow worst case)

still watching for weaker RUB & MXN + TRY @ 7, BRL @ 5

looks like there are futures for Brazil, we can likely do standard alloc for ■■/■■ when we do the OTC for ■■ in $1mm

5:29 PM Alex Gurevich Is CNH total positon currently balanced between portfolios?

I decided to reduce our bet against Chinese currency. Notice, I said, "China is now in the best position." This was insightful, if I may say so myself. I realized that China had already taken the brunt of the pandemic disruption, and the US economy, not yet affected by COVID, was more vulnerable.

Have you ever been at the beach, trying to walk to the next cove, with a narrow strip of sand being intermittently swept by waves? You have to start running when the water is still high and just beginning to recede. Running into the swirling flow is counterintuitive, but you can't wait for the ocean to retreat all the way if you want to give yourself more time before the next wave comes.

The human mind tends to project the events of the near past into the future. This is not always wrong; trend-following can be quite profitable. But the ability to draw the distinction between trends, which may continue, and patterns, which have no choice but to shift, is paramount for macro trading.

5:41 PM **CK** all $12   March 11th, 2020 ⌄

5:42 PM Alex Gurevich Let's reduce. Unwind about $5mm. Also take down risk in ■ but about $5mm

China is now in the best positon.

By $5mm to $18mm in ■.

Will be left with 18/9/7

5:44 PM **CK** re Asia upcoming rolls, elaborated somewhat earlier but to reiterate:
1. CNH roll carries anywhere from 0.8%-1.2% ann. against us, barely unch'ed from where we've rolled it since last year....pts are more elevated vs 2019 levels but on the lower end of the range of the post GFC era so not particularly prohibitive carry...longer dated points have popped somewhat meaningfully in the last few weeks

2. HKD 3mth roll is back to carrying positively for us so less burdensome but still on the 'high' side of the range in terms of points which as you know were negative for a handful of years...longer dated pts are high
3. Ultimately the carry isn't meaningful enough whereby it should sway us one way or the other but gun to head I'd rather not be sitting long USDAsia after they've survived the massive headwind of COVID w no problem

5:44 PM Alex Gurevich I'll keep HKD.

5:44 PM **CK** cool

i'll unwind $5 of the OTC in ■

leaves us w $5 OTC fwd + $2 fut in ■ ($7 total)

and then $5 worth of ■ futs

all CNH

6:08 PM **CK** CNH is rebal'ed, Trump made it a bit easier on me

 1   ☺⁺

6:56 PM QZ Expect quite large P&L divergence between ▮▮▮▮
and ▮▮▮▮, largely due to the under-performance of off-
the-runs vs treasury future, 3-4 bp or even more.

For 3/11

7:37 PM **CK** working bid 60x PEH0 @ 4.54 (22 equiv), working bid
30x NKH0 18,000

8:21 PM Alex Gurevich We might gap down a lot on DEDZ open.
Make sure not leave orders there...

8:26 PM **CK** no active orders, i agree

would we rather leave our NK and MX orders out of the
market?

8:27 PM Alex Gurevich I am offering EDH0 at .325

8:27 PM **CK** *no active DEDZ orders

i see you

Tokyo governor FYI: *KOIKE: DON'T THINK
CANCELING OLYMPICS AN OPTION

8:28 PM **Christopher Lutton** Weird comment

8:28 PM Alex Gurevich They will cancel Olympics

8:28 PM **Christopher Lutton** I agree with Alex

I feel like oil is going to 15

It is hard to imagine now that at this stage, the Summer Olympics
was even a subject of discussion.

Meanwhile, financial markets continued to unravel, heading
for a massive down day. It seems none of us was getting much
sleep. Not content with leaving overnight orders, I continued to
accumulate positions, including dividend futures and Canadian
bonds.

MARCH 12: THURSDAY

March 12th, 2020 ⌄

1:54 AM Alex Gurevich I bought a bunch of DEDZ and sold some EDH0 at 35!

2:08 AM Alex Gurevich I grabbed some Canadian bonds cheaply but there was no liquidity only 5 at a time from algos.

2:23 AM Alex Gurevich Looking for chances to add to that and to XMA. But that's relative to US performance. Working 300 more DEDZ4 at 75.

5:24 AM Alex Gurevich Covering 180 AUD. Reduce roll amount when you get to it.

5:24 AM **CK** Roger

5:32 AM **CK** BRL highly illiquid, briefly flashed 5 indicatively right at open but couldn't get anything done. Still working $1mm ■ (then ~$2 and ~1 ■/■ on the futs side for classic alloc) at that level

5:33 AM Alex Gurevich FFH0 trading at wrong price again?

As panic continued to rise, I tried to reassess various paths of the Fed response. With only six days until the policy meeting, it seemed natural for the Fed to wait for the next easing, but the market was increasingly pressuring them and pricing the Fed Funds futures as if the cut had to be made immediately. EDH0, the Eurodollar contract, was not pricing much relief.

5:33 AM Alex Gurevic **March 12th, 2020** ⌄ ng price again?

5:33 AM **CK** Seems like it. Same as we saw a few days back

5:37 AM Alex Gurevich How can FFs trade at 38? They've been 1.09 and 1.69 at the beginning. Can you model if they take them to .09 at the meeting?

5:38 AM QZ 99.30

1.58 fo 2, 1.09 for 16, 0.09 for 13

99.38 would have to price in emergency today??

5:54 AM Alex Gurevich High chance of happening but emergency 50 today - barely gets us there and EDH0 performs much better then

Selling all FFH I can ...

5:56 AM QZ 100bp cut today does get FFH0 above 99.4 🙂

Sure. makes sense

5:58 AM **CK** great

6:01 AM Alex Gurevich What are people who are buying them thinking?

Sorry I bought so few CAd bonds only 5 at a time. Without algos I would get any

6:04 AM **CK** so thin at that time of night, something is better than nothing

6:05 AM Alex Gurevich I am confused - did I have another 300 DEDz4 working at 74?

No 75 2was just filled. Put another 300 at 74.

6:06 AM **CK** correct

also take a look at NZD, CAD, NK, RUB and lmk if you have levels in mind to unwind/add

---

6:08 AM Alex Gurevich Nikkei trading 17,370. Weren't we targeting 18,000?

Did we get done on that

6:09 AM **CK** yea order seems to have been cxld...NKM0 equiv for 18k is 17,800

no we did not, not sure why we got cxld o/n, i'm checking...but in the meantime we can work something better here

6:10 AM Alex Gurevich Are you sure I see 30 pending in NKH0?

Sort it out

6:10 AM QZ BMA/3mL run:
1Y   100.2500%
18M   100.0000%
2Y   99.7500%
3Y   98.7500%
4Y   98.0000%
5Y   97.5000%
6Y   97.1250%
7Y   96.7500%
8Y   97.1667%
9Y   97.5833%
10Y 98.0000%
12Y 98.5000%
15Y 99.0000%
20Y 99.5000%
25Y 100.0000%
30Y 100.50 ↓ Latest messages

There were separate interwoven conversations happening during the very early Thursday morning in California. I was still accumulating risk assets, working orders for Nikkei and dividend futures.

Municipal Swaps

At some point, I must have requested a run of municipal index swap quotes from Qin, which she provided. Reading it now, I am amused that she used the old nomenclature of BMA/3ML. Nowadays, the index is usually referred to as MUNIPSA.

There is quite a bit of history and even nostalgia there. My first job on Wall Street was at a swap desk at Bankers Trust in 1997. I had just gotten my PhD in mathematics. Besides trading "vanilla" interest rate swaps, as we encountered earlier, my desk also specialized in basis index and municipal index swaps. I am not going to discuss what all of those are; it is sufficient to know that some of them are fairly esoteric instruments that trade infrequently but often in huge notionals when they do. They are designed to capture minute differentials between movements of various types of floating interest.

Municipal swaps are a thing apart because they have tax sensitivity. Just as LIBOR swaps are indexed to interbank borrowing rates, municipal swaps are indexed to the short-term borrowing rates for municipalities. And since municipalities borrow tax-free, their paper becomes more attractive when the margin tax rate goes up. To put it very simply, if MUNIPSA trades at 70% of LIBOR, it implies a marginal tax rate of 30%.

Although theoretically, those swaps should mostly be driven by tax policy projections, the actual drivers are multiple other factors. For example, when rates go down, people pay less attention to avoid taxation on their interest income and so muni paper becomes relatively cheaper—that is, percentages go up. Even more important is the factor of general risk aversion.

In times of crisis, municipal funding becomes more precarious and short-term muni rates spike, infecting the long-term funding projections as well.

Jumping a bit ahead, I will show you how the swaps played through 2020 and into early 2021. Notice that the one-year swap shot up to 100% in March, but so did the thirty-year! Whereas the former calmed down fairly quickly, the latter gave us a second chance a few weeks later. We will get back to it in Chapter 8.

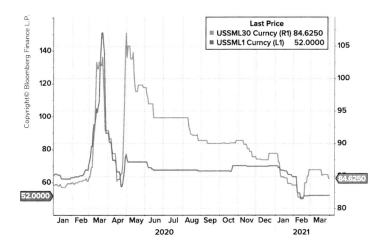

Unlike the Ratio on One-Year Municipal Index Swap (Red), the Ratio on Thirty-Year Swap (Blue) Jumped Back Above 100% After the Shock of March 2020.

The spectacular funding spike in the worst week of March accounted for considerable deterioration of muni carry in the short maturity. But spread over a thirty-year horizon, the effects of one bad week were minimal, and I started to look at an opportunity to capitalize on the panic in longer maturities.

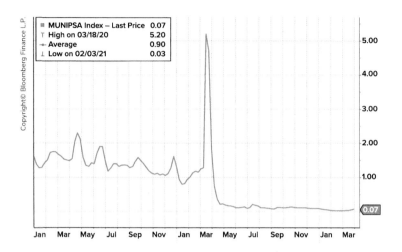

SIFMA Municipal Swap Index 2019–2020: SIFMA Municipal Swap Index (a seven-day yield) spiked for three weeks in mid-March 2020.

You will not see me executing any trades in munis at this juncture. I knew that the crisis would pass, but why was I hesitating? It was the ghost of negative interest rate policy (NIRP). With precipitous policy easing occurring and negative rates having already become a standard in much of the developed world, how was I to know that the United States would remain "immune"?

And the concept of being in a swap transaction where one negative rate is compared to another in *percentage terms* was making my head hurt. This is the good part of being a discretionary money manager: if you can't wrap your head around a certain transaction, you always have the option of sitting it out. Move on to something you *can* understand.

In the end, I didn't increase my muni positions till later in May, when I became more comfortable with the idea from ▓▓▓   March 12th, 2020 ⌄

6:11 AM **CK** that was loaded but cxld (not by me, seemingly by the exchange or dealer) though I'm double checking before we load another order in

6:12 AM Alex Gurevich Ok do another 30 when sorted

Should I go short March funds here?

So many things I can buy against it

6:13 AM QZ if they do 100bp today, 99.49

6:13 AM Alex Gurevich Even April funds are a buy against March?

100bp today?

6:18 AM QZ If funds rate brought down to 17bp (as April funds) by friday, FFH0 could be 99.38, I suppose

6:20 AM Alex Gurevich Well at least thé gréât March fed funds trade is over...

6:21 AM QZ yea, fabulous one

6:24 AM **CK** 74 is done DEDZ4, 73 bid?

6:28 AM Alex Gurevich Nikkei done?

Qin check risk limits before putting more in

6:28 AM QZ doing it now

6:28 AM **CK** haven't executed Nikkei since I haven't gotten final confirm on last night's (non) trade

6:29 AM Alex Gurevich March funds are creeping up again...

6:29 AM QZ For muni, there's a 97 bid in 10y (just 1 dealer), no offer

6:29 AM Alex Gurevich Is it color from ▓▓▓?

6:29 AM QZ yes

They can work something for us,

6:30 AM Alex Gurevich 120%?

6:30 AM QZ They checked market, that's what came back

showing on 50m 10s?

6:31 AM Alex Gurevich Thinking? Should we take a stab?

6:32 AM **CK** ntg done NK, going to do the 30x here

6:32 AM Alex Gurevich Ok

6:32 AM QZ

image.png ▾

---

image.png ▾

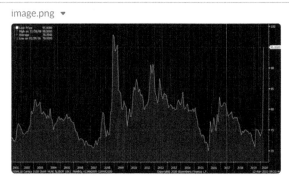

10y muni

but we are at zero bound on rates

6:34 AM **CK** NK done

6:36 AM Alex Gurevich How are we on risk limits? For DEDZ4?

6:37 AM QZ I think we are full on DED

total 1800 done today?

6:38 AM **CK** agree

300 2, 600 3, 900 DEDZ4

6:38 AM Alex Gurevich 100% risk limit? Even with the value
adjustment?

6:39 AM QZ slightly under,

6:41 AM Alex Gurevich I put last one in at 71.5

6:41 AM **CK** see

6:42 AM QZ Still has a little room, since price down

calculating

The Dividend Futures

The dollar continued to rally, which was good for my long dollar positions but also meant trouble for all assets priced in dollars. In previous years, I had gotten so used to rooting for stocks to go down that it was hard to get alarmed when my existing positions started to slide. I was happy for a chance to rebuild my position on Nikkei futures, where I felt I had taken profits too early in the past. I was also methodically buying dips in European dividend futures (DEDZ), which had been my strategy for the past decade.

Due to certain market participants hedging their future dividend income, the dividend curve was chronically in *backwardation*—that is, the companies were projected to pay in aggregate less dividends in the future than they were paying now. That was a persistent market dislocation, especially if you assumed even a modicum of economic growth. Just buying deferred dividend futures and earning positive slide as they rolled into closer maturities had been very lucrative.

Euro Stoxx 50 Dividend Future Curve as of June 28, 2019: The deferred dividend future contracts were cheaper compared to the front contracts.

The trick was not to load up at the top. Because of low liquidity and one-way flows, the corrections were vicious.

The first time I entered this trade was during the European debt crisis of 2011–2012. The future became priced for a *Forever Armageddon*, which didn't make any sense.

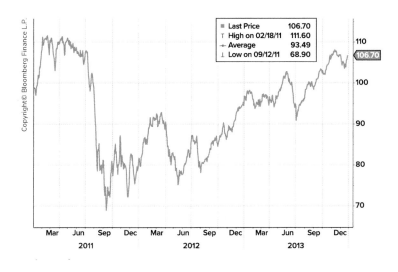

The Fourth Euro Stoxx 50 Dividend Future Price 2011–2013: European debt crisis of 2011–2012 priced in dividends being permanently cut.

It paid to wait patiently for the next big scare, load up when it arrived, and then just sit on the carry and roll up. Having successfully executed that strategy several times, I had no intention of failing to take advantage of the pandemic crisis.

However, as I kept accumulating and pushing toward risk limits, it dawned on me that it was all well and good to think that dividends would be cut when everything in shutdown was restored, but with everybody receiving a bailout, would any dividends ever be paid? What if companies were not allowed to pay dividends anymore? Could the interest rates go so negative that companies would merely strive to not lose money and 0 percent yield would be all one could hope for, thank you very much?

I had already addressed this point in my market note[14] from July 2019:

> Taking this thinking to an extreme, an investor may line up to buy shares in any company which has a long-term perspective of non-negative earnings, regardless of how high the valuation is. Theoretically, any perpetually non-losing money concern becomes of infinite value.

Back in my early days of trading (it must have been 1997 or 1998), I heard a veteran trader say something like, "The price goes from 'cheap' to 'cheaper' to 'really cheap' to 'unbelievable value' to 'GET ME OUT!!!!'"

Indeed, in markets you have to be careful what you ask for. When prices continued to collapse, the pressure on the portfolio from the direction of equities started to mount. I stayed the course but now with a sense of trepidation.

Experience Counts

calculating   March 12th, 2020 ⌄

6:42 AM Alex Gurevich April serial is probably a bit if we are going 0 rates

We should just buy 5yr futures... they'll go much higher if we cut to 0 today...

6:53 AM Alex Gurevich Thinking of buying back front March sold overnight...

---

14   https://honteinv.com/negative-in-perpetuity/

6:59 AM QZ To clarify on DED, still has room. We set $1.5 mm
notional per risk unit. I was looking at number of
contracts. But price went down. Still safe to say 20%
capacity left

7:06 AM QZ small short on FFH0 now, right?

wrong chat

7:11 AM Alex Gurevich Cover 120 JPY currency here standard

Also cover 120 AUD standard

7:11 AM **CK** k

JY done, AD partial

AUD & JPY done

7:22 AM Alex Gurevich Thx

Being able to buy April's seems like easy buy against
March FF and finding pressure will likely diminish by
then... otherwise Libor + 45 good for spreads...

But afraid to load up because of course can go wider...

Like in 2008.

The discussion in the chat above reached a most important
point, which would prove to be critical to our performance in
the month of March and the whole of 2020. Notice, I was looking
to switch my bet on easing on the funding pressure from March
Eurodollars (EDH0) to April Eurodollars (EDJ0). The flaw in
my thinking was that unlike most of my other strategies, this
one relied on a certain outcome occurring *within a certain time
frame.*

Counting on the Fed to get things under control *eventually* was correct, but counting on it to get things under control on a *deadline* was unreasonable. There is a saving grace in that conversation. I said that I was afraid to load up heavily on that position because based on my experience in 2008, it could prove to have unlimited downside.

This was the definitive "experience counts" moment of 2020. I liked a trade idea but recognized its vulnerability based on a very similar debacle my portfolio went through in the early days of the GFC. Without that visceral memory, I would have proceeded with much less caution.

7:24 AM **CK** yes   March 12th, 2020 ⌄

quickly re FFH0

as currently allocated from your trades o/n, FFH0 is +1124 ▓▓ / -312 ▓▓ / +70 ▓; in aggregate we are long 882x) -- how would you like that to look?

looks a bit funky as is

7:27 AM Alex Gurevich Also afraid to leave sell orders they can cut any moennt

Maybe last batch use to flatten...

The panic and tension in the market reached a point at which I was afraid to leave any limit order. Another emergency rate cut or other market shock, which would make prices gap, seemed possible any second.

looks a bit f·

7:27 AM Alex Gurevich Also afraid to leave sell orders they can cut any moennt

Maybe last batch use to flatten...

7:31 AM **CK** cool we'll sort it when we have a sec...as long as you know you are long 882x FFH0 and working 1500x order to sell, thats all that matters

*long 605x, working ntg per your recent cancellation of the order

7:39 AM QZ Running a risk snapshot as of now

8:09 AM **CK** done on the EDH0 btw

8:14 AM Alex Gurevich AUD below 63. Unwind another 120 there...

8:14 AM **CK** unreal

k

8:15 AM Alex Gurevich When Fed cuts to zero and introduces more repo. Dollar rally maybe over so taking advantage now.

I stayed the course, taking profits on my dollar longs.

now.

8:16 AM **CK** yes, agree

note NZD too btw

8:17 AM Alex Gurevich NZD is getting expensive on the cross. AUD to go first...

8:17 AM **CK** agree w you there

1.02 cross is obscene

AUD got done btw

8:18 AM Alex Gurevich K

8:18 AM **CK** (I'm assuming you have EMSX up in front of you today)

8:28 AM QZ

image.png ▾

---

image.png ▾

	Limit				Limit			
95				60				32
1.43	(1,899,486)	62.5%/23.1		30.92	(4,070,657)	68.7%/45.0		16.49
1.44	(167,091)	14.9%/23.1		7.39	(358,259)	16.4%/45.0		3.94
	(2,066,577)				(4,428,917)			

I mean DEDs

image.png ▾

		Limit				Limit			
95	14		110	60	30		100	32	
36.74	(1,223,717)			78.87	(2,626,753)			42.09	(1,401,974.4
9.04	(439,585)			19.35	(941,014)			10.30	(500,885.9
2.79	(250,854)			5.98	(538,084)			3.19	(287,140.3
48.57	(1,914,157)	87.6%/55.4		104.19	(4,105,851)	96.5%/108.0		55.58	12,190.00

image.png ▾

	Leverage	Limit			Leverage	Limit			Leverage
142.02	1.49			169.45	2.82			89.72	
40.15	0.42	32.2%/124.7		86.03	1.43	35.4%/243.0		45.86	
35.98	0.58	38.9%/92.4		77.17	1.29	42.9%/180.0		41.15	
49.87	0.52	36.0%/138.6		·				·	
21.50	0.23	38.8%/55.4		18.00	0.30	16.7%/108.0		9.00	

Long EM

image.png ▾

MXN	(4.08)	(145,629.89)	-44.2%/9.2	(8.75)	(311,995)	48.6%/18.0	(4.67)	(166,397)	-38.4%/12.2
RUB	(1.45)	(35,726.98)	-15.1%/9.2	(2.99)	(72,272)	-16.6%/18.0	(1.80)	(38,545)	-13.1%/12.2

Risk file in email

image.png ▼

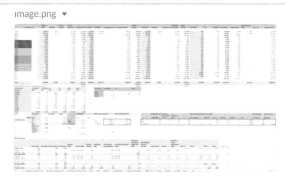

8:34 AM Alex Gurevich Let's put in 70 bid on 300 DEDZ4 just in case

8:35 AM CK k

8:36 AM QZ This is based on last night's P&L. Adjusted for today's P&L, there is around 20-25% capacity left for equities

9:09 AM Alex Gurevich Add to Nikkei. Next 30.

9:09 AM CK see you

done

DEDZ4 @ 70 is done

just your EDJ0's & the PEH0 you put in this AM working

9:28 AM Alex Gurevich What about TIPs - cheap again for outright buy. If can't do off the run (.40 yield on bbg) try buying on the run .22 yield). We can switch later when things come down

9:28 AM CK i'll see if we can get a refresh

9:28 AM QZ ▉ axed on 42

9:29 AM Alex Gurevich Wow axes to sell? Let's buy them!

9:29 AM QZ on 242, 243, according to them

but price is wide, checking now

9:30 AM Alex Gurevich Wait which ones are those? If they are axes ahouldbe wide...

9:30 AM **CK** ■ showed an 'axe to sell' that was 1.5pts above market yesterday

just to temper expectations

9:32 AM QZ ■ offer 106-14

0.41 yld

9:35 AM Alex Gurevich Yes let's take $10mm

9:36 AM QZ outright

9:36 AM Alex Gurevich Yes

9:36 AM QZ repo?

9:36 AM Alex Gurevich Just buy it! And repo too

My responses in this chat are about as testy as you will ever see me get. I was chasing the inflation-indexed bonds again.

9:36 AM Alex Gurevic' ___ March 12th, 2020 ∨ ___) too

9:36 AM CK we are, waiting on them to come back

9:37 AM QZ refreshing price one sec

106-19 now

do it?

9:37 AM Alex Gurevich Yes

9:38 AM QZ done

9:38 AM Alex Gurevich Took a lot... thx.

We may come to increase but need to look at balance sheet first...

What was the total size of their axe?

Did they say?

9:40 AM QZ checking repo right now, ballance sheet is quite full

1.24 repo

9:41 AM Alex Gurevich We could switch out of something but all off-the-runs are very cheap. If anything not too cheap to futures switch out of it.

For example If WN is fair to cash bonds - switch out...

In any sector. Assume everything is very cheap to futures but if not switch out to free balance sheet.

9:43 AM QZ every future is very expensive relative to cash, will check if there is anything marginally reasonable

9:55 AM QZ

https://www.newyorkfed.org/markets/opolicy/operatin g_policy_200312a

9:57 AM Alex Gurevich Well it's getting fixed now!

9:58 AM QZ yes

Re. Tips, more to go, that's all we can get out of him

9:58 AM Alex Gurevich Did we just snap 10bps on tips

9:59 AM QZ seems that way

10:01 AM Alex Gurevich Spreads are really moving / I hope

10:01 AM QZ yes

10:02 AM Alex Gurevich Look at funds Libor going in the opposite direction. Did I nail it!

Reduce another 120 jPy here

10:06 AM CK got it

done

---

needless to say things are all over the place so all of this covering is best efforts around the levels when you make the initial request

(or better, but not chasing worse)

10:13 AM Alex Gurevich	Yes
	Are we net short March funds now?
10:13 AM **CK**	small long in aggregate
	(had we finished the entirety of the clip from earlier we would have been short)
	+605
	FFH0
10:15 AM Alex Gurevich	I thought I sold the last clip entirely?

10:16 AM **CK**	you did 277x at 99.3375 and then pulled the remaining 1223
10:17 AM Alex Gurevich	I am confused don't see any partials left
	Are you sure that's not what I see in my EMSX
10:17 AM **CK**	sorry my apologies
	that last clip is in there
	it was the same one you pulled earlier, not sure why that wasn't updating for me
10:18 AM Alex Gurevich	Phew..

As you can see from the pace of the chatter, fast-paced trading was conducted simultaneously in several markets. As I have mentioned, it was natural for some confusion to occur. However, as I read through this almost a year later, I observe uncharacteristic irritability in my remarks. This stress of sleepless nights had to be getting to me, and all I could do was try to keep a clear focus on my strategic principles.

The market had become disappointed in the possibility of an instantaneous rate cut and March Fed Funds (FFH0) started to sell off. I wanted to make sure that we had already gotten rid of our position.

10:18 AM Alex Gurevic   **March 12th, 2020** ⌄

10:18 AM **CK** i know, better me wrong on that one than you given the direction that has headed

you should be -618 net short

managing bookings right now

10:19 AM Alex Gurevich Let's cover the shorts and get square. Don't want to be short under 25.

10:20 AM **CK** ok so i am going to buy 618x FFH0 here, agree?

(under 99.25)

10:20 AM Alex Gurevich Yes

10:20 AM **CK** great

you'll be flat

sec

10:22 AM Alex Gurevich Looks like we are 4 points up on TIPs

10:23 AM **CK** yea BBG screen was a bit high earlier when we got our quote from where dealers saw so give or take but uhhh yea nice ITM haha

10:24 AM Alex Gurevich I'll be driving for a few minutes. Moving to Sausalito office.

10:24 AM **CK** kk

FF thin so we are sitting on the bid 24.75 right now

It's hard to imagine that after all that activity, it was still morning. I was heading *to* the office.

10:24 AM **CK** kk   **March 12th, 2020** ⌄

FF thin so we are sitting on the bid 24.75 right now

10:55 AM Alex Gurevich Spoke too soon March is going back down - buying more here...

10:56 AM **CK** cool

12:51 PM Alex Gurevich Roundtripped 30bps on tips. Do they they to sell is another $5mm at 52 yield or better?

12:57 PM QZ checking

can work it

not offering there

1:01 PM Alex Gurevich Where are they?

Bouncing a little here...

1:02 PM QZ 105-17

105-18

you there?

1:03 PM Alex Gurevich Thinking

Long bonds bounced a bit. Should be better now. Check agianX can they do 105-08?

1:05 PM QZ checking

can he worrk it?

says thru mid

1:06 PM Alex Gurevich Bouncing again.

Where is he now?

Moving away. Tell him to work 105-08 till close.

1:15 PM QZ doen

done on tip

1:27 PM Alex Gurevich Good. Let's call it a day.

I got cocky too early when they did QE

1:27 PM QZ What a day

1:28 PM Alex Gurevich Thought it was all over in our favor. Little do we know. Think they cut tomorrow morning?

Losing My Innocence

Those last comments reflect that I had begun to lose my pre-COVID innocence. I started the day expecting the huge sell-off in the stock market and overall chaos to work in my favor. The Fed didn't cut outright, but they added liquidity via accelerated purchases of Treasury bills and repo operations. I was expecting the funding pressure to ease, but it kept ratcheting up.

We were losing on our equity positions, on precious metals, and on swaps; the only bright spot on that day was our long dollar position, where I kept taking profits.

The trading day for Thursday was closed for operations purposes and we tallied a significant loss. My guess is, it was the worst day in my portfolio since early 2018. I wasn't worried yet, as the year-to-date performance still looked very strong.

Once again, there was not much of a break. We discussed our strategy about the approaching opening of Asian markets.

do we know ˈˈˈˈˈˈˈˈˈˈˈˈˈˈˈˈˈˈ ˌrrow morning?

March 12th, 2020 ⌄

1:29 PM QZ Hmm, i doubt. might need the market to cool down before they do more, no?

1:29 PM Alex Gurevich Cooling down seems not what the markets are doing

1:30 PM QZ but whatever they do is washed out by headline of famous people getting virus

US is not at the peak of the bad virus news yet...

1:35 PM **CK** insane day

1:36 PM QZ Maybe tomorrow morning, E-mini down anther 200 pts before market open, FED capitulates..

1:37 PM   **CK** i mean stock market is gonna keep probing lower o/n

alex we only got 5 done on the FFH0 < 99.25 from earlier so we remain short 613x...i've killed the order given its moved away and EoD

1:38 PM   QZ Going to run another risk snapshot as of now

1:39 PM   Alex Gurevich It's all right with FFH0 if they don't cut on Friday it's not going anywhere. If they do we have al it to make.

1:42 PM   **CK** yup agreed....ntg done on the PEM0, so i've killed it (3% off market)...just small partial left working on your EDJ0

AUD 62.30 Alex, shall we take some more off?

just gave you a ring but AUD bouncing a bit now, definitely able to work something into EoD if it suits

2:01 PM   **CK** lmk if you have a AUD level in mind that you'd like me to work once market opens up again in an hour

4:37 PM   Alex Gurevich I think CAD is to look at now. Could take off 60 above 1.39.

4:38 PM   **CK** ok roger

doing that here ish

4:47 PM   **CK** done

5:33 PM   Alex Gurevich K

9:45 PM   **CK** AUD rates getting thumped

thin liquidity + this: https://www.news.com.au/lifestyle/health/health-problems/coronavirus-vaccine-canadian-company-claims-to-have-found-a-cure-and-could-do-human-tests-in-weeks/news-story/8652a2d98759d609cf8e73e07d7058fc

     NewsComAu
     Coronavirus: 'We've got the vaccine', says Canadian company

A Canadian company has claimed it's found the cure
for the deadly coronavirus.

Mar 12th, 2020 (17 kB) ▾

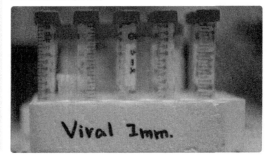

10:28 PM **Christopher Lutton** i saw that making it's way around as
well FROM MY KIDS...defense One has that story which
i think came out very early Thursday but not 100%

That evening, virus-related rumors made it into our chat. I
usually don't like clogging up our work channels with banter, so
HonTe has a separate channel for sharing general market news.
At some point, we also created a "life and safety" channel, where
we would share pandemic information as it pertained to employees and their families.

MARCH 13: FRIDAY

March 13th, 2020 ⌄

5:42 AM QZ Hmm, 3m libor jumped 10bp. Libor ois spread in the
70s!

7:03 AM QZ Slightly overextended in duration. But EDH0 rolling off on Monday. 1y VaR jumped up. Will double check calculation. But given market condition, not suprising

image.png ▾

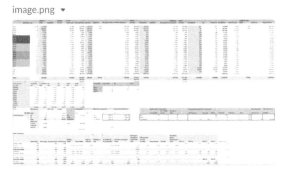

number before % is percent of max limit, number after / is max limit

image.png ▾

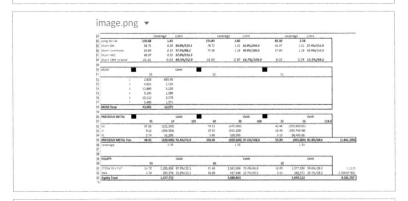

7:11 AM Alex Gurevich It's probably going to be a bit messy with var. my gamble in Mar over the last few days went bust. But so far I am betting they'll bring funding under control. Hence buying April. And yes only one day with somewhat limited downside, then regroup and wait for the Fed.

Early morning brought the news of further funding pressure. I know, by now you've read this phrase too many times. LIBOR jumped higher, and I had to admit that my latest bet on March Eurodollars (EDH0) had failed. Remember, I had still made a large profit on my options on EDH0, but doubling down at the final stretch had backfired.

I had to be increasingly careful allocating risk and thinking of downsides.

March 13th, 2020 ⌄

7:11 AM Alex Gurevich It's probably going to be a bit messy with var. my gamble in Mar over the last few days went bust. But so far I am betting they'll bring funding under control. Hence buying April. And yes only one day with somewhat limited downside, then regroup and wait for the Fed.

Keep an eye on any short end treasuries normalizing to create space for TIPs.

7:12 AM QZ copy

7:14 AM Alex Gurevich Added a little Australia too. Will reassess after Fed seems very cheap, no way rates there are going up.

7:15 AM CK like that scoop, thing completely unraveled last night any dips are a buy there for the indefinite future

8:28 AM CK ADM0 back down at 50 area

(62.50)

8:28 AM Alex Gurevich Where did we last reduce?

8:29 AM CK 63.32 looks like

ADH0 but roll is negligible

*was negligible

****63 last

8:30 AM Alex Gurevich We didn't catch the last drift down?

8:30 AM **CK** 63.68 / 63.32 / 63

8:30 AM Alex Gurevich Ok let's reduce another 120.

8:30 AM **CK** k working around here

done at 40

8:33 AM Alex Gurevich Good.

8:48 AM **CK** 62.00 gone in AUD just now

metals only just now finding a temporary base

8:55 AM Alex Gurevich Can reduce more here.

8:55 AM **CK** buying 120x ADM0 here

done

its 4PM LDN close in 3min + what seems to now be standard pre weekend price insensitive risk reduction

8:58 AM Alex Gurevich Getting on ▮▮▮▮▮ call now

8:58 AM **CK** i would suspect we get even slightly crazier moves in next 2min

ill do more ADM0 if i see 61

---

going to be on that ▮ call too in a moment

8:58 AM Alex Gurevich Yes

8:58 AM **CK** another thing to note as we head into the weekend, but mainly for liquidity next week:

08:48:57 REMINDER FOR MONDAY: CME Pit Trading Floor will be closed at end of business today, the trading floor is shut indefinitely until further notice due to coronavirus. This will affect liquidity in ED options mainly.

> underlying ED will definitely be less liquid as a result so
> we will need to tread more cautiously
>
> 9:02 AM   Alex Gurevich   Add 60 to silver standard

Precious Metals

Guess what? Precious metals are priced in dollars. And every-thing priced in dollars was cratering. By March 2020, I had been long gold for a while, and I had already been diversifying into silver and platinum.

This was a long-horizon play that I initiated in 2016. The logic was that gold plugged a major hole in my portfolio. I was long dollar and long US Treasury bonds with a smidgen of long equities. What was I afraid of? The inflationary collapse of the USD. I was not expecting it—back then, the interest rate differential was very supportive of the dollar—but I didn't rule it out.

My logic was that gold was cheap, and it likely would not get really expensive till the next cycle occurred, but if something were to go sideways, I didn't want to have to chase the price of gold as it moved higher. This is how I presented my portfolio construction at the Global Macro Investor (GMI) conference in 2017:

Portfolio Construction Pyramid: Underscores why long gold, long bonds, and long dollar against Swiss franc constituted a balanced portfolio.

Even though it was not my entire portfolio, I felt that those three positions (long gold, long bonds, and long dollar via short Swiss franc) represented a balanced combination able to withstand most economic scenarios. As it happened, this structure came under a lot of pressure in early 2018 (as discussed in Chapter 1) but eventually withstood the test of time. The dollar rebounded in late 2018, bonds took off in 2019, and as interest rates started to fall, gold gained traction after a multiyear slump.

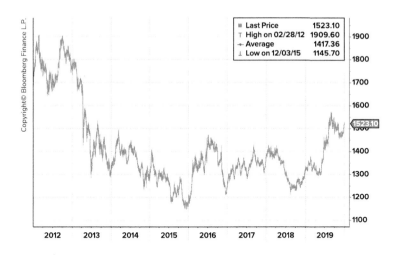

Roll-Adjusted Gold Future Price 2012–2019: After a multiyear slump, gold gained traction in 2019.

On the surface, that made sense. When the yield on cash holdings declines, zero-yielding (or negative-yielding if you account for storage costs) assets like gold become more attractive.

However, in past cycles, the initial easing was not the time when precious metals had their strongest performance. Such price action is a product of the broad strength the dollar tends to exhibit when the Fed starts to cut rates. This phenomenon trips up many traders who bet on the "obvious" causality of lower rates leading to a weaker dollar.

In fact, two other paradigms dominate:

- **Causality:** When rates are being cut, US treasuries become more attractive to foreign investors due to potential for price appreciation. Thus, cross-border

flows into bonds drive the dollar higher via capital
account surplus.

- **Concurrency**: Initial cuts tend to respond to tightening of financial conditions, often caused by recession
  or crisis. Thus, the beginning of easing is almost by
  definition concurrent with a shortage of liquidity.
  Until this shortage is fully alleviated, the dollar
  goes up.

The following charts show how gold performed around the two
previous easing cycles. The circled areas are early in the cycle; the
rest is the subsequent uptrend.

*Roll-Adjusted Gold Future Price 2001–2002: This chart illustrates gold perfor-
mance during 2001–2002 Fed easing cycle.*

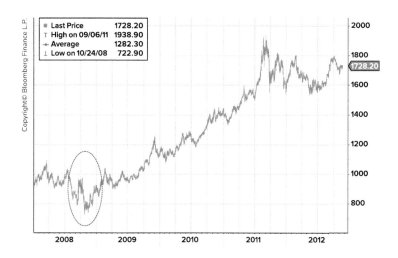

Roll-Adjusted Gold Future Price 2007–2012: The 2007–2008 easing cycle and the subsequent Fed-on-hold years.

Hence, in 2019, I was not expecting any gains on gold and was surprised by the early rebound. My strategy, however, doesn't rely on me guessing the exact trajectory of the price. Both charts shown above demonstrate that *eventually* the liquidity was provided, and precious metals went into a multiyear bull market.

Here is an excerpt from my Macrovoices interview:

"I see a secular bull market involved. I see we are at the beginning of secular bull market. I think the move that occurred so far, depending upon whether you think if from $1,200 to $1,500 is just a minor blip, is the beginning of a move which could be several times higher in magnitude

And I think that, given how we measure the previous bull markets in gold and how we are in the cycle, I would be surprised to find gold below $3,000 five years from now.

...

And, yes, we might get a better entry opportunity. But it's not relevant because the upside is way too big to wait.

...

But if you think as you and I do, I think you absolutely have to rush to the screen and buy gold.

You need to, like, stop this conversation, pause in the middle of this interview, and buy gold — if that is the view you subscribe to."

"Pause this interview and buy gold" ended up being frequently quoted. It was not a universal trade recommendation; I try to avoid those. Rather, it was a strategic suggestion for a particular group of long-term gold bulls.

What I was saying was that if you did hold the opinion that the continuing flood of easy money from the Fed would put pressure on fiat money and eventually precious metals would have no choice but to stage a massive rally, the correct strategy would be to buy gold at that moment and not wait for some technical or fundamental catalyst.

This had to do with the idea I discussed in TNPT about muddying your P/L profile from a very high-expected-value trade by overlaying it with lower edge short-term bets.

...opportunities to capture a massive move of a developed market currency are very rare. You will only have a few of those in your career.

So if you have a profitable short-term technical strategy - by all means, trade it on its own value. But overlaying a rare and valuable long-horizon macro call with tight stops and technical entry points will only "muddy-up" your risk profile and create a potential for missing your move.

This was written in the context of trading currencies but could be applied to any asset class including gold. Let's look at what gold did in 2020.

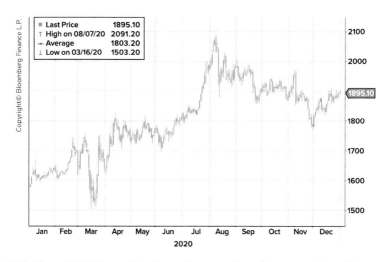

Roll-Adjusted Gold Future Price December 2019–December 2020: A few spikes prior to March 2020 due to geopolitical events, a crash in March 2020, and a takeoff after the Fed injected liquidity.

Even before the epidemic fear became central to financial markets, one sitting on the sidelines could have been spooked into buying gold at higher levels. Remember the brief Iran crisis after the drone strike on January 3, 2020? Like all market events on the other side of March 2020, this one feels very long ago.

The subsequent intraday spike on January 8 could have made you worry that you had missed the boat and sucked you into buying. Or would you sit it out? Would you hold out till early March when you would become sure that gold *had* to go up... only to get trashed a few days later? Or would you only have gotten into gold after it broke out later in July 2020 and ridden it all the way back to your entry point?

I am stating those hypotheticals to show how difficult it is to wait for a good entry point and how much easier it is just to be in the position if you are confident in the long run.

When the COVID recession started to loom on the horizon, I wasn't expecting it to be an immediate boost for my precious metals. In fact, on March 2 I tweeted (and pinned it for a while):

Alex Gurevich ✔
@agurevich23   ...

Repeat after me:
Gold hedges inflationary shocks like wars
Gold doesn't hedge deflationary shocks like epidemics

7:08 AM · Mar 2, 2020 from Tiburon, CA · Twitter for iPhone

222 Retweets   **45** Quote Tweets   **1,279** Likes

Rather, it benefits from later Fed actions.

Later, when gold did go up, some people gave me a hard time for that tweet. But I held to my statement. This is how I responded to critics:

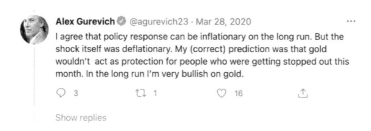

Indeed, gold and silver were not helping my portfolio (or anyone's portfolio) in the sequence of several painful trading days starting from March 9, 2020.

I have to confess, even though I didn't expect positive price action fireworks, I wasn't ready for the extreme price collapse either.

Why did it happen?

In my article[15] from a few years ago, I drew a parallel between precious metals and cryptocurrencies. I explained that no one actually *needs* to own gold. The industrial and jewelry demand for the metal is negligible relative to above-ground supply. Its monetary worth is derived from its consensus rating as a store of value. The performance of gold can be viewed as an indicator of excess liquidity. If people have a lot of cash, they'll buy some

---

15 https://honteinv.com/in-quest-for-digital-gold/

gold with it; otherwise, they won't. It's that simple.

There is, however, a broad perception of gold as both a risk hedge and an inflation hedge. Indeed, it does usually jump when geopolitical concerns rise. Investors turn to the "safety" of gold when their domestic currency gets severely debased or in the event of an imminent war.

Wars tend to be inflationary in themselves, almost by definition. Accelerated spending and production, coupled with actually destroying *physical* wealth, would naturally lead to increasing amounts of money relative to available goods.

It is natural to buy gold in such situations, but its functionality can be reduced to being just an inflation hedge or, if you wish, an excess liquidity hedge, not a risk hedge.

By Friday, March 13, investors who were holding gold as a hedge had begun liquidating.

9:02 AM Alex Gurevic   **March 13th, 2020** ˅   ıdard

9:02 AM **CK** k

9:09 AM **CK** super choppy, still working, partial done

done

still looking to unwind remainder of CAD at 1.40? we are back at 1.3950

9:45 AM Alex Gurevich For now maybe reduce another 120 JPY.

9:45 AM **CK** k

done

12:30 PM QZ Sorry to bother. We have an issue here.

Due to big move in EDH0, ■■■■ equity is -3.5 mm as of now.

Heading into the weekend, pandemic disruptions were beginning to mount and the developing funding crisis was making me nervous. Stocks were rebounding sharply, diminishing the likelihood of immediate policy action. My portfolio, however, continued to tank as the drag from treasuries, spreads, LIBOR setting, and precious metals overwhelmed the gains from the dollar and equities.

We were still comfortably up on the year, but our capital was increasingly tied up, and margin pressures started to surface in some portfolios.

done   March 13th, 2020 ⌄

12:30 PM QZ Sorry to bother. We have an issue here.

Due to big move in EDH0, ■■■■ equity is -3.5 mm as of now.

Waiting on timeline when we have to shore up the amount

If it is EOD today, we may have to sell collateral or option.

12:32 PM Alex Gurevich Free up on Monday anyway?

12:32 PM QZ Option expiration on Monday should free up 2.8 mm assuming 56 ticks

yes, getting exact time, hopefully by EOD Monday

12:33 PM Alex Gurevich Selling collateral won't get cash in today anyway

12:35 PM   QZ Will update shortly once we have a clear deadline

12:39 PM   Alex Gurevich I could wire money in - but that requires
           subdoc?

12:40 PM   QZ Copy, will give ▇▇▇▇ a call

12:44 PM   QZ A small piece of money, we can exercise 600ish
           EDM0 option. leftover from last time. Doing it now

           👤 1 reply 1 year ago

1:53 PM   QZ EDM0 98.375 exercise is in. We communicated with
           ▇▇▇ on EDH0 option expiration as of Monday morning
           8 am. Unless market moves against us drastically, in
           theory we should be ok. Subscription does not make the
           cutoff. In worst case, we may have to sell collateral.

           👍 1   ☺️⁺

Everything we do as a hedge fund depends on funding and leverage. This is what allows us to take aggregate positions far in excess of the cash value of our AUM (assets under management). I have explained earlier our dependence on borrowing via repo (repurchase agreements). The borrowing is explicit when we take positions on bonds funded by repo and implicit when we buy futures.

The reliable funding (ability to borrow against) for safe Treasury bonds and liquid exchange-traded futures is the bedrock of our operations—or, if you wish, the rug that was being pulled from under our feet.

Friday, the 13th (can't make this up!), ended with a loss even greater than the previous day's. Heading into the weekend of the Ides of March, I was starting to feel that my super-successful portfolio was a giant with clay feet.

CHAPTER 6

WEEK 3: THE DARK DAYS

Back in my days at J.P. Morgan, my colleagues used to think of me as superhuman for my ability to stay calm and measured in the face of any market volatility or financial losses. In fact, I have always been good at *appearing calm*. I have never thrown my phone, cursed brokers, or screamed at junior traders. A thirty-million-dollar loss has always been less likely to set me off than a glitch in a computer system.

Speaking of glitches, when my Wall Street career took off in the 2000s and I became known for my equanimity on the trading floor, I started to have glitches in my personal life. The stress of being a senior trader responsible for all the decisions in my portfolio seeped into my personal life. I became completely unable to make even the simplest decisions in my daily routine. A traffic light turning red just in front of me felt like the cruelest blow of fate, frustration rendering me incapable of driving.

Since then, I have learned to cope with my stress a bit better. Although I haven't become (and am unlikely to ever become) an easygoing, low-stress person in my daily life, I am at least more consistently functional.

A good way to clear my mind and to calm my nerves is to put myself into a situation where I don't have to make any decisions. The pressure of the first two weeks of March was getting to me, so over the weekend, I went to my favorite hot spring resort. Whether to begin with *hot pool* or *cold plunge* was about all the management responsibility I could handle.

Hand sanitizers were everywhere, and temperatures were taken at the entry. But masks had not yet been introduced into our routines. My extra justification for going there: I believed the boost to my immune system outweighed the risk of infection.

There were definitely no hugs or handshakes. I soon realized it was hard not to touch anything other people were touching, such as pool railings. Despite the contact concerns, I still enjoyed the water and even chatted with some friends. We talked about travels, life plans, and various other non-COVID topics.

MARCH 15: SUNDAY

I packed early on the afternoon of Sunday the 15th, getting ready to pick up my kids from their grandparents' on my way home (even having them stay with grandparents had been a cause for trepidation).

As I stepped into an area of better cell reception, I received the message I had barely allowed myself to hope for. The Federal

Reserve had executed an emergency rate cut of 1% (or 100 bps) and promised a major asset purchasing program. The timing could not have been better—as far as I was concerned, it was just under the wire.

To my embarrassment, when I purchased the options on the March 2020 contract (EDH0), I hadn't thought through one technical issue: the Federal Reserve policy announcement was happening Wednesday, March 18, but the contract settlement was calculated against the LIBOR rate published on Monday, March 16 at 11:55 a.m. London time, two days earlier. All my options were about to expire before the easing could be fully priced in.

In my defense, when I entered the position, I hadn't expected the COVID crisis. If the contract price had been driven by a more predictable easing path, such as in 2019, this timing discrepancy would have been less of a problem.

Up to this point, there has been a lot of talk about a "relief from the Fed." I realize that some readers may feel cynical about the central bank bailing out hedge fund managers. I urge you not to apply this resentment indiscriminately. There were undoubtedly asset managers in trouble, and an easier policy would help them, as it had in previous recessions. Whether in recent history, monetary policy has been used correctly to stabilize asset prices during times of crisis is a question of politics and economics and is way beyond this book's scope.

Macro managers like myself don't have a mandate to hold assets such as stocks and bonds. Rather, we use all available tools to capitalize on any direction the financial markets might take. I focus not on what the Fed *should* do but on what the Fed *will* do. If I thought they were going to fumble, nothing was stopping me from liquidating the risk positions (yes, the markets on the week of March 9–13 were still functioning well enough to allow that) and book profits.

I chose to bet on the Fed stepping in. As with all market judgments, you make money when you are right, and when you are wrong, well, you know...This is a very different reality from being stuck in positions and hoping for a rescue.

Having said that, LIBOR had been frustrating me by creeping up. My sallies into fading this move by buying March and April Eurodollars were only causing more aggravation. So it appeared the cavalry had arrived just in the nick of time, only hours ahead of the LIBOR reset.

The original chat related to this event is not in this book. Indeed, at 2:00 p.m. on Sunday, I was not anywhere close to a computer screen. I had to put in my earbuds and try to make sense of the situation as I drove. Fortunately, my team members *were* at their posts and were filling me in on the phone.

I am kind of glad I didn't look at the screen at that first moment. My portfolio P/L was probably flashing the greatest gain in my career in absolute dollars and possibly in percentages as well. Not actually seeing the numbers with my own eyes reduced my disappointment afterward.

What the market giveth, the market taketh, and I am used to it. Profits evaporating on occasion is the price of trying to pyramid one's gains. After over twenty years of trading, I have the fortitude to withstand gyration, but something different fell over me on that drive home.

The Point of No Return

I got the sinking feeling that we were not out of the woods yet. As I mentioned, it is theoretically possible to cross the event horizon of a supermassive black hole and not even notice it.

Some part of me must have known. The Ides of March was the point of no return, and the world would never be the same.

oops, typo, 99.3125

3:25 PM QZ That includes 9000 in options

closed at 99.065 on Friday

short 613 FFH0 in ■■, right now 99.38, I don't see much mispricing

3:26 PM **CK** updated FX:

image.png ▾

Ticker	Last Price	%1D
EURUSD	↓1.1168	+0.55%
CCFREUR%	20.07y	
USDJPY	↓106.15	-1.37%
EURJPY	↓118.57	-0.75%
GBPUSD	↑1.2378	+0.81%
EURGBP	↓.9020	-0.15%
EURCHF	↑1.0568	-0.03%
USDCHF	↓.9466	-0.54%
USDCAD	↓1.3822	+0.12%
AUDUSD	↓.6168	-0.56%
NZDUSD	↑.6032	-1.66%

Copyright© Bloomberg Finance L.P.

Qin sent over ED, here is FF:

image.png ▾

Ticker	Last Price	Net
▸ US MACRO (18)		
▸ EURODOLLAR (23)		
▾ FF & SOFR & FRA/OIS (24)		
▸ FF1	99.3800	+0.10
▸ FF2	↓99.910	+0.07
▸ FF3	↓99.910	+0.04
▸ FF4	99.920	+0.04
▸ FF5	↓99.920	+0.03
▸ FF6	↓99.925	+0.02
▸ FF7	99.935	+0.03
▸ FF8	99.925	+0.02
▸ FF9	99.920	+0.03
▸ FF10	99.910	+0.02

Copyright© Bloomberg Finance L.P.

US bond futs:

image.png ▼

Ticker	Last Price	Net	Volume	%1D
▸ FFA	↓99.910	+0.07	9428	+0.07%
▸ TUA	↑110-13⁷	+0-08³₄	32367	+0.25%
▸ FVA	↑125-08½	+1-02¼	70150	+0.86%
▸ TYA	↑137-31	+1-22	57703	+1.24%
▸ USA	↑179-14	+2-25	7395	+1.57%
▸ WNA	↑218-14	+6-00	514	+2.82%

Copyright© Bloomberg Finance L.P.

metals:

image.png ▼

Ticker	Last Price	%1D	Net
▸ COMMOD INDEX (12)			
▾ METALS (24)			
XAU	↑1554.35	+1.60%	+24.5.
▸ GCA	↓1553.40	+2.42%	+36.7(
▸ GCGC	-.70	+30.00	+0.30
▸ SIA	14.915	+2.86%	+0.42
▸ PLA	750.30	+0.86%	+6.40
▸ PAA	1592.00	+5.49%	+82.9(
▸ HGA	245.70	-0.28%	-0.70

Copyright© Bloomberg Finance L.P.

4:19 PM Alex Gurevich curve flattening slightly but not catastrophically it seems. we should start getting ideas how treasuries are performing vs. eurodollars?

4:21 PM QZ I think 8 pm, should have some picture on spreads

For off the run, unlikely any clarity

4:22 PM Alex Gurevich i believe Libor setting will be reflexive with EDH0. Markets are so thin maybe we can't sell or we'll drive the Libor up? Crazy?

You saw me joining the chat the moment I was settling in front of my desktop at home. EDH0 was up 25 bps, implying that LIBOR setting a few hours away would be 0.25% lower than projected at Friday close. But the bid was beginning to fade. With trading just opening in Asia, there was no real liquidity to take profits. I expressed a notion that was likely a bit silly.

You must understand, though, that the process of LIBOR setting is extremely opaque and subjective—murky even to those who, like me, have spent decades trading LIBOR swaps. There is a reason why LIBOR setting scandals swelled up in the aftermath of the GFC and why the swap market is currently in the process of moving away from using LIBOR.

There is a notion out there that the bankers who submit LIBOR settings watch the futures and are influenced by the price action. Could it be that by selling a few thousand contracts into a thin market I could drive the price and influence the bankers to set the rate higher and hurt my remaining position?

Given the scale of that multitrillion-dollar market, it was doubtful that my portfolio alone could affect the price. However, the fact that I even considered this testifies to how unstable the market was at that time.

Sorting through the chaos, we tried to find value. CK pointed out that Australia was lagging in the rate-cutting bonanza, and I decided to build up a position in Australian bond futures (XMM0 was the front contract at the moment).

drive the Li! **March 15th, 2020** ⌄

4:22 PM **CK** here's short term idea: what about more AUD bonds? they aren't from from where they are the past few days

aren't far

4:24 PM QZ yea, that's crazy

4:24 PM **CK** XMM0 @ 99.09

4:28 PM Alex Gurevich Still cheap

4:29 PM **CK** yea feels like it...all these rates markets feel a bit at the mercy of being at the lower bound so we have to decide if worthwhile in the very short term given some of the squeezes...but that feels kinda wrong even still

RBnZ and Fed act emergency on Sunday...doesn't RBA have to do something? and thats beside the point that we know where those yields have to go in the medium term

agree re EDH0

4:47 PM Alex Gurevich Add 120 XMA at 99.075 or better.

4:47 PM **CK** k

99.12 right now

will get the bid in

staged for 120x, but only 60x working at 99.0750 currently....order book is thin so no reason to telegraph our interest to the market until it gets a bit more liquid

BoJ policy meeting at noon Tokyo time (3hrs +)

The cut provided some much-needed relief for the swap spreads. Our discussion was the measure of our uncertainty over any pricing.

BoJ policy r   **March 15th, 2020** ⌄   time (3hrs +)

4:57 PM   Alex Gurevich I see. Saw it trading down there earlier. Not to worry. Watch KRW if it weakens further and forwards I assume moving more in our favor may be worth starting to take profits.

4:58 PM   **CK** yea it was down there for like 20mins

anything close to 99 is definitely worthwhile, maybe we get lucky in the overnight liquidity spasms

sounds good re KRW, local spot market hasn't yet opened (think in 1min?)...any level in mind?

JAPAN MOF OFFICIAL: MUST LOOK AT FX MARKET GOING AHEAD

5:02 PM   QZ Treasury market just opened

I mean cash trading

5:02 PM   Alex Gurevich Any sense what TIPs are doing among other

5:02 PM   QZ no market there

On cash curve, 7-10 best performer

5:04 PM   Alex Gurevich Let me know when you have a sense of cash. It seemed to me that five year futures were ahead of Eurodollars but not certain of anything...

5:06 PM   **CK** take with a grain of salt but ballpark starting levels:

image.png ▾

image.png ▾

Ticker	Last Price	Net
USGG3M	↓.1220	-0.12
USGG2YR	↓.2994	-0.19
USGG3YR	.6001y	+0.04
USGG5YR	↓.4266	-0.29
USGG10YR	↓.6261	-0.33
USGG30YR	↑1.2951	-0.23
USYC2Y5Y	↓11.923	-9.93
USYC2Y10	↑31.876	-14.33
USYC2Y30	↓98.489	-4.62
USYC5Y10	↓19.327	-4.71
USYC5Y30	↑85.940	+5.00
USYC1030	↑65.497	+9.40

(3yr point is stale)

5:06 PM QZ Your sense is right, I see FV rallied around 21bp, while 5y bundle around 18.5

short end spread has widened, 5-9 bp, but obviously fluid

5:13 PM QZ Hard to tell exactly, but i think cash bonds are outperforming treasury future by quite a bit now, in other words, implied repo appears to converge towards ois.

Hope it is not illusion

5:13 PM Alex Gurevich :) watch the basis if it gets fair can start taking profits...

5:15 PM QZ Not sure if we can trade basis right now, but definitely tomorrow morning

5:18 PM CK 10bps 2y futs, 22bps 5yr fut, 30bps 10yr fut, 26bps 30yr fut vs this recent cash update validates what Qin saying:

image.png ▾

Ticker	Last Price	Net
USGG2YR	↑.2855	-0.20
USGG3YR	↓.3610	-0.24
USGG5YR	↓.4234	-0.29
USGG10YR	↓.6308	-0.33
USGG30YR	↑1.2934	-0.24

but again, hard to know what is real still

5:19 PM Alex Gurevich I am not even certain we'll be up money
by Tomorrow morning

5:20 PM **CK** i'm not counting on it

Given our positioning, the very idea of not making money on an emergency 100-bp cut seemed preposterous.

Again, the black hole comparison is apt. Once you pass the event horizon, there is no escape velocity, not even the speed of light. No form of propulsion, no force in the physical universe could reverse your trajectory to the central singularity.

The Only Future You Can Have

In my recent forays into the science of black holes, I acquired a deeper understanding of that inevitability. Time and space become interchangeable within the event horizon. Time itself flows into the singularity. The singularity is not just a point in space ahead of you. It is your future. The only future you can have.

Furthermore, one might think that by firing your engines, you may slow down your fall, make yourself linger a bit before the final collapse, but this is not the case. The way I think of it: since all directions lead toward the singularity, accelerating in any direction will only speed up the fall. The Fed had definitely fired its engines. But what would be the impact?

5:20 PM **CK** i'm not cc   March 15th, 2020 ⌄

5:37 PM **CK** 2s seems fickle on ▆▆ but rest of USGG tickers seem accurate vs ▆▆ indications: ▆▆▆
▆▆▆▆▆

17:31:40 23.65 (2) 33.6 (3) 41.7 (5) 58.3 (7) 64.7 (10) 129.5 (30)

5:53 PM QZ If my screen is right, we should have made 15bp or more on 10/23. But trading now is a stretch. Will likely pay away 1 bp to do 3y bundle vs FV, unlikely to get a tight quote on FV vs 10.23 or any quote at all. May have to just unwind the basis in the morning. Let us know if you want to do it now.

5:54 PM Alex Gurevich We don't have to unwind. I am just trying to gauge we we are

5:57 PM QZ Copy

6:00 PM **CK** any level / amount you'd like to unwind in the AM if it's there? figure it can't be bad to have marching orders on this when we wake up in the AM since market has been so whippy

also, just now: 18:02:08 *RBA STANDS READY TO PURCHASE AUSTRALIA GOVT BONDS

*RBA: WILL ANNOUNCE FURTHER POLICY MEASURES ON THURSDAY

8bps move 10yr

6:14 PM Alex Gurevich Did we get the extra ones?

6:15 PM **CK** no unfort

slipped back down to 99.10 or so before exploded higher

99.21 now

the upsize last week looks good though!

6:19 PM　Alex Gurevich　Yes can't get them all

The Royal Bank of Australia (RBA) stepped in with verbal easing and we missed our bond purchase. Oh well. On the other hand, the AUD weakened further, and I continued to take profits. I had implemented the strategy of incrementally reducing my positions once they reached preset target levels for years.

It can be frustrating because as the market keeps moving in my favor, I feel that I am giving up profits. Conversely, when the price snaps against me, I question why I took off only a small piece. The fact is, I haven't come up with anything better. Incremental reductions seem to work out for me in the long run because they allow me to feel in control of my position and give me a sense of better navigating market swings.

Another trader may achieve a similar result by running a full position with a trailing stop, for example, or by using some technical indicator of when to take profits. My sense is that all reasonable exit strategies have similar mathematical expectation, so I apply the one most suited to my psychological makeup.

This is an important point. I cannot claim to always make decisions in a perfectly dispassionate, logical way. Human thought is inevitably affected by emotional stresses and cognitive biases. I try to pursue strategies that keep me most isolated from my idiosyncratic emotional vulnerabilities. In other words, all else being equal, I choose the approach that stresses me least. I would go so far as to say that it may be worth sacrificing incremental value in the market for the option value of guaranteeing your clear thinking through future market events.

Hence, incremental reductions.

6:19 PM Alex Gurevic   March 15th, 2020 ⌄   ‖

6:19 PM **CK** AUD back lower though if we want to pick back up there

we mentioned 61 on Friday, at 6109 now

6:24 PM Alex Gurevich Yes can Cover another 120.

6:24 PM **CK** k

30 done, not chasing, will stay at 61.15

6:37 PM **Tony Peng** Trend portfolio rebalance for Monday 3/16/2020: No signal changes. Leverage is further reduced from 5.63 to 4.79 amid high vol in the past week. Rebalance occurs in multiple positions due to large price movements as well as changes in Model recommendation in overall asset classes: FX weight 39%-> 41%, Bond weight 45%->42%, Equity weight 16% ->17%.

image.png ▼

FX futures	Contract Value	CRNCY	xrcy	Score	Signal	Theoretical Positions	Theoretical Exposure	Trade Position Positions	Existing	New	Exposure	Tracking Error
JY1 Curncy	116,283	USD	1	1	3	14.91	1,733,888	14	16	-2	$1,627,675	-6%
CD1 Curncy	71,800	USD	1	1	3	24.15	1,733,888	24	26	-2	$1,725,200	-1%
RN1 Curncy	60,320	USD	1	3	1	-86.23	(5,201,665)	-86	-92	6	($5,187,520)	0%
AD1 Curncy	61,450	USD	1	3	3	-84.65	(5,201,665)	-84	-88	4	($5,161,800)	-1%
SF1 Curncy	131,588	USD	1	0	2	0.00	0	0	0	0	$0	0%
EC1 Curncy	139,056	USD	1	0	2	0.00	0	0	0	0	$0	0%
BP1 Curncy	77,065	USD	1	1	1	-22.50	(1,733,888)	-22	-24	2	($1,695,375)	-2%
Total					8			230	248	16	$16,966,570	
Bond futures												
TY1 Comdty	138,281	USD	1	2	1	-33.92	(4,622,254)	-34	-42	8	($4,833,563)	0%
JB1 Comdty	153,280,000	JPY	0.00927	1	1	-1.63	(2,311,127)	-2	-2	0	($2,842,731)	23%
XM1 Comdty	148,067	AUD	0.8203	1	1	-25.16	(2,311,127)	-26	-28	2	($2,387,990)	3%
CN1 Comdty	146,990	CAD	0.7243	1	1	-21.71	(2,311,127)	-22	-26	4	($2,342,227)	1%
RX1 Comdty	174,170	EUR	1.1107	2	1	-23.89	(4,622,254)	-24	-30	6	($4,642,815)	0%
Total					7			108	128	20	$18,049,323	

> 10:09 PM **CK** BoJ action...kept policy rate unch'ed but seem pretty
> willing to act if things go haywire....up'ed their ETF
> purchase target and adjusted corp bond / CP buying

MARCH 16: MONDAY MORNING

The monetary engine failed to bring down the LIBOR setting or to
assuage the market panic.

> March 16th, 2020 ˅
> 4:59 AM   QZ 3m libor 0.88938, rose 4.62bp
>
> Fear reigns
>
> SPY down -10%, silver -14%, gold -3.2%, margin calls...

I assumed that LIBOR would have been higher without the cut.
It did set a bit lower than where it had been projected on Friday
afternoon. Going back to the black hole theory, I don't know if the
policy action made any impact on the price trajectory. Any effect
on the market so far would be purely psychological—it takes time
for liquidity to "seep" into the market and even longer to affect
the real economy.

> SPY down -´   March 16th, 2020 ˅   ' -3.2%, margin calls...
> 5:43 AM Alex Gurevich Count our. Blessings. Where would have
> Libor set without the cut?
>
> 🐦 1   ☺⁺

5:44 AM QZ Sorting out margin for ████████, should be ok, finger crossed

5:50 AM Alex Gurevich Surprised AUD and CAD bonds are not moving.

We'll look at TIPs some more today.
1. Do you know why 2042 look like having the highest yield any reason. Maybe ask some else other than ████?
2. Does ████ have more of those to go?

5:54 AM QZ Reserve Bank said it was ready to buy the nation's sovereign bonds to support the market. But, it said a

---

policy announcement will only come on Thursday. Aussie bonds still aren't keeping up with the rally in U.S. government securities

████ does have more to go, I think. Can't trade with ██ yet on cash bond. asking now

Also gearing up to unwind 2023s to free up room

6:07 AM QZ I was wrong, ████ is no longer axed to sell 242,243. Trying to get some color on the kink of TIPs curve

6:13 AM Alex Gurevich We also can switch some cash 30yr into TIPS but was more interesting last night (though not executable) cash 30 rallied more than TIPs

6:28 AM QZ sorry, dealing with ████ right now, they still ask us to sell collateral, Going to talk to margin dept, will update

---

Our gains on Sunday had faded, primarily because of the collapse in precious metals. The overall portfolio was holding up, but increasing margin requirements and sharp price movements were causing margin calls in certain subportfolios.

Portfolio Collateral

This might be a good time to talk about portfolio collateral. When a macro manager like us receives $100 million from investors, it doesn't mean that we go out and buy $100 million worth of assets such as stocks. Rather, this cash is mostly used as collateral (or margin) requirement to trade exchange-traded futures, over-the-counter derivatives, foreign exchange forwards, and other leveraged instruments.

Only a fraction of this cash is needed on a typical day. Indeed, if we built up our risk to the point that all our cash would be tied up in margin, even the smallest drawdown would cause margin calls and position unwinds. Thus, much of the money ends up sitting there as a reserve. It improves the fund's performance to earn at least some interest on the excess cash, but it has to be kept safe and liquid.

As far as I know, most managers tended to keep their cash in short-term instruments like Treasury bills of three months or shorter maturity. I, however, preferred holding medium-term Treasury notes (six to seven years maturity). It worked for me, as it satisfied my position preference to long Treasury bonds in general (short maturities wouldn't have much price upside) and to be long bonds versus swaps. That is, I would hold bonds as collateral and regulate my duration (my exposure to movement in interest rates) via various swap instruments. Without going through all the math, take my word that it led to a better cash flow than keeping cash in short instruments and replicating the asset swap exposure separately.

There is a transaction cost to buying and selling assets, which creates a downside to my approach. As you may have read in the chat a bit ago, we used some of our free cash to buy extra notes. Now we were forced to sell some of that collateral back in a hurry to raise the required cash.

---

executable) **March 16th, 2020** ∨ 'han TIPs

6:28 AM QZ sorry, dealing with █████ right now, they still ask us to sell collateral, Going to talk to margin dept, will update

6:34 AM QZ looks like we need to sell 3mm treasury. They used start of the day number which show negative equity of 5.5 milion

Looking at selling 3 mm T 2.25 11/25, curr yield 0.625

6:44 AM QZ If agreed, will go ahead to do this

7:01 AM QZ We will have to go ahead with this.

8:09 AM Alex Gurevich Ok if it fixes the problem

We could exerci more option later

8:22 AM Alex Gurevich Can you get me some color on what's going on with Canadian bonds? I want to buy more. Are they having funding issues like US?

8:22 AM **CK** sure, will check now

8:30 AM QZ haha, Fed bought 100m of our 10/23

8:37 AM Alex Gurevich Did it move them?

8:40 AM QZ not much. But 12+ bp richer from where we bought

Everything I said earlier notwithstanding, the Fed had started to buy some Treasury issues as part of their liquidity program, and when they bought what we owned, it provided some incremental relief.

Currency Gains

Despite the pressure on our portfolio, there was still enough going right. When the Canadian central bank joined the party, there was an opportunity to take profits on Canadian dollar short (long USDCAD) and to look to buy more Canadian bond futures.

8:40 AM QZ not much   **March 16th, 2020** ⌄   om where we bought

8:48 AM QZ ***FED TO CONDUCT ADDITIONAL O/N REPO OP. MONDAY; MAX SIZE $500B**

👍 1 ☺

8:52 AM **CK** still waiting on further color, but initial feedback is similar to what we expected...BoC announced buybacks & switch buybacks...seeing a bit of relief in the cash market after the recent measures...unwind flow of past few days is starting to turn to cash buyers here at these levels on the back of the BoC shifts

---

Trend done a short while ago:

image.png ▾

EXECUTION					
Security	Action	Qty	LH	OA	Fill
JYM0 Curncy	Sell	-2	-1	-1	94.9125
CDM0 Curncy	Sell	-2	-1	-1	71.59
NVM0 Curncy	Buy	6	3	3	60.8667
ADM0 Curncy	Buy	4	2	2	61.47
BPM0 Curncy	Buy	2	1	1	123.33
TYM0 Comdty	Buy	8	4	4	137-20+
XMM0 Comdty	Buy	2	1	1	99.005
CNM0 Comdty	Buy	4	2	2	146.43
RXM0 Comdty	Buy	6	3	3	172.53
DFWM0 Index	Buy	6	3	3	8783.167
NHM0 Index	Buy	2	1	1	16512.5
Z M0 Index	Buy	6	3	3	5098.083

9:00 AM **Tony Peng** Confirmed on Trend trades.

9:03 AM **CK** USDCAD back up near 1.40, only have a few $$ left (94x) if you have a level you want to unwind (last we discussed was 1.40)

9:04 AM Alex Gurevich Cover CAD

9:05 AM **CK** BoC just announced funding market measures

9:05 AM Alex Gurevich I'll be buying more CN bonds

9:05 AM **CK** k

CAD is covered, we are now flat

(excluding Trend)

posted the statement on #general chat

BoC is buying CAD MBS & expanding collateral eligibility to ease funding constraints in non-mtg mkt (in summary)

9:11 AM Alex Gurevich Feel free to pull out my routez and put in small pieces. Exact price not important. Hard to get liquidity in CNM0.

9:11 AM **CK** sounds good, its def thin

yea our bid was supporting the market

going to work in clips of smaller

its alll algos in CNM0 right now so as you suspected, can't show anything big in t h eorder book

100/600 done

Canadian bond futures (CN) are usually liquid, despite their trading volume being much lower than that of the US ten-year note futures (TY). The size we were trying to execute in this chat should have never made a dent in the trading. The markets were very thin.

There was some discussion of repo funding, and then I turned to buying Brazilian currency, which was washing out along with other emerging markets.

100/600 dc   **March 16th, 2020** ⌄

9:24 AM QZ reg on GC last trading 0.95, on the screen one week 0.42 (unverified), off the run still trading around 5 bp wide.

TU implied 0.94(?) FV implied repo 0.75

9:26 AM **CK** 250/600 done...giving it a breather...see if it drops out then i can aggres in 100

9:30 AM Alex Gurevich Still very high repo I am sure it'll come much lower...

Hoping when front end will get relieved on repo - long end goes down tips with it and we can buy it.

9:36 AM QZ Hear you on high implied repo. Just trying to get a sense where we can get out on the basis as off the run is still wide.

9:38 AM Alex Gurevich I think we wait for Gc to collapse.

As Fed keeps liquefying

9:38 AM QZ roger

9:38 AM **Christopher Lutton** Be interesting to hear what ██████ ███████████ sees these days?

9:48 AM **CK** we've done 320/600 on the CNM0, hoovered up a good amount of liquidity despite the algos...not chasing here since its basically 5 x 5 liquidity and one way higher past 10min

146.38 average

10:01 AM Alex Gurevich It's fine don't chase. We have a lot.

10:01 AM **CK** exactly

gets back below 146.60 we'll revisit

10:06 AM QZ GC trading back to 35

10:07 AM CK $CAD peeking above 1.40 for first time since '16...roll
adj highs then look to be 1.43...that might be one of the
better USD shorts in 6-12mths pending US growth & oil
higher (probably go somewhat hand in hand since OPEC
not racing to support oil when there is no chance of
price snap during zero demand)...stash it in the ideas
drawer for later

11:23 AM Alex Gurevich BRL is at our level.

Are there futures? Carry seems very low in front and
hump up into longer maturities...

11:26 AM Christopher Lutton Jan 21s are 3.84%

11:26 AM CK there are futs

BRA

11:27 AM Alex Gurevich Liquid?

11:28 AM CK double checking, think we could probably do some in
our size

11:28 AM Alex Gurevich If so let's do $3mm in proportion.

11:28 AM CK BRL markets trade as futures on Bovespa so I'd
suspect it to be more liquid on CME too compared to
your typical EM which trades to 1mth NDF so a future
is rarer

yup, sec, confirming liquidity and sizing

in ▇ you want to do OTC or futs?

▇/▇ futs obvi

11:34 AM Christopher Lutton finally at least you have some people
willing to pay a ton for the topside. This risky is quite a

bit higher than when  recommended the one year digital puts

image.png ▾

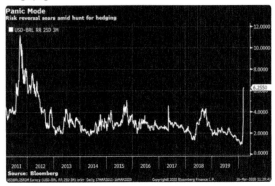

11:36 AM **CK** yea, def better, but we need to keep in mind that

Brazil almost always completely blows out before it gains momentum agai to the strong side

so lets do some and save ammo for when they have to jack rates to save the FX

Alex, I'm going to work 4.99 equiv in BRL

█████ will be OTC (its 5x more liquid than fut) and will work the corresponding futs levels once ███ is done, cool?

11:37 AM **Christopher Lutton** I just couldn't believe how much jan 21s were down today. I just didn't see it

11:43 AM **CK** waiting on prices, but will be doing $0.7 OTC in ████...remaining $2.3mm will be futs on best efforts...

11:44 AM Alex Gurevich If doing forward in ███ can do $1mm.

11:44 AM **CK** thanks

they'll hate me less with the round amount haha

With all EM currencies selling off, there were opportunities to both continue building positions in other countries, which I thought were long-term holds, such as Turkey (TRY) and Mexico (MXN), while taking profits on my short positions such as in Korea (KRW). Remember that in the following charts, the prices are presented from the dollar perspective, so a higher number means weaker foreign currency.

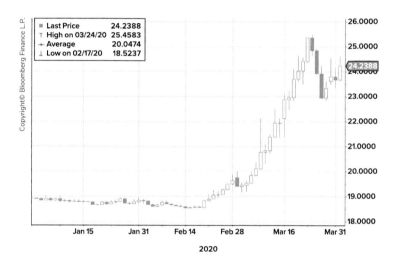

Mexican Peso (MXN) Spot Price January 2020–March 2020: MXN depreciated over 25 percent in March 2020.

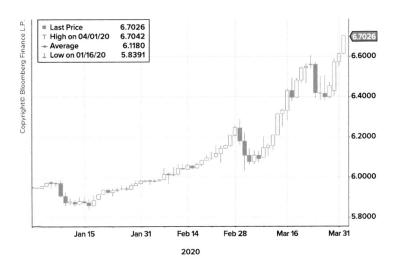

Turkish Lira (TRY) Spot Price January 2020–March 2020: TRY depreciated over 14 percent in the first quarter of 2020.

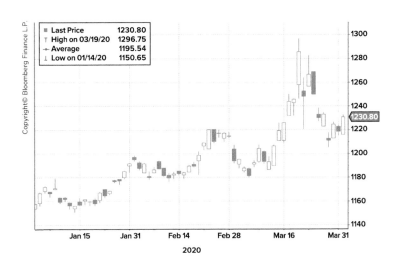

South Korean Won (KRW) Spot Price January 2020–March 2020: KRW depreciated nearly 9 percent at one point in March 2020.

Turkey is a particularly interesting case since, in the long run, it seems that it is always rapidly devaluating. However, due to high domestic interest rates, the carry on owning Turkish lira is so good that it makes money in the long run, nonetheless. It is particularly lucrative to buy it after any major sell-off.

MARCH 16: MONDAY AFTERNOON

they'll hate · **March 16th, 2020** ˅ 1 amount haha

11:45 AM Alex Gurevich I am cautious though about building too much forwards exposure. Should consider taking off 1/2 KRW.

11:45 AM **CK** yup, will revert on that in a sec...doing BRL first

11:45 AM Alex Gurevich Ok

11:48 AM **CK** thats done

call it 5 where we did it

makes me nostalgic for the 1.5 USDBRL days....

11:58 AM **CK** BCB will be in today almost certainly (they were last at 5 the other day)

if there are really USD funding issues, TRY will be at 7.5 in the next week

(and thats even w crude where it is)

CNM0 is back to our levels, going to re-engage

12:01 PM QZ Please be reminded outright duration risk is around 91% for ████, that includes stub (EDJ0)

12:57 PM **CK** MXn thru 23

only little more CNM0 done, painful/phantom liquidity

1:06 PM **CK** re KRW, we obvi have the $10 left....we are at multi year highs more or less exclusive of GFC...my inclination would def be to take off half here

> not only is Asia somewhat on a better trajectory on COVID, but most of Asia has had enormous surpluses (piling up reserve in $) up until recently which get recycled in the form of off balance sheet forward interventions/sterilizations + in these funding crises the KRW/SGD curves of the world tend to flatten (local banks need to s/b KRW x b/s USD out of need for front end USDs that don't exist in the system)...as such I dont expect us to get much of a kicker on our far forward points

In the last screenshot, CK reiterates that Asian economies had already taken the brunt of the COVID crisis and were now in a better position than Western ones. I was correct to start unwinding any short Asian currencies position, but in retrospect, I wish I had taken that thought even further and acted more decisively.

> only little m. **March 16th, 2020** ⌄ ;ul/phantom liquidity
>
> 1:06 PM **CK** re KRW, we obvi have the $10 left....we are at multi year highs more or less exclusive of GFC...my inclination would def be to take off half here
>
> not only is Asia somewhat on a better trajectory on COVID, but most of Asia has had enormous surpluses (piling up reserve in $) up until recently which get recycled in the form of off balance sheet forward interventions/sterilizations + in these funding crises the KRW/SGD curves of the world tend to flatten (local banks need to s/b KRW x b/s USD out of need for front end USDs that don't exist in the system)...as such I dont expect us to get much of a kicker on our far forward points

so even though USd longs somewhat hedge us in an extended USD funding crisis...i Don't think USDKRW longs do that given the specici local dynamics...so as a portfolio position, as a margin, and as an individual trade...probably worthy of reduction

lmk! can unwind at Asia open tonight if we want

1:12 PM Alex Gurevich Yes I think the plan is to take 1/2 off and go down to core position of $5mm for now.

1:13 PM CK k cool, will plan to handle that this evening unless i hear otherwise

The day ended with surprisingly flat P/L after a crazy session. Our significant gains on US and Canadian bonds were offset by a crash of precious metals and losses on equities. The price action left me feeling unsettled.

hear otherw   **March 16th, 2020** ⌄

5:06 PM CK KRW popping at the open, trying to get a px so we can unload...

*USDKRW popping higher

5:25 PM Alex Gurevich K

6:49 PM CK normally this would have taken 10mins but hilariously bad liquidity for the KRW tonight which is normally the most liquid Asia FX (which is telling in its own right)...there is basically no bid in the long end forward curve (dealers are stopping out of long positions in panic fashion) which is an exaggerated version of what I was mentioning earlier today

we can trade to our date and be done with it @ circa 1200 but more reasonable points should put it at 1210/1215 level (USDKRW spot exploded to 1240 and trades there currently) so I'm hesitant to do so...another option is to sell 1s KRW and put ourselves into a steepener at quite wide levels and then unwind the curve trade once things calm...the problem in all of this being that KRW curve can flatten further

for the time being I have left an order to our specific date w █████ and if liquidity gets better (such that I'm not trading 2% wide bid/offer) or even if moves back to reasonable level, I will transact on best efforts

in other news, NZD curve is steepening on back of fiscal news if we have any interest there, will post curve in a sec -- they probs QE at some point so may not be as long lasting sell off....

6:58 PM Alex Gurevich I think do a short duration hedge and square forward curve when it calms down.

6:58 PM **CK** great

doing

1mth2y chart (spread is the bottom one) shows it well vs history:

image.png ▾

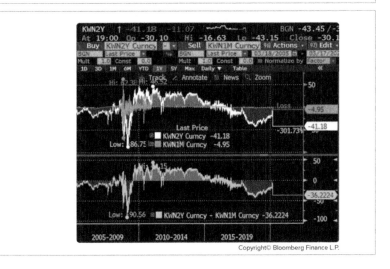

> 7:05 PM **CK** $5 covered, we'll manage 1s18mth curve in the coming days

> 7:35 PM Alex Gurevich I will look at NZD curve in a bit
>
> 8:37 PM Alex Gurevich Yes upward slope in New Zealand curve is of course a joke. Probably very hard to trade and we kind of full on DV01. Let's monitor it for when we have something g to take off...
>
> 8:37 PM **CK** Sounds good to me. Def can't sustain itself. Stash it away for later

Aside from bemoaning pure liquidity in Korea, we didn't have a particularly notable night session. From the break in our chat, it appears that we may have even gotten some sleep.

The morning brought new fireworks.

MARCH 17: TUESDAY MORNING

Stocks rebounded sharply overnight, but LIBOR jumped much higher, reflecting the relentless funding pressure.

> March 17th, 2020 ⌄
>
> 5:09 AM QZ 3m Libor jumped 16 bp to 1.05188!
>
> GC last traded 0.55.
>
> Stock gain diminished overnight.
>
> 5:29 AM QZ ▆▆▆ may be short of cash again

6:01 AM QZ Yesterday BOC announcement of buying mortgages drove CAD swap spreads won 20+ bp. CDSS10 not marked at 27.5

6:07 AM QZ Div futures on EUREX needs cash collateral. As our positions grow and market moves against us, this poses the problem. We will have to sell another 5mm treasury. NOT ideal. But has to be done.

The request has to be in before 9 am central time. I will have to send this out shortly.

6:43 AM Alex Gurevich Ok.

At that moment, P/L on the day looked close to flat to me (which would prove to be optimistic), so I was a bit frustrated by continuous margin problems in various accounts and the continuous need to liquidate collateral.

have to sen   March 17th, 2020 ⌄

6:43 AM Alex Gurevich Ok.

Only ▮▮▮ problem?

6:46 AM QZ yes, ▮▮ has enough cushion

6:50 AM Alex Gurevich We are not losing money though? Flat on the week as a firm? Maybe a little down in ▮▮▮?

Why can't we move cash around?

Time take off another 120 AUD (I did 120 last night).

6:52 AM CK k doing

thats done

6:55 AM QZ Nikkei and Eurex needs cash for collateral, can't pledge treasury. Those adds up to 6.6 mm cash. We also bought treasury last week.

with regard to ▮▮▮▮

> 6:59 AM Alex Gurevich Ok. Selling out $5mm is not really such a huge deal. Annoying bid-offer. Probably a wash with last but.
>
> 6:59 AM QZ Last week plus 3/16, ▓▓▓ lost 8.7 mm

The original stock rally was fading a bit, but treasuries were beginning to rinse off massively in a steepening fashion (long-dated bonds were selling off harder than the short-dated ones). The US dollar continued to strengthen, and our AUD position was reaching new profit-taking targets.

> 6:59 AM QZ Last wee' **March 17th, 2020** ˅ t 8.7 mm
>
> 11:41 AM **CK** fyi alex CLN0 Comdty back below the levels you bought it at the other day though only 5% down on the day so less of a blow out fade kinda trade like it was the other day 30% down
>
> 12:05 PM Alex Gurevich Yes I faded the original blow outX but now prefer to own RUb and MXN
>
> 12:05 PM **CK** roger that
>
> 12:06 PM Alex Gurevich I am going to take it easier now and not try to fade every move...
>
> 12:06 PM **CK** yup great
>
> will keep you posted on AUD & JPY for the time being, those are closest in mind given our portfolio prefferences and currentt levels

> 12:27 PM **CK** AUD at the lows again if any interest
>
> 12:52 PM Alex Gurevich Let's look for close to 59 now.

12:53 PM **CK** sweet

5:56 PM QZ Just a heads-up. ███████ is still thin in cash as it stands
right now. I see only 1-1.5 mm cushion.

We ended up with the worst sell-off in long-dated bonds in this
cycle (and one of the worst ever).

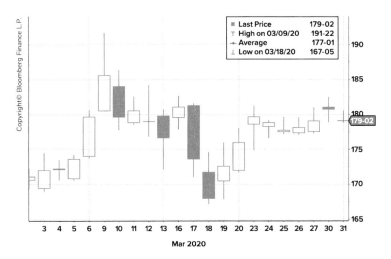

Roll-Adjusted US Classic Bond Future: Lost over 10 percent from peak to trough in
March 2020.

The fact that we no longer had a long bond position helped us survive
the day. Medium-term bonds were in trouble, though. Also, despite
the modest equity rebound and various additional measures the
Fed had announced, the funding pressures were building, and our
April Eurodollar (EDJ0) position was starting to give us trouble.
The day ended with a sizable loss, which, together with the previous week's losses, were accumulating to a very sizable drawdown.

MARCH 18: WEDNESDAY MORNING

QZ started the day bright and early, checking the funding levels. A little later, LIBOR was set, creeping up further. Most of the chat was a tranquil discussion about adjusting our Treasury and asset swap position. The thinking was to take advantage of the steepening of the yield curve to take profits on some shorter term treasuries and shift the risk into long-dated TIPS.

March 18th, 2020 ⌄

4:22 AM QZ FRA/OIS before Libor sets

J20: 55.625

K20: 42.625

M20: 33.625

U20: 25.750

Z20: 28.250

H20: 21.250

Fed's primary dealer credit facility helped, but longer dated swap spread still tightened 2-4

According to current market, ████ may call for another 3.5 mm cash. ██ has 16 mm cushion. ████ should have enough cash for now, will update once getting reports

4:53 AM QZ Apparently a wild run on WN overnight, following poor trading in late Tuesday afternoon, sold off as much

---

as 30bp from close o/n at one point

5:04 AM QZ Libor is out, 3m libor 1.11575 up 6.387 bp

EDJ0 trading down to 99.29, as high as 99.39 o/n

7:03 AM QZ GC is trading down to 20c. Looks like FED's PDCF is working.

7:10 AM **CK** front end Fed (and coordinated G3 policies) seems to have at least temporarily normalized 3mth basis as well. HY EM still taking a beating since USD is still in shortage there but more liquid LY EM like KRW showed some initial funding calm last night...doesn't mean out of woods but hopefully headed in the right direction

JPY still has room to go...EUR/GBP already back to Feb levels

---

10:09 AM QZ With curve steepening, tempted to sell 1.5 1/15/23 outright to free up room? TU implied at 0.92, FV implied 0.88

10:13 AM Alex Gurevich Hmmm; where they on asset swap now? (how much of it is stub - there is so much in the first roll - numbers for short treasuries are very dépendant on stub - standard swap stub is probably worth 10bps on 2yr)

10:13 AM QZ libor - 0.5

10:17 AM Alex Gurevich ,how much is stub to April 31st worth?

We can probably let them go at so close to Libor...

Can we line up offer on TIPs:, I was thinking sell 100mm 10/23 buy $25mm TIPs?

10:20 AM QZ we were funded at .6 yesterday, not sure where we will be funded going forward, .2?

10:20 AM Alex Gurevich TIPs??

10:21 AM QZ yesterday was .75, very high, i think today will be down, but anywhwere .2-.4

10:22 AM Alex Gurevich We'll probably get to much cheaper soon... CPI Will go negative with oil price for a while.. but long-term I think it'll bounce hard...

Is it possible to line up an offer on TIPs?

10:23 AM QZ will be hard, likely two separate trades

can check

10:24 AM Alex Gurevich Yes two separate. First need to get an offer for TIPs...

10:24 AM QZ looking at 1/31 because it appears to be 5bp wide market on BBG, 10/23 seems 7bp wide

checking now

10:25 AM Alex Gurevich Maybe get indications for both?

10:27 AM QZ have 76.3 1/23, how many tips if 2/42?

10:27 AM Alex Gurevich Say 20...

Not sure what actuel duration is for TIPs

10:29 AM QZ if duration neutral, about 10mm

2/42

10:30 AM Alex Gurevich But TIPs don't have regular duration..

Let's set $15mm

10:31 AM QZ I was using like 0.7 beta

ok 15 mm

10:34 AM Alex Gurevich Are you on chat with ███?

10:34 AM QZ let me invite you

if you are on bbg

10:36 AM Alex Gurevich Yes

Am I not on this chat?

10:36 AM QZ you see invtie?

10:37 AM Alex Gurevich Yes what should I do to get in?

10:37 AM QZ Then you are on chat

you can type in

I am asking 10/23 vs 2/42 TIPS

10:38 AM Alex Gurevich I don't see it on my chat list

10:39 AM **Christopher Lutton** you can uninvite him and invite him back.

10:39 AM   Alex Gurevich   Oh found it

10:39 AM   **Christopher Lutton** nice

10:39 AM   QZ   do you see the response in chat?

Great, you found it!

107-19 bid on bbg

10:42 AM   Alex Gurevich   Also ask him for 1/31/23?

10:43 AM   QZ   I see 100m 10/23 roughly matches 15mm 2/42 tip

10:44 AM   Alex Gurevich   Is 107-19 bid already super wide

10:44 AM   QZ   yes, 28 offer

10:45 AM   Alex Gurevich   Can we work screen on that one? Or give them an order?

10:45 AM   QZ   we can give them an order, screen not reliable yet

10:45 AM   Alex Gurevich   BBG say it's trading at -28

10:46 AM   QZ   could try 1/31 as well, but on 10 mm 2/42 tip i see

since we have only 76.3 mm 1/31

20-28 1/4 market for o/23

10:47 AM   Alex Gurevich   We don't have to exactly neutral my concern is not that but how many tips we can afford to own - they already dropped 10%...

So can we electronically offer on the screen?

10:47 AM   QZ   No

10:47 AM   Alex Gurevich   Or ask them to work 107-28?

10:47 AM   QZ   that's fine

the other leg contingent on this one?

if 10/23 done, then look at 2/42 tips?

10:49 AM Alex Gurevich Yes let's work offer on 10/23 then worst case scenario - we lost them up on the day and reduced risk....

Wait do we have any issues they are axes to buy?

10:50 AM **CK** no not on our books

10:50 AM Alex Gurevich Ok

I am giving them order

10:51 AM **CK** great, seems best approach...BBG screen & liquidity in general make aggressing at bid completely pointless

---

10:51 AM QZ Sure

███ called, says in this environment, they can only try on best effort basis

We will watch it, my guess is won't get done unless through bid side

10:55 AM Alex Gurevich An order is an order? Why can't they work an order all they have to do is sit on the offered side for a +.

10:57 AM QZ too swamped, I guess...

10:57 AM Alex Gurevich Technically we could sell an issue they are axes to buy short/long will reduce our net balance sheet - can you check if any of the issue they want to buy are a little more expensive

10:58 AM QZ sure

11:00 AM Alex Gurevich We can also stay on holding pattern. Our TIPs positon is not insignificant. And the short term bonds will carry extremely well.

11:02 AM QZ holding pattern for now, unless it gets to our level

8:28 PM **CK** shifting back to this chat. order to buy 120x ADM0 @
55.00 in market for RBA meeting in 2min

25bp cut to 0.25%

👍 1   ☺⁺

and Fed launching MM liquidity ddXRILIRY

*FACILITY

RBA targeting 3yr govt bond 0.25%

The gap in the Slack chat for the next few hours was symbolic of what happened to our portfolio. On that day, we completed our descent into the singularity.

Defiance to Risk Parity

So what really happened that day? Equities sold off overnight limit-down and then rebounded to a "modest" by March standards sell-off of 5 percent, which erased the previous day's gains. In further defiance to *risk parity* (the idea that you can construct a portfolio in which bonds will cushion your stock volatility by moving in the opposite direction), the treasuries sold off as well, pushing swap spreads further into negative territory. This time, medium-term maturities led the way down, which was much worse for my portfolio structure.

Precious metals, after the previous day's respite, moved further down. All our LIBOR positions continued to leak money as well.

The day ended with one of the worst losses our current trading program had ever suffered in absolute and percent terms.

The one bright spot was the collapse of the Australian dollar. It declined so rapidly that I started to put unwind orders at every figure (59, 58, 57, 56, 55...). Jumping ahead, the incremental unwind strategy with AUD proved very effective.

Had I had to pick a single profit-taking level, I would probably have given up my position too early. As it was, I covered most of my short when AUD traveled down about 20 percent on the year.

The residual position stayed in for a few more weeks. When the dollar reversed (spoiler!), I vowed not to give up too much of my gains on Aussie and put a stop buy of 0.60 for 50 percent of my residual and 0.65 for the rest. It didn't take very long for those stops to be triggered.

The following chart shows the points at which I bought back AUD.

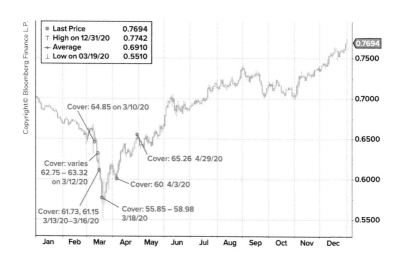

Australian Dollar (AUD) Spot Price 2020: The marked price points were the levels at which we covered our short positions on AUD versus USD.

You can see that after the massive sell-off, AUD established a strong uptrend and actually ended positively for the year. Riding this position down and then covering it in a patient and disciplined manner was the *true move* of our most successful repositioning of 2020.

Now back to the black hole.

MARCH 18: WEDNESDAY EVENING

The RBA eased and introduced yield control (capping the yield on three-year sovereign bonds at 0.25%). What happened next was one of the most dramatic moments of 2020.

11:02 AM QZ holding p   **March 18th, 2020** ˅   it gets to our level

8:28 PM **CK** shifting back to this chat. order to buy 120x ADM0 @ 55.00 in market for RBA meeting in 2min

25bp cut to 0.25%

👍 1   😊⁺

and Fed launching MM liquidity ddXRILIRY

*FACILITY

RBA targeting 3yr govt bond 0.25%

8:32 PM **Christopher Lutton** !!!!

8:32 PM **CK** YCC has been imported from Japan

XMM0 is getting wrecked

97.50

do we want any?

eh 98

https://rba.gov.au/media-releases/2020/mr-20-08.html

Reserve Bank of Australia
Statement by Philip Lowe, Governor: Monetary
Policy Decision | Media Releases
The coronavirus is first and foremost a public health
issue, but it is also having a very major impact on the
economy and the financial system. (3 kB) ▾

RESERVE BANK
OF AUSTRALIA

50bps in 10yr now, but i mean, this is a ridiculous
headline in a world of CBs heading to 0: *AUSTRALIA
10-YEAR YIELD SURGES 128BPS, MOST ON RECORD

8:41 PM Alex Gurevich Unfortunately we can't catch any falling
knives here...

8:42 PM **CK** sadly not, but wow

3s10s since '01:

image.png ▾

Copyright© Bloomberg Finance L.P.

8:52 PM **CK** 10pm PST RBA conference...i've left the order at 55
for now in EMSX, feel free to cancel if it suits

Who could imagine the headline following the introduction of
yield curve control in the the chat above would be "AUSTRALIA
10-YEAR YIELD SURGES 128BPS, MOST ON RECORD"?

This is somewhat arbitrary, but I choose this to mark the market
continuum folding into the infinitely dense singularity. Liquidity disappeared completely, and sovereign debt of developed

"riskless" countries collapsed through a fluke of order flow, despite very positive news on the policy side.

Was I a buyer taking advantage of this remarkable opportunity? Unfortunately not. I was tapped out on risk. Our losses reached the point that it was not possible to put on any more risk position, regardless of how favorable the levels were.

And honestly, if I was out of risk capacity, it was likely that almost all other risk players were too. This is how such price action can occur: a couple of forced sellers and all buyers out of oxygen. This was a classic instance of the portfolio paralysis I described in TNPT.

Whatever the reason, portfolio stops are always very painful and always, in my experience, perfectly mistimed. That is, you always get stopped out at the very bottom, from your portfolio perspective. You end up being flat at the point when your positions would have proved to be most profitable if initiated.

There is a reason why it tends to go this way. Involuntary portfolio stops tend to hit multiple money managers simultaneously when an unlikely market dislocation occurs. When everyone is done stopping out, the market starts to normalize.

Portfolio paralysis is the edge of this cliff; the anticipation leading up to a portfolio stop. The market is in chaos, and great opportunities pop out on the screen one after another, beckoning like the chiming of an ice-cream truck. All you can do is hold on by the skin of your teeth and hope the market will give you a reprieve tomorrow. And "hope" is an ugly word in the world of investments. It is something that is always getting dashed.

Usually, portfolio paralysis is only a painful delay of the inevitable portfolio stop.

At such times, one may be able to regain traction by forcefully liquidating much of the portfolio and freeing up space to focus on the one position that is currently going haywire. I have to confess, such decisive repositionings are not my forte. I am generally afraid to mess things up even worse and choose to stay the course, while observing the risk limits, as the path of least resistance.

There is a classic maxim about cutting your losses and letting your wins run. It has two very separate foundations.

The first is that markets are inclined to trend. Assets that are going down tend to continue going down, and assets that are going up tend to continue going up. It is a special case of the statement that historical patterns have a tendency to persist.

The second point has to do with a poker analogy (which I will discuss in more detail later): you are much more likely to make good decisions when you are up money. Counter to the common instinct, you are better off quitting a losing session early and continuing to play on when you are winning. Similarly, when your portfolio is under pressure, it is often better to square everything up and regroup.

Both of those points have an element of wisdom, but I question their universal application. In fact, I often wonder if accepting the "cut losses/get flat/take a break" maxim has become a source of many macro portfolios' underperformance.

I discussed in TNPT how some asset classes tend to trend and some don't. Often, reducing positions that go against you is the opposite of what you should be doing. I will get to examples in later chapters.

The psychological advantage is real and tangible, but within my strategic approach, it doesn't automatically merit the "cut losses" approach. When the overall portfolio is doing well, cutting a losing trade is not a requirement. A more measured and rational decision about the poorly performing trade in question is allowed. At the poker table, it is equivalent to deciding whether to push a specific hand or let it go.

In a drawdown, risk management parameters may mandate broad risk reductions. But getting flat to regroup doesn't have to be warranted. After all, it is a decision in itself—and making decisions is exactly what one is not supposed to do when psychologically disadvantaged.

Note that I have pretty much accepted this mental impairment as a given, and I have not even tried to make the argument, "I can be cool as a cucumber and perfectly rational in any market situation."

Long ago, I discovered it is useless to deny your own emotional biases, and it is beneficial to trade in a style compatible with your own psychological makeup.

Stick to Your Plan

The best approach I have discovered is very simple: make a plan and stick to it. Obvious though it seems, it is in many ways counterintuitive because another ingrained maxim is, "Be nimble." We traders are taught that we need to continuously process all the new incoming information and be ready to change our views and positions. Some of the traders I know like to speak of, "strong opinions, lightly held," a phrase introduced by technology forecaster Paul Saffo.

I take issue with this maxim as well. I think it is one of those catchy phrases that has limited use. For some investors, it might work, but if anything, I prefer the opposite, "weak opinions, strongly held."

I tend to stay agnostic about specific market or economic forecasts. I have often been asked questions like, "Where do you think the euro will be at the end of the year?" In response, most of the time I draw a blank. I don't even offer the ubiquitous, half-hearted, "If it holds above the 1.16 support, the path of least resistance will be upward toward 1.25, but even if it breaks below, there might be considerable downside," a statement tantamount to, "If it goes up, then it goes up, and if it goes down, then it goes down."

No, I don't typically have strong opinions. My strategic system, described in TNTP, helps me select superior dominant trades. So I am in a trade because I judge the odds to be in favor of its eventual success. But I have no conviction or even opinion on the time horizon or circumstances in which the favorable market move will eventually occur.

I rather like to think of a trade as a "bullet out of a gun." You think, evaluate, and aim very carefully before taking the shot, but once you've pulled the trigger, the trajectory is no longer within your control.

There is a Russian saying that can be roughly translated as, "The victory is forged behind the lines." You can develop the best strategy = through calm, deliberate study and contemplation. Your thought process when you research a trade is inherently superior to what you may come up with in the middle of a market commotion.

This doesn't only apply when you are losing money. Imagine you are a stock investor. You picked a stock that is currently trading at $100; you think the company is well managed and you set a $150 target for your position. A few months later, the company reports good earnings. The stock jumps to $150. At this moment, it is too easy to start thinking, "Well, with the results this good and all the excitement about the stock, I can run it to $180." However, you no longer have the advantage of your original analysis. The strong report has made public what you anticipated. Now that everyone has the same information, it's better to stick to your original price target.

My handling of the Aussie dollar short described above was perfectly in line with this approach. My other positions were well sized and well thought-out.

The Bathroom Floor

The truth is I was terrified. It didn't matter that I was still considerably up on the year. It didn't matter that I was confident my trades were correct and would make money in the long run. It didn't matter that I was staying within position limits and observing risk management discipline.

All of those constructs and ideas could melt away as we passed into the black hole. Bonds could trade at *any* price and banks could withdraw all access to the balance sheet, forcing us to liquidate our holdings at *any* price. Precious metals didn't *have* to trade at any specific level either, and as for the dividend futures... What dividends?

The *Shield against Uncertainty* was protecting me; I knew that all of those things would return to normal once liquidity overwhelmed the crisis. But even under the cover of that shield I was being seriously battered.

I can't pinpoint the exact night that saw me immobile on the bathroom floor. It is as easy to imagine it happening on the night of the singularity as on any other night in March.

I managed to get up, hands shaking, legs weak, and stumble into bed. I recovered after getting some sleep, but for days afterward I felt faint and queasy in the afternoon. This unfamiliar weakness made me feel strange, unsure, and bizarrely unsafe in my body. I was fearful of going to bed because as soon as I would lie down, my heart would start beating heavily, and my chest felt constrained. I wasn't able to sleep for more than an hour at a time.

I was correct to assume I didn't have COVID—no antibodies were found in the subsequent test. My collapse may have been caused in part by a reaction to the supplement I had taken to help myself relax and sleep better. But stress had to be the main culprit.

Something like this had happened to me once pre-pandemic. That experience prevented me from being convinced I was infected and stopped me just short of checking myself into a hospital.

Being able to sleep well at night and not worry about our health is a privilege that many of us, blessed with a good situation in life, take for granted. In another lesson of 2020, the strain of dealing with the pandemic market deprived me of that privilege.

MARCH 19: THURSDAY MORNING

The next morning brought another bout of funding pressure with EDJ0 (April Eurodollar) selling off 20 bps, now down 35 bps from its high point over the previous twenty-four hours.

We were dealing with the fallout of the previous day's setback— still up on the year but now having gone through our possibly largest ever intra-month swing. I had gone from what looked like a record month in the first few days of March to what was beginning to look like one of my worst months ever.

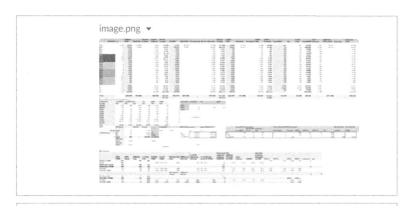

image.png ▾

March 19th, 2020 ⌄

4:58 AM QZ EDJ0 99.0475/99.05

EDJ0, EDM0 both moving down, FRA/OIS widening relentless

5:10 AM   QZ ▬▬▬▬ calls for 4mm cash, will sell 5mm treasury this morning to cover.

5:29 AM   QZ 10y TIPS auction today. $12bln reopen

WHITE HOUSE MULLS 50-YR, 25-YR BOND TO FINANCE $1.3T STIMULUS

Curve steepened >6bp and 30yr spread tightened with the headline

6:11 AM   QZ Fed expands dollar swap lines with central banks

60 bln for 6 months includes Aussie, NZD, Korea, Mexico, Brazil..

Simple cash management via selling collateral was no longer sufficient. I had to start some meaningful risk reduction to follow our risk guidelines. I sounded full-on retreat in April Eurodollars (EDJ0).

March 19th, 2020 ⌄

6:58 AM   Alex Gurevich Let's start trickling out EDJ0. It keeps going against us, negative carry and dangerous. And correlated to the rest of our port.

6:59 AM   QZ agree

6:59 AM   CK K

7:00 AM   Alex Gurevich Try to sell 1200 at .02 if works or.0175 if doesn't. Liquidity is bad so may have to do it slowly. Driving down selling doesn't help.

If Libor calms down we'll still make money in Junes.

7:01 AM   CK K

7:04 AM   Christopher Lutton TIPS #1: 01/15/2024 maturity w .625% yield   and TIPS#2 07/15/22 maturity w .125% yield. Both have shitty yields bc I bought during '08 crisis & aftermath

---

ignore above

7:17 AM **CK** got 49x done then someone hit 99.0125 bid...going to be a slog....if bigger bids pop up above 01 ill take advantage but for now its very thin so no point pushing

8:07 AM **CK** in case you aren't in front of screen, its trading at 9950 now, have done 131x so far today

8:08 AM QZ GC is under .2 now. Front end spreads recovered somewhat from late Wed selloff. 1/23 around Libor flat. Understand it has a lot of carry, and not ideal to sell. But EDJ0 is tough going, and risk is over. Any thoughts?

I wrote earlier about how the experience of 2007 taught me to proceed cautiously with LIBOR bets. I sensed that EDJ0 was the direction where the most danger lay. Also, being a short-term bet, it threatened me with unrecoverable loss, even if I would eventually be proven correct about funding.

Another point I raised concerned something else I addressed in TNPT.

> When confronted with an untenable drawdown, I had previously tried to selectively reduce. I disposed of positions I felt were less important and kept (or even increased) the positions, which contained the most value. However, that approach typically backfired. The problem is that the positions which I most believed in, and had in the largest size, were typically the ones giving me trouble. And as they went against me, I perceived them to have more and more value (if you like a stock at $30, you would love it at $20, right?). And, of course, as I gave up on the less paramount positions, which proceeded to perform well, the core positions continued their downward momentum.

I had to cut what was giving me trouble.

EDJ0 is tou   March 19th, 2020 ⌄   er. Any thoughts?

8:10 AM Alex Gurevich Thé problem is we need to sell what is a problem not what has stabilized. I don't know if 1/23 will reduce our risk problems effectively. EDJ0 Will.

8:12 AM QZ Understood. Balance sheet could be an issue down the road, But agree with FED's injection, probably not imminent.

8:17 AM Alex Gurevich Carry on our favor on 10/23 against us on April. And if April turns after we sold it we still make money on other things.

I'm portfolio is stable today so let's look for opportunities to trickle out April. Doesn't have to be exact price. But can't slam it down. Anything we do will result in real risk reduction.

8:20 AM QZ Yes, a little tricky on April

8:24 AM CK yup i hear you...someone else is slamming it down as we speak...given our position the best opportunity to unload will be when we see chunkier bids (starting to appear at 97.5/98 level) or better yet when a buyer starts paying offers....if I see that I'll act more aggressively...in the absence of that though it will be a waiting game of very passive & small offers

9:00 AM QZ Short end spreads are moving in meaningful way

After the big loss on Wednesday, the portfolio was fairly flat on the day. This gave me some breathing space. Risk still had to be reduced in some pockets, but there was also a chance to take some profits.

Ending the Great Yen Trade

As the dollar continued going up, the time had come to end my great yen trade. I initiated long USDJPY (long dollar/ short yen) as far back as 2010. Back then, I was convinced that sooner or later, the yen had to collapse under its own weight. It took over two years for the trade to gain traction, but eventually, with Abenomics in the end of 2012, it did collapse, and my steadfast position launched the success of my current trading program.

I wrote in TNPT:

> Let's go back to my short yen trade of 2010-2014 and focus on a particular moment: the spring of 2013. The DPJ government had collapsed at the end of 2012 (this is what it took!), Abenomics had arrived, and the yen had started to tank. By May 2013, it had completed an over 25% decline against the dollar from its highest point.

> As the yen leveled off and pulled back some, the question was — should I call it a trade, take profits and move to greener pastures? I suspected the trade could go further, but I had a lot of profits at risk.

> The decisive factor for me was to look at the historical pattern. The trends in USDJPY had never turned around in such short time, so I felt relatively safe to persist.

> It worked. In October of 2014, the Bank of Japan surprised the markets with a dramatic new expansion of the monetary base and the yen decline re-accelerated.

My ability to run portfolio efficiently over those two years was enhanced by observing the historical pattern.

The story of my first book ended in early 2015, but the story of my yen trade continued even though it didn't dominate my portfolio in the last few years. I remember myself saying ten years ago or so, "USDJPY will touch 125 before 75." Back then, it was around 81 or 82. The chart below will show you that I was proven right by a very narrow margin.

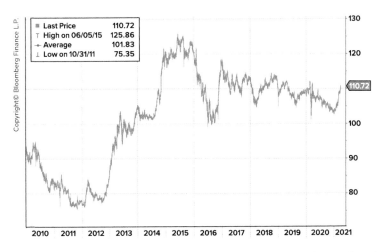

Japanese Yen (USDJPY) Spot Price 2010–2021: A peak (weakest yen) around 125 in 2015.

In observance of my price target, I took profits on the majority of my position in 2015, but I continued to run a small residual, just in case the yen bear market should entirely spin out of control. The trade underperformed later in 2016, proving inferior to being long Nikkei (this is a longer discussion beyond the scope of this book). However, when USDJPY touched 100 again in the wake of Brexit and it sold off again on the night of the 2016 US election,

I used opportunities to rebuild the position again, though still in much more modest size than my strategic commitment of 2016.

At one point, I tweeted:

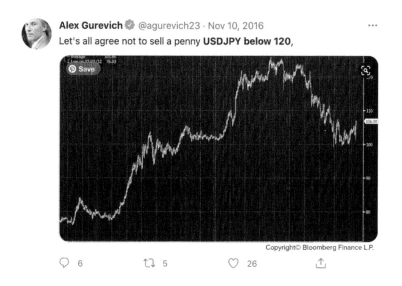

Alex Gurevich ✔ @agurevich23 · Nov 10, 2016   ...
Let's all agree not to sell a penny **USDJPY below 120,**

Copyright© Bloomberg Finance L.P.

♡ 6   ↻ 5   ♡ 26   ↑

Now, as dollar interest rates plunged, I realized the dollar rally was transient, and it was time to close the position down. USDJPY didn't touch 120 again, so I had to prioritize my portfolio performance over social media credibility (hey, compliance people, this is a joke).

Looking at the price chart in the following graph, one may conclude I was pretty far away from the 2015 peak. But when you take into account the carry from higher US interest rates and the cross-currency basis swap, the true economic price was, in fact, very close. This is how the roll-adjusted chart of yen futures, which reflects the actual economics of the transaction, looks (notice it is inverted because yen futures are quoted with yen being the numerator).

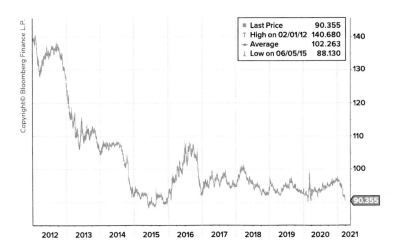

Roll-Adjusted Japanese Yen Future Price 2012–2021: To buy USD versus JPY is equivalent to short Yen future. The future price reflects the actual economics of holding the position.

9:00 AM QZ Short en͡ **March 19th, 2020** ⌄ ͡ meaningful way

9:00 AM Alex Gurevich Reduce USDJPY by 120 above 110

With finding moving Libor pressure may relief as well.

Funding

9:01 AM **CK** k

thats done

9:09 AM QZ I see us did fairly well on T 1.5 1/23 (the shorter piece) vs ED bundles, now it seems around L-4.5 (moved 4 bp better from earlier). Also appears tighter bid/offer, 3 bp instead of 5-6 yesterday. FED appeared scooped up 400m today. Your call if you want to sell.

we have 76.3 mm

Understand this is not the pressure point, just an opportunity to take some profit

9:28 AM **CK** little pop here in EDJ0, we've done 600 @ 99.0070 all day, pulling back for a sec...good buying interest right now

9:39 AM **CK** we've done 1000x, offers that were pent up from the AM sell off are getting very thin very quickly, i expect a shock pop here if we get thru 05.5

9:44 AM Alex Gurevich Ok you have discretion to work out of another 1200.

9:44 AM **CK** great thanks

9:44 AM Alex Gurevich But you can choose levels and work gradually..

9:46 AM **CK** sounds good, not being too picky about levels, just optimizing for liquidity based on order book

9:54 AM **CK** first 1200 done @ 99.0130...next 1200 dripping in

10:27 AM **CK** 1500 done all day

1:03 PM **CK** we've done 2400x all day

seems to be a firm bid at 99.0075 if you want to do more right now

1:16 PM Alex Gurevich I think can look for a further bounce now with funding stabilizing. Let's see what it does tonight/overnight.

1:16 PM **CK** great

working ntg

AUD order going to kill for now

1:27 PM Alex Gurevich Yes

4:21 PM **CK** $JPY 111

that and USDCHF full round trip down and back up to late Feb levels

5:00 PM   Alex Gurevich We have only one batch JPY left? Let's
          unwind it around 112.

5:00 PM   **CK** yea 154x

          sounds good

The day ended with more cleaning up in currencies and April Eurodollars.

Notice CK's remark about USDCHF (long dollar/short Swiss franc). Short CHF (against both dollar and euro) was the unsung hero of March 2020. We tend to celebrate trades that make outsized profits and bemoan those that accrete large setbacks. Not enough attention is given to failures to make money, nor to narrow escapes from losses.

Swiss franc, even more so than yen, is traditionally a safe-harbor currency. USDCHF performance had much to do with the dollar liquidity squeeze, but my larger exposure was EURCHF (long euro/short Swiss franc). When you go long EURCHF, you are, in effect, buying risk (or in other words, going long beta). As I discussed earlier, I was comfortable with having such trades in my portfolio because my interest rate position made me biased toward the risk-off environment.

It would be natural to assume that a crisis of such scope would lead to considerable losses on that position. The result, however, was relatively benign, and toward the end of March, I found myself losing less than 1 percent on EURCHF from earlier in the year, when I had accumulated the position between 1.06 and 1.07. The entry point ended up being so favorable that we went through a major crisis and *didn't lose significant money* on the short CHF position, which was a huge success.

EURO (EUR) versus Swiss Franc (CHF) Spot Price 2020: CHF appreciated only moderately against EURO, despite being regarded as a safe-haven currency.

At the end of the day, US interest rates were a minor loss for us due to pressures from rising LIBOR. Still, the rising dollar and the modest rebound in dividend futures offset those losses, ending the day with a small but much-needed positive number.

The dark days were coming to an end.

MARCH 20: FRIDAY MORNING

Stocks sold off further on Friday, but the singularity was behind us. If the singularity is the only future an object falling into a black hole may have, that means that once you fall into the event horizon, you are taken out of the timeline of the outside universe. However, it is theoretically possible to go through the center of a black hole and emerge in a *white hole* in an entirely different universe.

After Wednesday, I was in that new universe. And in this new universe, stocks were still going down. Dividends, however, did well overnight. LIBOR stabilized, setting up less than 1 bp, and spreads went wider (less negative). The Treasury bonds rallied enormously—as they should, in a normal universe, when equities are in a bear market and the Fed is adding an ocean of liquidity.

There is a precedent to the market traversing a funding singularity. In the GFC, the day of singularity was Friday, October 3, 2008. The funding markets were reeling in the aftermath of the Lehman bankruptcy and the destabilization of other financial institutions. I remember buying two-year bonds of Morgan Stanley for sixty cents on the dollar that afternoon. Over the subsequent weekend, the Fed announced TARP, a cash injection for major domestic banks. The lenders quickly realized that the Wall Street credit was now equivalent to the sovereign credit. The said bonds rallied immediately over ninety cents and were soon trading above parity.

The funding pressure eased out after that weekend and never came back. Stocks went much, much further down, bottoming a few months later in March 2009.

S&P 500 Index Price 2008–2009: After the TARP announcement in October 2008, the stock market fell further and didn't reach the bottom until March 2009.

Back then, knowing that the liquidity problem was resolved gave me confidence to build my equity position, as the entry points were getting better and better. In 2020, I had a similar conviction.

March 20th, 2020 ⌄

5:11 AM QZ 3m Libor set up 0.9bp to 1.20413, short end loosened up after the setting, EDJ0 bounced 9 bp to 99.115

5:17 AM QZ 8:15 snapshot: Treasury curve rallied 6-15bp with bull flattening, spread widened 1.5-6, WN limit up overnight

Still think prudent to sell EDJ0. Obviously, 1y VaR is still very high. EDM0 and plenty of other positions should work well if libor is tamed.

Asset swap snapshot: T 1.5 1/23 L - 3.8, T 2.875 10/23 L+3.5, T 2 5/8 1/26 L+12

Off the run b/o is wide 5-10bp

6:03 AM QZ

image.png ▼

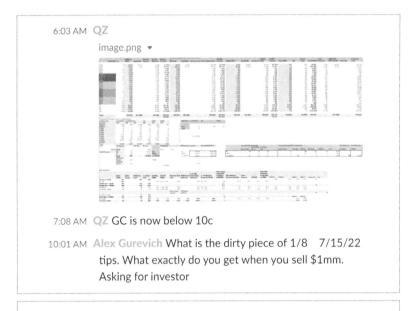

7:08 AM QZ GC is now below 10c

10:01 AM Alex Gurevich What is the dirty piece of 1/8   7/15/22 tips. What exactly do you get when you sell $1mm. Asking for investor

10:11 AM **CK** one sec, just confirming actual price in mkt

its ballpark 1.103mm

10:23 AM Alex Gurevich Thx!

Interestingly, on the day we were at last significantly up, there was much less chatter and very little trading. When the boat is on course, there is no need for course correction.

Qin pointed out some measures of risk were still high, however, and I took advantage of the relief bounce in EDJ0 to reduce our weak spot.

I cruised into the following week with my sails full of the storm of energy from the white hole.

CHAPTER 7

WEEK 4: THE AGE OF WONDER

A FEW WEEKS BEFORE THE SHUTDOWN, I CAUGHT UP WITH A friend whom I'd lost touch with for a while. Among other things, she claimed to be psychic—something I hadn't known about her. The pandemic was just beginning to affect global stock markets, so it must have been the end of February. She predicted that equities would bottom out on March 23.

I have an uncanny memory for any type of market calls, which comes from years of following various analysts and strategists and evaluating whether their research has any predictive power. So I marked it in my mind. Apparently, she noted the date as well.

For our investors' benefit, I will categorically state I didn't trade based on her forecast. But if you look at the chart of the S&P 500...

S&P 500 Index February 2020–March 2020: S&P 500 Index bottomed out on March 23, 2020.

Just saying...

MARCH 23: MONDAY MORNING

March 23rd, 2020 ⌄

5:04 AM   QZ   3M Libor set at 1.21563, up 1.15bp

Fed Signals unlimited QE

•• 1   ☺⁺

https://www.federalreserve.gov/newsevents/pressrelea
ses/monetary20200323b.htm

> **FRB Board of Governors of the Federal Reserve System**
> Federal Reserve announces extensive new measures to support the economy
> The Federal Reserve is committed to using its full range of tools to support households, businesses, and the U.S. economy overall in this challenging time. The

The Fed announced an unlimited QE program with a comprehensive range of asset classes eligible for purchase. This drew, and would continue to draw, criticism for impeding the natural price discovery. Most investors, however, welcomed the aggressive intervention by the central bank.

The important point at this juncture was that while the market's texture was beginning to gain some coherence, the funding pressure and the risk aversion were not yet relieved. LIBOR set higher, despite all the liquidity. Stocks plunged intraday to complete the fastest bear market ever.

Emerging markets continued to plunge. The portfolio gained traction, so I had risk space to add Mexican peso at what would prove to be an excellent level.

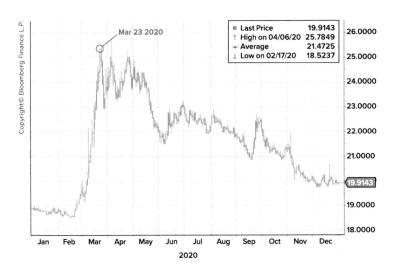

Mexican Peso (MXN) Spot Price 2020.

time. The   March 23rd, 2020 ∨

8:15 AM Alex Gurevich Add 120 standard allocation to MXN.

8:15 AM CK K

Done

1:07 PM QZ FYI. Mid market on TII 3/4 2/42 113-17+ , .123 yield

1:49 PM Alex Gurevich Let's check tomorrow if they can provide a reasonably tight bid for $5mm especially if they are up further...

1:50 PM QZ Sure, will do. Crazy, BBG showing mid yield under .11!

1:55 PM Christopher Lutton *CITI-LED GROUP STUCK WITH BILLIONS OF DEBT AS MGM CMBS FALTERS

sorry, wrong thread

3:39 PM CK forgot to post earlier but here are this week's Trend trades:

image.png ▼

EXECUTION					
Security	Action	Qty	LH	OA	Fill
JYM0 Curncy	Sell	-2	-1	-1	91.05
COM0 Curncy	Sell	-4	-2	-2	69.3275
NVM0 Curncy	Buy	12	6	6	56.3017
AOM0 Curncy	Buy	12	6	6	57.49333
BPM0 Curncy	Sell	-16	-8	-8	116.325
TYM0 Comdty	Buy	2	1	1	137-22
ESM0 Index	Buy	26	13	13	2197
DFWM0 Index	Buy	2	1	1	8316
NHM0 Index	Buy	2	1	1	16510

trades were completed at 7PM last night as part of a
trial run to see if this time would work better for some

operational challenges associated w Pac Rim exchange
allocations... we'll reassess after a few weeks!

3:47 PM QZ Thanks!

Notice how sparse the chatter was on Monday—there was minimal trading and no crazy around-the-clock activity. When things
go well, there is, in fact, very little to do. March 23 ended up being
the best day in the history of this trading program. Lower equities
and continuous pressure on LIBOR were overwhelmed by the
huge gains on bonds and precious metals.

MARCH 24: TUESDAY MORNING

LIBOR crept up further again! But stocks rallied. A critical transition had occurred. I wrote before that due to my interest rate
positions, I started the year very comfortable with any risk-nega-
tive events. Even my precious metals could be viewed as amelio-
rating certain kinds of risk.

This perception worked very well in early 2020 and through the first week of March. Then, during the "dark days," the correlations broke down. Treasuries started to go down instead of up, and to make matters worse, precious metals cratered. I found myself (me, the perpetual negative beta guy!) rooting for funding relief and recovery in risk assets.

This Tuesday confirmed that "good news" was "good news." To be clear, the news on the pandemic front was not good at all, with New York City already descending into a nightmare. But the white hole of central bank liquidity was pouring in cash, and Congress was moving forward on the stimulus.

Precious metals surged with equities, and inflation-indexed bonds started to recover pricing in some return of inflation.

March 24th, 2020 ⌄

5:17 AM QZ 3m Libor still set up 1.6 bp at 1.23238

        ██ is axed to buy 2/44. 2/45 through 2/50 TIPS. 2/42 yield slightly higher at 0.132

6:16 AM QZ Now funded below Fed effective for a week.

8:10 AM Alex Gurevich Qin, can you send the current IRBD spreadsheet ahead of meeting as soon as it's ready?

8:10 AM QZ Sure. Sending now

8:12 AM Alex Gurevich Seems our tips are reasoning 0.06 yield now.

8:13 AM QZ yup, you want to sell 5mm? ██ was axed for 2/44 earlier

8:17 AM Alex Gurevich Thinking. What yields are they bidding?

8:18 AM QZ Probably, 114-21, 0.075, my guess

can check

8:19 AM Alex Gurevich If they have higher bid on 2/50 we can look at it too... the curve will probably normalize eventually...

8:20 AM QZ 2/50 looks negative 4, let me check where they bid on either one

is it 5mm equivalent only or more?

Getting bids now

They only bid 113-27

revised to 114

We can give them a target to watch if you prefer

8:28 AM Alex Gurevich If we sell 2/50 then it'll be Smaller than $5mm weighted to 42s

8:29 AM QZ yes

8:30 AM Alex Gurevich Wait 114 was what issue?

8:30 AM **Christopher Lutton** 2/42s

8:31 AM QZ That was 2/42s. Unlikely there anymore.

But we can have them watch a level

8:32 AM Alex Gurevich Let's sell 600 April's EDJ0.

The easiest time to make good risk-management decisions is when you are making money. TIPS recovered a lot, and I was leisurely contemplating taking some profits before concluding that my position was not big enough. Simultaneously, the pain on April Eurodollars (EDJ0) was not going away, and I took some more off without any pressure from risk limits.

8:32 AM Alex Gurevic   March 24th, 2020 ∨   EDJ0.

8:32 AM **CK** K

8:33 AM Alex Gurevich Yes came off a bit I still love TIPs and not in a hurry. Because when we dilute at EOM it'll be hard to get them back from perspective of bid-offer.

8:33 AM QZ for 2/50s, equivalent 4 mm

114-3 bid now

for 2/42

8:35 AM Alex Gurevich How did you weigh TIPs in IRBD?

8:37 AM QZ BBG MARS used 40k for 15m

Probably too high

8:41 AM Alex Gurevich For $25mm?

8:42 AM QZ we only have 15mm

8:48 AM **CK** Done 600x EDJ0

More liquidity than usual at 98.9950 if you want me to do another clip

9:08 AM Alex Gurevich Ok do another 600

9:09 AM **CK** It is lower now 98.9800/50 at the lows of the day. I'll hang on the offer at 50 in small clips, not pushing it

9:10 AM Alex Gurevich I don't think you need to chase it down. We are fine here. Can work to sell on a bounce close to figure.

9:11 AM **CK** Roger that

10:19 AM QZ 2/42 mid market yield 0 if my screen is right

10:24 AM Alex Gurevich Yes seeing whole TIPs curve jump another 10bps

10:25 AM   QZ This thing is quite amazing

10:27 AM   Alex Gurevich 30yr breakeven back to 1.5%

10:28 AM   QZ Yup

Quite Amazing

Qin used the word "amazing," referring to the speed of recovery of the inflation-indexed bond. The reference issue was TII 0.75 2/15/42. We chose it because it traded very cheap relative to the rest of the TIPS curve. That in itself would be a source of value.

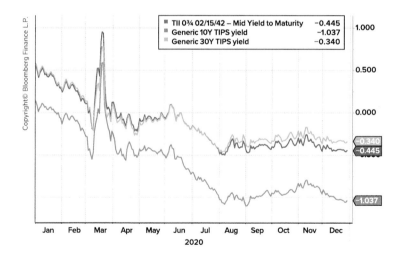

Yield Chart of TII ¾ 02/15/42 TIPS (Red), Generic Ten-Year TIPS (Blue), Generic Thirty-Year TIPS (Green): TII ¾ 03/15/42 presented more relative value as its yield spiked even higher in March.

The 0% yield referenced in the last chart pertains to a bond that jumped in price to yield exactly inflation (inflation + 0%) while we bought it at 0.497%, which was far from its intraday low of 1.07%.

After three days of extremely good P/L, we were back to a solid performance on the month and feeling in control of our destiny.

To be fair, the feeling of control applied strictly to my professional life. For all of us caught in the vise of the pandemic shutdown and stuck homeschooling kids, the personal aspects of our lives felt very much out of control.

MARCH 25: WEDNESDAY MORNING

Wednesday was my daughter's seventh birthday. Her party was one of the pandemic's early social casualties and had to be done over Zoom. She was very stoic about it.

As far as work went, there was little to do but wonder how fast TIPS were recovering. This time, CK used the word "unreal" to describe TIPS' price rebound.

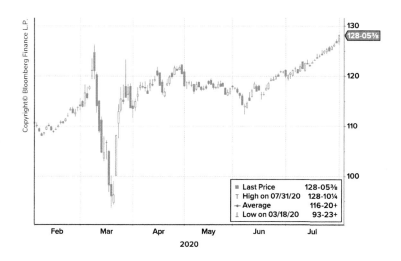

TII ¾ 02/15/42 TIPS Price Chart 2020: TIPS staged a remarkable recovery post-March 2020.

March 25th, 2020 ⌄

10:19 AM   Alex Gurevich -0.07 on 42s

10:20 AM   **CK** unreal

10:21 AM   Alex Gurevich Unreal - were the prices they were at earlier this month. Still very cheap.

10:27 AM   **CK** don't disagree with that either, the pace and nonlinearity of the moves is wild but ultimately makes sense given the price insensitive unwind short term versus enormous liquidity to hit medium term....

The stimulus passed through the Senate. The portfolio booked a hefty gain from European dividend futures, which overnight caught up with the previous day's rally in the United States. Bonds sold off a little and LIBOR positions both in April and June continued to drift against us. But the swap spreads continued their recovery with immediate funding issues being solved and the carry benefiting from high LIBOR settings.

Overall, another good day. After accruing a record month after the first week of trading in March and then reversing to face significant intra-month losses, I round-tripped again to a record month in the four trading days starting from March 20.

MARCH 26: THURSDAY MORNING

LIBOR jumped higher again, once again missing the memo that the funding crisis was over. TIPS rallied further in our favor.

In another embarrassing moment, I realized that in my head, the notional of our TIPS position was much lower than I had imagined. To be fair, I was well aware of my *duration* exposure. That is, I knew how much I stood to lose or gain when the yield on the relevant bond went up or down by 1 bp (0.01%). Not only were those now premium bonds, but convexity had extended their modified duration as they moved toward negative yields.

> 7:05 AM QZ Bloomberg Risk us using 2733 dv01 for each million right now.

image.png ▾

Copyright© Bloomberg Finance L.P.

9:02 AM QZ

image.png ▾

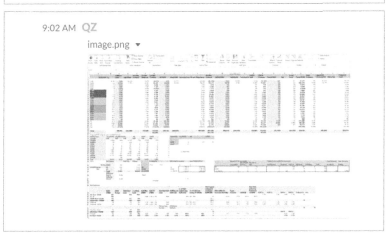

March 26th, 2020 ⌄

6:45 AM Alex Gurevich -0.18 on 42s

6:57 AM Alex Gurevich For some reason in MAV I see our positon on TIPs being 15mm I though it was 25mm

6:58 AM QZ No, it was always 15mm

> 6:59 AM Alex Gurevich Why is DV01 so high then?
>
> It's only 22 years
>
> (should have bought more)
>
> (not complaining it was a big contribution to our p/l vol).

Although I might have been too optimistic about the timeline for the end of the pandemic, the core of my approach was valid. Sooner or later, one way or another, the world would go back to normal. Hence, no matter how much travel was suppressed at the moment, it had no bearing on where travel would be two years later. It was natural to buy long-dated oil contracts below $40 a barrel (WTI), assuming the price would revert closer to the equilibrium of at least $60.

> **March 26th, 2020 ⌄**
>
> 11:27 AM Alex Gurevich Work 35.on June 2021 oil WTI. 60contracts. And 38 on June 2022 60 contracts. Open to switching if you think Brent is cheaper. Standard allocation.
>
> 11:28 AM **CK** see you
>
> CLM1 Comdty working to buy 60x @ 35.00
>
> getting '22 up in a sec
>
> 11:34 AM Alex Gurevich If I liquidity can double down in '21 but I think that contract is liquid.
>
> 11:34 AM **CK** quarterly crude contracts should be fine...Dec is always most liquid but we aren't big enough to matter

orders are staged and pieces are working depending on the typical order book size in the market (20x and 6x respectively)....if the offer gets down to our levels i'll get a bit more aggressive

no material view difference on Brent/WTI right now but ill look around and see if anything catches my attention...for now this is a good start

2:04 PM **CK** nothing done on crude today, will revisit it tomorrow AM

As often is the case, nothing was done on our first hunt for oil. Stocks ended strongly that day. The portfolio ended close to flat with some losses on the long position being offset by the gain on precious metals.

MARCH 27: FRIDAY MORNING

Despite the relief on risk assets and the Fed specifying that they were not out of ammunition on the previous day, LIBOR still jumped 7.5 bps higher. My trading of April Eurodollars (EDJ0) continued to be a case of throwing in the towel in slow motion.

In conversations with investors, I always emphasize the difference between portfolio risk management and position risk management. When a portfolio suffers significant losses, reducing risk is unavoidable. Indeed, even if you don't try to specifically manage volatility and drawdowns, you still have to face the absolute reality that when your portfolio loses money, it becomes smaller, and smaller portfolios can sustain smaller positions.

Position risk management, on the other hand, has to do with how much you are willing to lose on a specific trade. It usually involves stop losses or option strategies to limit the downside. In my opinion, too many traders focus on position stops, while portfolio risk management is paramount.

My approach has always been to institute rigorous rules for portfolio risk management but view managing position losses as a matter of strategy. This does not mean I don't have position risk limits. Quite the opposite: I use various stress tests and risk parameters to ensure that a given position can't damage the portfolio too much. Hence, it's a matter of portfolio risk management.

When it comes to a specific trade, this is what I wrote in TNPT:

> One of the classic instructions shared with beginning traders is "always trade with stops".
>
> This stop-loss practice can be invaluable to some trading strategies and completely detrimental to others. Traders too often find themselves stopped out of their correct and profitable positions because of a mismatch between the reasoning behind a trade and the strategy of execution.
>
> The world of trading is dominated by the mentality that cutting your losses quickly and letting your profits run is *the* key to success. Of course, doing the opposite is rarely a good idea. But just managing your losses on an individual trade is not a sufficient or even a necessary condition for profitability.
>
> I suspect that the idea of tight stops came from the days of the market's youth when information was slow to be disseminated

and it took time for prices to adjust to new inputs. In that world of such gradual adjustment to the news, it made sense to get out as soon as you realized you were wrong-footed.

But modern information flows are nearly instantaneous; adjustments happen faster and the market overshoots more frequently, especially when a multitude of players act on the same price triggers. The result is that "tight-stoppers" frequently get whipsawed by the price action.

Notice, the worn-down maxim "cut your losers, let winners run" is not without use. This is not so much a matter of controlling losses as one of going with the trend. The concept of information dissemination notwithstanding, certain asset classes tend to trend.

There was no doubt that LIBOR was trending upward and EDJ0 trending against me.

A version of myself very different from that of a few days prior was now selling the contract. I was no longer forced to control risk and reduce vulnerable positions to control the drawdown. Rather, I reached an obvious conclusion that the whole sally into April Eurodollars was not a great idea, and the odds of the contract recovering in the few trading days before expiration were bleak.

March 27th, 2020 ⌄

6:54 AM Alex Gurevich Let's trickle out some more EDJ0. 1200 at 85. I've no idea what is going on there

7:00 AM CK K

7:03 AM Alex Gurevich Sold most of it. Let's see what happens next seems bid...

7:05 AM **CK** great, good move on the small clips

thing just refuses to meaningfully bounce

7:06 AM QZ Japanese YE effect for the past few days? Should be over ? Don''t know either...

7:08 AM **Christopher Lutton** JPY x-ccy basis (1yr)

image.png ▾

image.png ▾

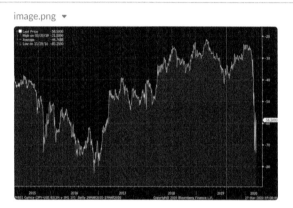

7:10 AM **CK** yea, front end has recovered a bit more, though hopefully April 1 some of that clears itself up...have definitely seen V shaped moves into/out of JPY YE in the past

7:12 AM **Christopher Lutton** yep, 3month x-ccy is here

image.png ▼

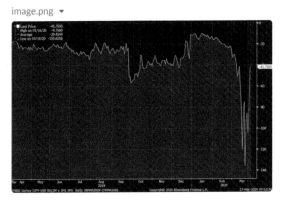

7:28 AM **CK** just making sure the CLM1 & CLM2 remain firm orders? retracing back a bit closer to our buy levels at 35 & 38 after the o/n pop

7:54 AM QZ

image.png ▼

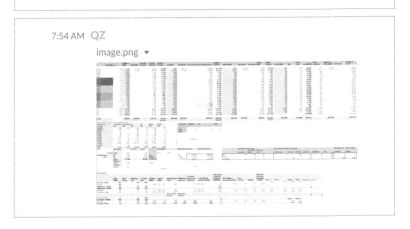

image.png ▾

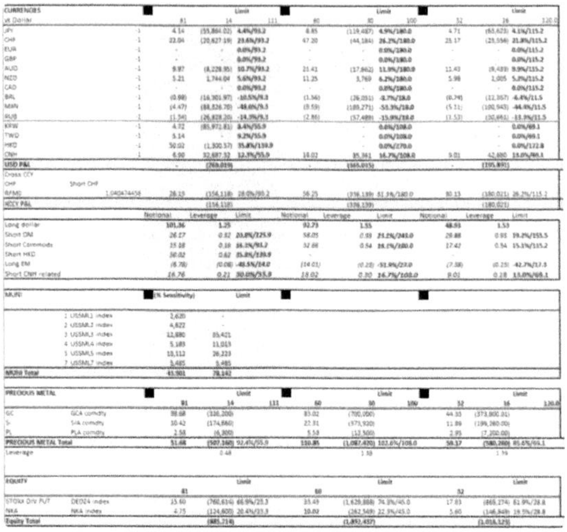

[table image — financial risk report, largely illegible]

8:25 AM   **CK** EDJ being stubborn, just printed <80

8:38 AM   Alex Gurevich Yes back with oil orders…

8:38 AM   **CK** roger that, about 1% away

10:28 AM   Alex Gurevich When does oil close trading? With the rest of futures?

10:30 AM   **CK** yea WTI closes at 2pm PST but if i recall it gets illiquid after settlement or so, let me confirm that time

10:31 AM   Alex Gurevich I think if it does not move down at all by EOD we should just lift our size. To establish core position. Will increase later…

10:35 AM   **CK** yea so official crude close is 11:30 PST but liquidity fine until 1pm PST or so give or take…Friday's probably a bit worse

it is worth highlighting that the CLM2 will be a challenge so the earlier we get started on that the better if you definitely want some on before the weekend my recommendation would be to have me work 30x best efforts around here (35.45/55 and 38.50/60 zone)...and then we can be opportunistic on the last 30x or lift as best we can at EoD (lets say 12 noon to be safe)...that way we def have 30x each on even if liquidity falls off a Friday cliff

10:42 AM Alex Gurevich Ok

10:43 AM **CK** k working the first 30x and 30x....we will revisit the remaining portion at noon if it doesn't' come our way before then

11:46 AM Alex Gurevich Can I see the chart of gold in Aussie terms over the last several years?

11:48 AM **CK** sure, grabbing

this should do it:

image.png ▼

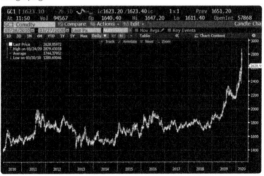

Copyright© Bloomberg Finance L.P.

12:17 PM **CK** 30x CLM2 finally done...still only 15x of CLM1 but coming back our way

going to push to fill the full 60x each by 1pm

30x done on both...working best efforts on rest into 1pm

12:22 PM Alex Gurevich Ok

Thx for the chart from the beginning on 2015 totally summarizes the performance of our portfolio.

12:22 PM **CK** haha yup

1:04 PM **CK** we are done on CLM1 & 2...35.75 & 38.66 respectively

1:14 PM Alex Gurevich Ok

1:14 PM **CK** for future reference, up until 1:15pm liquidity is OK for our volume but very one-sided so assuming that doesn't always work in our favor, sticking pre 1pm does seem best. CLM2 bid/offer doubled around 12:30...probs have to pay 5c and 10c respectively to get 30x done at 1pm

Aside from reducing EDJ0, most of the day was spent accumulating oil positions. Stocks sold off and bonds rallied; the dollar weakened. Due to losses on equities, LIBOR, and the dollar, the portfolio ended the day with a moderate setback.

Judging by the trading chatter, the week was relatively tranquil. Indeed, what is there to do when everything is going as planned? Propelled by the fountain of liquidity coming out of the white hole, my portfolio was set to cruise.

I am including the last two trading days of March (Monday and Tuesday) into this week that ushered in the age of wonder in financial markets.

MARCH 30: MONDAY MORNING

The full scale of the pandemic disaster unfolded in New York City over the weekend, but the markets felt a relief and the funding pressure abated.

TIPS had cheapened again after their amazing initial recovery. My focus of the day was to switch my positions away from long-dated nominal bonds and into TIPS. At the moment, I thought US inflation-indexed bonds represented such amazing value that if there was a way to manage the risk concentration, I would consider having nothing else in my portfolio. Note, the following chart is plotted in yield terms, wherein higher numbers mean cheaper bonds. I believed that those yields were heading deeply into negative territory.

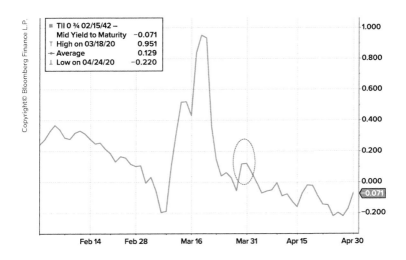

TII ¾ 02/15/42 Yield Chart February 2020–April 2020: Another buying opportunity toward the end of March 2020.

In the next chapter, I will talk more about the value and subsequent performance of those securities.

March 30th, 2020 ⌄

5:59 AM QZ

image.png ▼

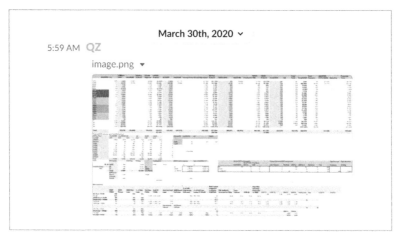

image.png ▼

7:10 AM **CK** trend model is now done for the week, inclusive of
CNM0 done @ 7AM today:

image.png ▾

| EXECUTION | | | | | | |
Security	Action	Qty	LH	OA	Fill	L
JYM0 Curncy	Sell	-2	-1	-1	93.4375	
CDM0 Curncy	Sell	-2	-1	-1	71.195	
NVM0 Curncy	Buy	12	6	6	60.23	
ADM0 Curncy	Buy	10	5	5	61.392	
BPM0 Curncy	Buy	6	3	3	123.953	
TYM0 Comdty	Buy	4	2	2	138-25+	
XMM0 Comdty	Buy	4	2	2	99.25	
CNM0 Comdty	Buy	4	2	2	148.02	
RXM0 Comdty	Buy	4	2	2	173.06	
ESM0 Index	Sell	-4	-2	-2	2508.56	
DFWM0 Index	Sell	-10	-5	-5	9534.3	
NHM0 Index	Sell	-6	-3	-3	18777.5	
Z M0 Index	Sell	-6	-3	-3	5420.8	

7:35 AM Alex Gurevich Qin, what is our oil risk limit? If not
established can you do some modeling by tomorrow's
risk call?

7:36 AM QZ Sure. Currently I set it at 0.9 million per risk unit. But I
am doing some stress testing to adjust

Will update once complete

8:03 AM Alex Gurevich Big move in break evens back to 1.3 in the
long end.
I want to consider the switch 46 treasuries to 42 TIPs.

Has this stuff gotten more liquid yet?

8:04 AM QZ slightly better, but liquidity issue still persists in long
end

Have 15m 2/46, you would like to switch all?

Have 5 mm 2/50 , might be easier switch

The issue trades slightly special

8:10 AM Alex Gurevich Yes can look at it. I think your model assigns too high DV01 to TIPs as it thinks of them as 0 yield bonds. In think in reality their modified duration can't be higher than bullets of the same maturity (1% yield). Probably lower based on historicals...

Very wide market on 46 on the s teen though not just TIps

Seems to trade on offered side putting the switch not far above 1.20% yield which pretty good break even...

Even 1.25%...

8:18 AM QZ On DV01, regression shows about 85% beta, so 15m TII 2/42 about 33k

8:20 AM Alex Gurevich 85% beta on yield?

I guess TIPs do have larger DV01 because they accumulate notional - my confusion that's what I was not taking Into account...

8:22 AM QZ Yes notional is indexed

8:23 AM Alex Gurevich Can you get a feeler how wide this thing could be trading - on a switch or I visually... alternatively we can use new cash to buy TIPs but that would really increase our risk...

8:24 AM QZ I think vs on the run 30s might be easier, want try that first or stick with 5/46?

Ok, feeling it out, will be back

8:34 AM Alex Gurevich Yes we could try on the run switch tool first...

8:34 AM QZ 5/46 seems not feasible at the moment, 11-13 ticks wide

trying to get a feel on the switch between ct30 and 2/42

8:35 AM Alex Gurevich Also monitor - cash basis maybe we could free up some balance sheet if cash becomes expensive to futures

8:35 AM QZ they see mid around 1.25-1.26, which i agree

roger on basis

trying to to get a quote of ct30 vs TII 2/42

8:38 AM Alex Gurevich If balance sheet want the issue we could switch TIPs with WNs.

Or even do more swap spreads vs. TIPs. If swap margins wasn't the issue as well.

9:04 AM Alex Gurevich What about implied repo? We finding very cheaply, right?

9:04 AM QZ But you are right, futures are cheaper, we could switch from cash to FV

FV implied under 30bp

9:06 AM Alex Gurevich Where are we funding?

9:06 AM QZ 10 c

9:21 AM QZ Roughly, i see the ct30 vs TII 242 mid spread 1.26, we probably could get it done around 1.275

Let us know if you want to do anything. CK reminded me we actually have 10m ct30, so could switch 10mm ct 30 equivalent

---

9:24 AM Alex Gurevich Yes let's just CT30 switch for those 10mm see what you can do...

Seems mid 1.245% feel free to give an order...

TIPs seem to be offered now maybe 1.25% switch is doable

9:26 AM QZ I think they will do about 1.6 bp from mid, checking now

9:26 AM Alex Gurevich But could pay al title more

9:27 AM QZ standby, waiting

126.e

126.3 bp

want to do it?

9:35 AM Alex Gurevich Yes

9:36 AM **CK** trying

9:36 AM QZ sec, refreshing

9:37 AM Alex Gurevich Should be better now

9:38 AM QZ 126.2976 is done

ok?

9:38 AM Alex Gurevich Ok

9:48 AM Alex Gurevich What's the weighting?

9:49 AM QZ 10m ct30 vs 10.25 TIPS

The gain on the LIBOR relief and swap spreads offset negative marks on dividends and commodities. The day ended with a small positive.

MARCH 31: TUESDAY MORNING

This was the last trading day of the first quarter of 2020; new investor cash was coming into the portfolio and it was time to tally the beans and adjust position sizes.

I am struck by the contrast between the frantic activity that transpired earlier in the month and the collected, even relaxed, manner in which I conducted the end-of-the-month rebalancing.

March 31st, 2020 ⌄

7:36 AM Alex Gurevich Good morning. Today at our risk call our
objective is to estimate portfolio sizes and funding of
the EOD. Décide New portfolio allocations.

7:36 AM QZ copy

7:37 AM Alex Gurevich We should spreadsheet ready for positon
adjustments. Take into account $15.5mm inflows in ■
macro as of tomorrow.

🗨 1   😌⁺

Thé won't be immediate sweeping adjustments as risk
will be taken down somewhat.

7:44 AM Alex Gurevich We should create a short-cut code to how
to positons.

ATL adjust to ■ (make all positons on this security
aligned with current ■ size)
ATO adjust or i
ATA adjust to ■

HCD highest common denominator: add to align with
with whatever port has the largest positon
LCD lowers common denominator: reduce to align with
portfolio which has the smallest position

Of course there will be other incremental adjustments.

7:48 AM CK will do

Qin and I both setup versions of that last time around to
help expedite the task

9:04 AM Alex Gurevich WRT interest risk comparison. can we
look at it excluding stub and AND excluding front June.
This is not for purposes of risk management - June is
still a risk but for purposes on risk balancing,

9:04 AM QZ roger

9:07 AM   Alex Gurevich What will be the reset trading level of ▮▮▮ as of tomorrow? Assuming today's P/l. (almost 2X cash I assume)

9:12 AM   QZ Estimate 91mmm

assuming no flows

9:25 AM   Alex Gurevich I am thinking right now: keep ▮▮ at 30. ▮▮▮▮ 22 units (slightl overfunded) and ▮▮ 18 units. Let me know if it feels right.

9:26 AM   QZ Agreed

10:00 AM   **Christopher Lutton** Ah, i thot ▮▮▮ might be coming down to 25

be interesting to hear your thoughts on risk-call

10:09 AM   Alex Gurevich It will stay at 30. But we will gradually make it less over-risked relative to 30 like it is now.

10:09 AM   **Christopher Lutton** copy

11:43 AM   **CK** we bought the $1mm TIPS 02/42 Alex

112-17...now comes the ops challenges...

11:49 AM   **CK** confirmed: no TIPS allowed for ▮▮▮

awaiting rebal instructions for futures into today's close

11:50 AM   Alex Gurevich CLM1 and CLM2: HCD

SIK0: HCD

11:52 AM   **CK** see you

11:52 AM   Alex Gurevich CNM0 adjust ▮▮▮▮ to ▮▮

CNM0 adjustment column for ▮▮ may need to be corrected because we need to incorporate swaps into the balance

PEM0; HCD

12:04 PM   QZ Copy on CN

12:04 PM Alex Gurevich DEDZ4: 25% of increase required for HCD accounting for shorter contracts as well.

12:08 PM **CK** k

12:12 PM QZ Can't buy TIPs for ■■■■. Rejected by ■■■

12:14 PM Alex Gurevich SFM0: LCD

12:15 PM **CK** k

12:28 PM **CK** all buys...CLM1 10x (6 ■■ / 4 ■■), CLM2 10x (6 ■■ / 4 ■■), SIK0 101x (61 ■■ / 40 ■■), CNM0 367x (all ■■) are all done

PE & SF next up...DEDZ4 not top priority given its virtually closed, so will loop back on that

12:28 PM Alex Gurevich K

1:16 PM **CK** bought 150x PEM0 (90 ■■ / 60 ■■)....have bought 50/110x SFM0 so far but mkt same way and liq a pain so still working (ultimately 99 ■■ / 11 ■■)

so everything except half of the SF & the full DEDZ4 is done so far

---

1:44 PM **CK** SF is done

for now we are repo'ing the $1mm TIPs done w ■■■, we will have to revisit the conversation around cash management w ■■■ tomorrow AM

1:53 PM Alex Gurevich Ok.

3:32 PM **CK** for tomorrow, DEDZ4 upsize will be for 337x (202 ■■ / 135 ■■), which is 25% of the 1350x upsize we need to satisfy HCD conditions...unless you have a specific level in mind, I will work this on best efforts basis when I'm up tomorrow

3:33 PM Alex Gurevich Yes if I am up tonight - I may put something in myself...

3:33 PM   **CK** k cool

market opens at 11:30 PM, ill stage the order for you now (and you can modify it if you want) assuming EMSX allows me

3:36 PM   Alex Gurevich K

I am often still up

3:36 PM   **CK** thats staged in EMSX as a limit order (max 73.00), just make sure you adjust the limit level if/when you route it tonight

kk cool

i'll work it at best tomorrow AM if i don't hear anything though will obvi check for any instructions you've left in advance

---

3:46 PM   **CK** 'classic' allocation has been updated on EMSX to: 30 /22 / 18 ■

7:44 PM   Alex Gurevich Executed HCD on RFM0 (sorry CK I know you have liquidity concerns...)

10:05 PM   **CK** haha if we like the position then we'll figure out the liquidity! 8% of open interest and climbing!

🐾 1   😄

We were only one quarter down, and already, people noticed how difficult it was to imagine that the Australian wildfires, which had horrified us in January and now seemed so distant, were part of the same fateful year.

In some ways, the battle of 2020 was only beginning. I had to deal with the accumulated exhaustion of sleepless nights, the stress of market swings, and the even greater stress of homeschooling children.

But I had no fear or doubt about charging forward.

CHAPTER 8

HITS AND MISSES

I UNDERSTAND THAT KEEPING COMPLETE TRACK OF THE TRADING chatter was probably not easy. I reiterate that my objective was to give you, the reader, the *feel* for what we were dealing with, rather than a comprehensive analysis of all executed transactions. Furthermore, the blow-by-blow narration might have obscured the bigger picture of what actually transpired in the month of March.

In this chapter, I will share the price charts again for principal asset classes. Some of what I show here will be repetitive; my goal is to demonstrate through visuals how different this month was from any other period in financial markets.

It will be easy to see the amazing price entry points for a plethora of trades. I got several right, but none perfectly right. There are many I missed entirely. Some of the missed opportunities were not within my mandate or expertise. Some escaped my notice in the commotion. Others I didn't have a chance to act on because my risk capital was tied up in other transactions.

I have acquired the psychological fortitude to go over mistakes without allowing "should haves" to ruin my mental state. Returning to the poker analogy, it is, of course, easier to dissect strategic errors after a winning night. However, I have proven myself able to do so after losing periods as well.

So after having tallied our wins and losses, let's recap what cards we had been dealt.

MARKET VOLATILITY

The most broadly appreciated effect of the pandemic on the financial markets was stock market volatility. Throughout the book, I have been referring to the S&P 500 as the common gauge of the US stock market performance. However, the NASDAQ index probably tells the purest form of the story.

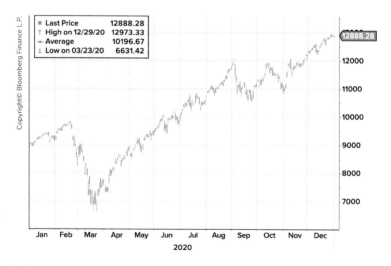

NASDAQ Composite Index 2020: Following a deep sell-off in March 2020, a re-markable steady rebound took the index to a new high.

Notice the index sold off very deeply in what was identified as the fastest (and shortest) bear market in history. However, what was most remarkable was not the rapid bounce but the relentless rally, which continued throughout the year and took us to decisive new highs. Part of this price action was the evolution of liquidity on which I have already elaborated. Seizing on that liquidity story, I have chosen to buy other equity indices such as Nikkei and dividend swaps.

The NASDAQ rally had another powerful component: the accelerated technology adoption, including the transition to online retail. I will not elaborate on this—the societal changes precipitated by the pandemic and ensuing benefits to the mega-tech sector will be well familiar to the readers.

I have to admit that specific opportunity was not at the forefront of my mind. I was not denying what was happening; I simply did not have a sufficient understanding of the scope of technology adoption to make it an integral part of my trading strategy.

As an amusing anecdote, a few years before COVID, I started to think that buying puts on Amazon could be a good strategy to prepare for the next recession. My logic was that should retail sales dip even incrementally, the company would face a painful choice between slowing its growth or erasing its slim profit margins. I hadn't foreseen that due to the nature of the recession, it would prove to be a tremendous windfall for the company.

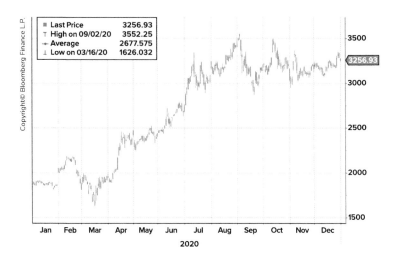

Amazon.com Inc Stock Price 2020: The pandemic resulted in a windfall for online retail.

Good thing I was aware that I had no expertise in the analysis of individual stocks and stayed away from such amateurish bets. The flip side of that was I also didn't participate in any other equities that benefited from the pandemic such as Zoom.

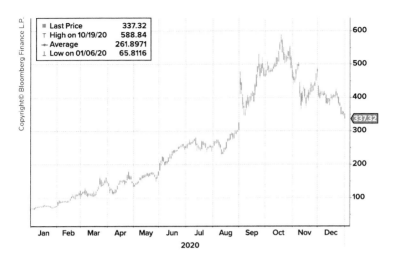

Zoom Video Communication Inc Stock Price 2020: WFH ushered in the explosive rise of online communication companies.

I also didn't buy the bottom on any stocks, such as United Airlines, which were hit hard and were bound to recover.

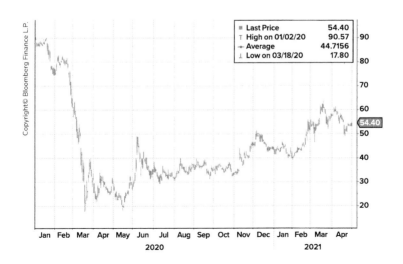

United Airlines Holdings Inc Stock Price 2020: A decent recovery following the COVID crash.

To be clear, I don't beat myself up over missing trades that weren't within my realm of expertise. My strategy was never meant to be the only comprehensive way of money management. Although I aspire to deliver superior and independent returns by taking advantage of macro opportunities, which do include levels of broad equity indices, I expect investors to rely on other managers to capitalize on sector rotation and single stock valuations.

As I mentioned earlier, whereas the stock volatility during the pandemic was most broadly understood, the price action in other asset classes was even more unusual.

TREASURY BONDS

Let's think about what should be the safest investment in the world: US Treasury bonds. Many laypeople think of bonds as a "safe, boring" domain. Bond traders, however, are subject to as much risk to their portfolio as they choose to take—it all depends on duration and leverage.

Furthermore, in a sense, bond portfolios, which are constructed with the expectation of lower volatility in the underlying instrument, can be the most vulnerable. Let me clarify that I am talking only about portfolios that have *long* positions in assets. Short positions are an animal in themselves, and I will mention them in the conclusion of this book.

Any asset that represents a claim of some future cash flows has a limited downside no matter how uncertain those cash flows are. Price can only go down to zero. So if you put your portfolio in very risky stock investments, you can only lose all your money if they all go bankrupt simultaneously.

Now, suppose you invest your portfolio in bond instruments. Assuming that those bonds can't lose more than 5 percent of their value, you can leverage that portion of your portfolio 10:1 (that is, borrow nine times the cash you have to buy, for example, $10 million worth of bonds with $1 million cash). You calculate that your leveraged bond investment is less risky than your plain-vanilla stock investment because your downside is $10 \times 5\% = 50\%$ of cash invested.

However, what if your initial assumption was incorrect and bonds go down 12 percent for whatever reason? Now your loss is $10 \times 12\% = 120\%$, and you are insolvent.

This exercise demonstrates that disruptions in instruments deemed safe are more detrimental to the stability of the financial market than disruptions in instruments already considered volatile.

Although Treasury bonds experienced a very rare level of volatility in March 2020, for the purposes of this recap chapter, I will focus on an instrument, which is supposed to be even safer than regular bonds.

Indeed, assuming that long-dated government bonds have no possibility of default, inflation is considered the greatest risk, as it would affect the value of future cash flows and cause yield to go up and price to go down. Hence, we have inflation-indexed bonds, TIPS, featured prominently in this book. Given you own the securities backed with the full faith and credit of the US government and protected from inflation, where would the volatility come from?

The answer is always the same: assets go down in price when there are more sellers than buyers. You can stand on the sidewalk shouting, "The price is wrong!" all you want. The price will do what it will do.

In the month of March, the volatility of this safe instrument surpassed that of the stock indices. Note that it took nine days for thirty-year TIPS to journey 31.4 percent from its intraday high on March 9, 2020 to its intraday low on March 18, 2020. Compare that to the month it took the S&P 500 to sell off 35.4 percent from its intraday high on February 19, 2020 to its intraday low on March 23, 2020.

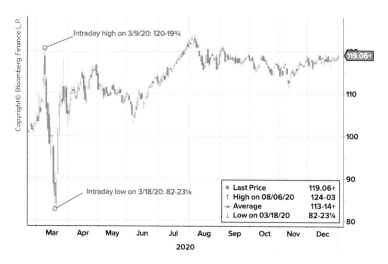

TII 0.25 02/15/50 TIPS Price 2020: TIPS price volatility in March 2020 was no less than stock price volatility.

TIPS VALUE

There are different ways to look at the TIPS value, including price, as above, real yield (yield in excess of inflation), or implied inflation breakeven (difference between the yield on nominal bonds and the real yield on TIPS). For the purposes of my portfolio, I often look at them on the asset swap basis, looking at the difference between the yield on the corresponding swap and the real yield on the bond. The following graph charts this asset swap.

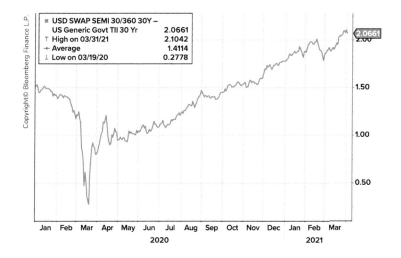

The Spread between Thirty-Year Swap Rate and Yield on Generic Thirty-Year TIPS January 2020–March 2021: Buying the asset swap in March 2020 was very profitable.

I didn't get in at the very bottom, which was 28 bps on March 19. However, executing it much higher at 92, I still felt that I was receiving an enormous gift. Think of what I was paying and what I was receiving:

I pay repo (the funding rate on the bond) + 0.92%, and I receive LIBOR + inflation. Repo is almost always lower than LIBOR, so for me to lose money, average inflation would have to stay way below 1%. Given my earlier thesis that the policymakers would keep adding liquidity until liquidity became excessive, such an outcome appeared extremely unlikely.

Even though I didn't get into the swap at the optimal point, it continued to rebound in my favor and headed toward what I considered to be the minimum economic value of 2.50%.

Readers not familiar with fixed-income markets might not be impressed by an almost 2% range on the asset swap. However, keep in mind we are talking about assets with a thirty-year duration. A change of payments by 2% per annum represents a total of 30 × 2% = 60% variance in cash flows. And although payments in the distant future typically have a lesser impact due to discounting, in the current environment of near-zero rates, they are quite weighty. Hence, the amazing stock-like volatility of "safe" assets in 2020.

MUNICIPAL BONDS AND SWAPS

Another "solid" investment that went out of whack in 2020 was municipal bonds and swaps. We have discussed this, and I won't repeat too much. The interesting thing about those swaps is that they first spiked in March, when the short-term funding blew out, and I missed the chance to do anything about it. However, the market gave me a second chance in May, and this time I acted, increasing my position. I didn't do as much as I should have, but at least I did something.

AUSTRALIAN GOVERNMENT BONDS

However, the March award for the "Strangest Bond Price Action" goes not to TIPS or munis but to Australian government bonds. On

March 19, 2020, the Royal Bank of Australia (RBA) announced massive monetary expansion, including yield curve control—officially not allowing the three-year bond below a certain price (0.25% yield).

In response to this extremely dovish news, bond futures had an unprecedented several-minute crash, which we have already discussed in the context of our trade transcripts.

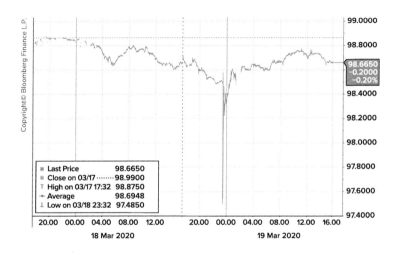

Intraday Chart of Australian Ten-Year Bond Future Price March 18, 2020–March 19, 2020: A mini crash following RBA on March 19, 2020.

Handling Australian bond future (XMA) has overall been a miss—up to the point when I am writing this book now, in the winter of 2021.

On the day of the yield spike in March, we had no risk capacity to take advantage of this obvious opportunity. Later in the year, as the market stabilized, I established a very substantial position in XMA. This worked well for a few months as Aussie bonds outperformed those of the United States and Canada, but then, starting in late 2020 (jumping quite a bit ahead here), they sold off very sharply again (this time, in a more typical manner), putting pressure on my portfolio.

Having missed the great entry and then chasing the bonds up led to a risk of being in a losing trade.

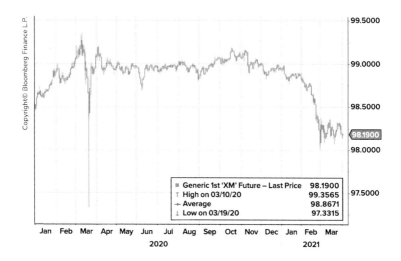

Roll-Adjusted Australian Ten-Year Bond Future Price January 2020–April 2021.

I am much more satisfied with my handling of the AUD short and my other long USD trades. I managed to ride a significant AUD position down without taking too much profit prematurely and to cover it when it turned in the opposite direction without giving back too much profit. This is all one can ask for.

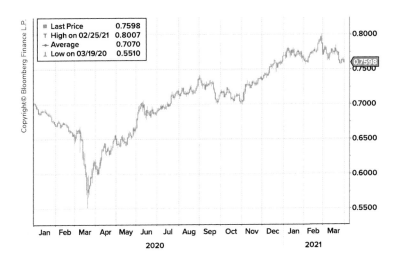

Australian Dollar (AUD) Spot Price January 2020–March 2021: We made the right decision to cover our short position on AUD as the currency appreciated substantially after the dip in March 2020.

EMERGING MARKETS

Expanding our view from the developed world, like Australia, to the emerging markets, it is easy to see that opportunities were abundant. Between bonds, currencies, and equities, I will not dwell on all the dips that could have been bought there. I felt reasonably satisfied, having accumulated Mexican peso at least at cheap levels (a higher number on the following chart means weaker peso).

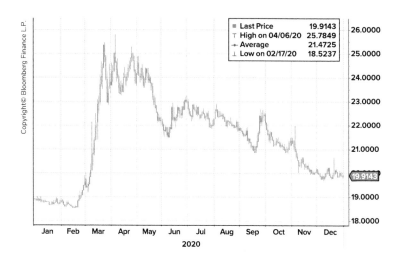

Mexican Peso (MXN) Spot Price 2020: We accumulated long MXN positions during the crisis.

PRECIOUS METALS

Precious metals are often viewed as a form of currency, and as such, they are subject to the vagaries of dollar funding. The silver crash in March and the subsequent rally of about 150 percent in 2020 were spectacular. Being already long precious metals going into March, I had somewhat limited space in which to maneuver, but I moved in the right direction, increasing my silver position. The metals ended up being a significant contributor to our 2020 P/L.

Precious metals traded weaker over the subsequent few months. I feel this correction is consistent with how the great gold bull markets, such as the one that started in 2003, proceeded. By the time this book is out, the reader may have a better idea of how this position is faring.

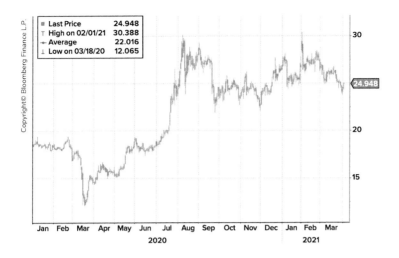

■ Last Price	24.948	
T High on 02/01/21	30.388	
◆ Average	22.016	
⊥ Low on 03/18/20	12.065	

Roll-Adjusted Silver Future Price January 2020–March 2021: Post-March crisis, we increased our position in silver, which appreciated significantly in 2020.

There is a bet on precious metals that gives one much higher leverage: mining stocks. Indeed, imagine it costs $1,000 to mine one ounce of gold. If the price of gold goes from $1,200 per ounce to $2,000 per ounce, the net profit goes from $200 per ounce to $1,000 per ounce!

Let's look at the Junior Gold Mining ETF (GDXJ). It had reached a high of 141.7 in 2010 when gold was strong. In March, it crashed down to 19.5. This presented a great buying opportunity, which completely escaped my attention at the moment. Somewhat similar to Australian bonds, I got into the trade later in the year and suffered when the asset class went into correction.

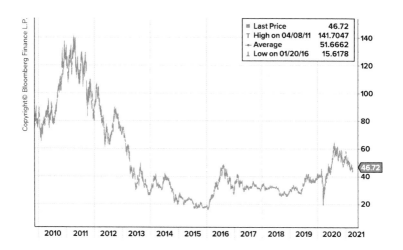

VanEck Vectors Junior Gold Miners ETF (GDXJ) Price 2010–2020: Potential upside could be several times higher than for the metal itself.

Precious metals are distinct from other financial instruments, as their supply is limited by the laws of physics, and they are viewed as "hard assets."

DIGITAL ASSETS

These days, it is impossible to talk of hard assets without mentioning the word I have successfully managed to avoid up to this point: Bitcoin.

There, I did it. Digital assets are assets and thus are subject to liquidity. Bitcoin crashed into the market singularity along with everything else in the month of March. It emerged buoyant and victorious from the white hole and, within a few months, made a new high.

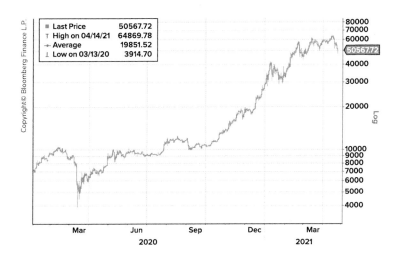

■ Last Price	50567.72
T High on 04/14/21	64869.78
-▲- Average	19851.52
⊥ Low on 03/13/20	3914.70

Logarithmic Chart of Bitcoin in USD Price January 2020–April 2021.

I am very careful when clients ask for my recommendation when it comes to investing in cryptocurrencies. Computers and software have never been my strong suits. Although I am fortunate to have a background in math, which makes discussions of crypto tenable, I still don't feel sufficiently educated or qualified. I certainly haven't yet figured how to fit dynamic crypto trading in my portfolio strategy.

I do understand the Pascal's wager[16] aspect of Bitcoin. If for some reason in the near future digital assets become the only accepted store of value, an investor may be incentivized to put at least a small portion of their portfolio into the crypto space. The idea is

---

16   "Pascal's wager" is the name given to an argument attributed to Blaise Pascal for believing, or for at least taking steps to believe, in God. Alan Hajeck, "Pascal's Wager," The Stanford Encyclopedia of Philosophy, Summer 2018 ed., https://plato.stanford.edu/entries/pascal-wager/.

that a very small allocation, which can easily be written off, can save you in the event of global collapse of fiat currencies.

My recommendation to investors who think along those lines has been "do it yourself." They don't need to pay me management and incentive fees for a simple "buy and hold" transaction. Some of my other portfolio positions are also long-term "buy and hold," but I believe that I add value by navigating dynamic position, selection, and size adjustments. "Do it yourself" might not have worked, for example, with the bond futures and all their swings that occurred over the last few years.

Lacking expertise, I didn't feel it was a particular miss not to buy Bitcoin in March. It was certainly on my radar as one of the liquidity indicators. But I felt there were plenty of assets (including those I mentioned) that had a similarly excellent risk-reward profile when accounting for a smaller downside and greater availability of leverage.

THE STRANGEST PRICE ACTION

I've gone through a bunch of successful and unsuccessful trades of March and discussed assets I understand and assets I don't understand, and I would be remiss not to mention the strangest market event of 2020, which, in fact, might have been the strangest event in the history of financial markets. Surprisingly, even though this event was rooted in the markets of March, it didn't actually happen until April.

The award for staging this event goes to—are you ready for it?— OIL. I have written about buying deferred oil contracts, and the trade panned out exactly as I expected. The June 2021 oil contract CLM1 traded as low as 29.09 on the travel shutdown and then rallied to as high as 67.29 in early 2021.

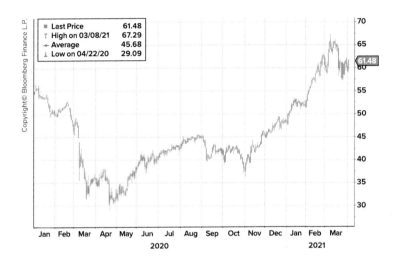

June 2021 WTI Crude Oil Future January 2020–March 2021: A reasonable dip and recovery in 2020.

However, this "reasonable" dip and recovery doesn't paint the picture of what happened to WTI oil, scheduled to be delivered on May 1, 2020, in Cushing, Oklahoma. Apparently, the storage facility was overfilled with unused oil, and the price crashed over the weekend of April 17, 2020 to levels not seen in decades. But that was only the beginning.

On the afternoon of April 20, 2020, I watched in astonishment as the contract went lower and lower until it crossed into the *negative* territory. People were willing to pay money for someone to take oil off their hands!

And even that was only the beginning. One could understand a mildly negative price for technical and regulatory reasons, but it didn't stop there. By the end of the day, the contract put in a low of almost negative $40 a barrel—a flip of what might have been a reasonable positive price in a modest demand environment. Somebody had to actually close their oil position at the equivalent of paying $40 to dispose of a barrel of oil!

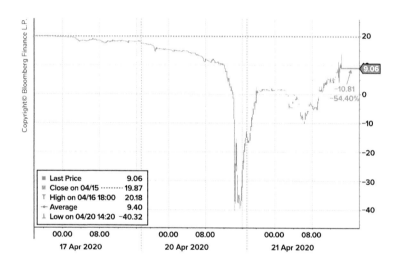

May 2020 WTI Crude Oil Future Price April 17, 2020–April 21, 2020.

I don't own freight trains or storage facilities. The issue with the May delivery had nothing to do with deferred contracts. To this day, I don't know if I had a sound way to take advantage of this dislocation.

Regardless, it was quite a show—as was all of 2020.

CONCLUSION

THINK OF A LONG, LONG POKER NIGHT. EVEN IF YOU ARE NOT A player yourself, you can probably conjure up an image from some old movies: tired, red-eyed gamblers, gulping coffee or alcohol, smoking cigars, cursing. Well, the picture no longer looks exactly like that—smoking has been mostly prohibited by now, cursing will get you banned, and most of even the dumbest gamblers avoid alcohol at the table. Even coffee is rarely needed because everyone is running on adrenaline. But the gist is the same. Ten, sometimes twenty, thirty, or more, straight hours at the table, during which everyone is sweaty, grimy, and worn.

Now think of yourself as the player who is "stuck," losing money on the night. You are desperately hoping to claw your money back—just one or two lucky hands to break even and you can go home. Because of all the coffee or soda, you really need a bathroom break, but you can't get up even for a minute because you may miss the one hand that could let you dig yourself out of the hole. So you hold it in, biting your lip against the pain in your bladder, and squint with your tired eyes at each new card, hoping it will be *the one.*

At long last, you are dealt a good hand and you commit most of your remaining stack, but an opponent is raising hard, and it looks likely you may be beaten. No, the other player is not bluffing, you know that, but there are still more cards to come and you could still get lucky, maybe, maybe...

Now let's look at a different poker experience. You are up a lot of money, your chip stack is so high you can barely see over it. You are tired and hungry. There is a strong temptation to cash in your chips and book a good win.

But you look around the table and see other players squirming. That's what you are here for: *to make them squirm.* The easy money is at the table, and you must keep playing. You go to the bathroom. You rinse your face. You order some herbal tea and scan (probably unsuccessfully) the casino menu for something light and healthy to eat.

There is no rush. When a hand starts breaking against you, you fold and minimize your losses. Who cares? You are still far ahead. You get outdrawn on the last card; you laugh it off. But when you see a weakness, when you smell an opportunity, you have no fear of committing your chips. Most importantly, you are having fun.

In the opening chapters of this book, I described the origins of my favorable setup for the pandemic. When the first quarter of 2020 ended, this is what I wrote in my investor report.

Looking from the outside at just our monthly performance over the last three months it is easy to form one of the following misconceptions:

HonTe is a perpetually long vol, tail-hedging fund, which usually loses money but benefits when "black swans" occur.

The HonTe investment team had identified early and correctly the pandemic risk and positioned accordingly.

HonTe was able to pinpoint all the major shifts in the market dynamics and take tactical advantage.

HonTe got lucky by having the right positions at the right time by pure chance

All those notions must be dispelled:

Over more than two decades of investment experience, we have managed to navigate multiple bull and bear markets in risk assets. Our current trading program performed through several years of economic expansion and periods of both low and high volatility. We have met our objective to have on average no correlation or negative correlation to the stock market in order to provide diversification to our investors. That is not to say that we have been invulnerable to correlation breakdowns. But from our long track record it is clearly not our intention to bet on extreme moves and lose money in more "normal" markets.

Ironically, in our non-professional assessment of the medical situation, we erred on the side of being too optimistic/ complacent. We certainly did not differentiate ourselves by any insights on the epidemic. Alex in particular feels that several of his early opinions and perceptions turned out to be wrong. The point here is that in our portfolio management we ended up relying not on our laypersons' speculations, but on our professional approach to portfolio construction.

Our trading volumes for this quarter and especially during the last month were much higher than usual and rapid risk adjustments were continuously required. But that does not mean our tactical trading was always effective. We will discuss the positioning in more detail in our investor letter but suffice it to say a lot of poorly timed trades were executed along with the good ones. The important thing is that we did what was needed to stay within our strategy framework and keep the portfolio going. The main source of P/L was strategic positioning, not tactical trading.

There has been a fair bit of good and bad luck in our team's combined careers. We have always strived to position to benefit from a sudden crisis. This does not always work out perfectly, but on average we do expect to make money on risk-off events. Such events do happen every few years (1998: Russian debt crisis, 2001: 9/11, 2008: GFC, 2011 European debt crisis, 2016: Brexit); performance during such events is an important contribution to the long-term track record, and we account for continuous risk of "black swans" in our portfolio construction.

To illustrate the scope of our gains on just one aspect of our portfolio—options on EDM0 (June 2020 Eurodollars)—I include our full trading logs for 98.375 on 98.25 strike calls. Notice the difference in price (right column) between all the buys, marked by B, and the sales, marked by S.

As of Date	Ticket	Security Description	B/S	Amount	Price
02/15/2018	5254	EDM0C 98.375	B	2500	0.06
02/15/2018	5255	EDM0C 98.375	B	3500	0.06
02/15/2018	6001	EDM0C 98.375	S	3500	0.06
02/15/2018	6000	EDM0C 98.375	S	2500	0.06
02/15/2018	6012	EDM0C 98.375	B	3500	0.06
02/15/2018	6011	EDM0C 98.375	B	2500	0.06
01/08/2019	7456	EDM0C 98.375	B	100	0.065
01/08/2019	7451	EDM0C 98.375	B	2000	0.065
01/08/2019	7452	EDM0C 98.375	B	400	0.065
01/08/2019	7455	EDM0C 98.375	B	500	0.065
01/10/2019	7512	EDM0C 98.375	B	1500	0.06
01/18/2019	7582	EDM0C 98.375	B	1500	0.05
06/03/2019	8907	EDM0C 98.375	S	400	0.32
06/03/2019	8908	EDM0C 98.375	S	100	0.32
06/03/2019	8909	EDM0C 98.375	S	100	0.32
06/03/2019	8885	EDM0C 98.375	B	800	0.24
06/03/2019	8887	EDM0C 98.375	S	800	0.24
03/13/2020	21127	EDM0C 98.375	S	617	1.105
06/15/2020	27157	EDM0C 98.375	S	6800	1.326
06/15/2020	27161	EDM0C 98.375	S	700	1.326
06/15/2020	27159	EDM0C 98.375	S	3283	1.326

As of Date	Ticket	Security Description	B/S	Amount	Price	Type
01/08/2019	7463	EDM0C 98.25	B	250	0.08	OA
01/08/2019	7462	EDM0C 98.25	B	1250	0.08	OA
01/08/2019	7470	EDM0C 98.25	B	250	0.075	OA
01/08/2019	7469	EDM0C 98.25	B	1250	0.075	OA
01/17/2019	7564	EDM0C 98.25	B	250	0.07	OA
01/17/2019	7563	EDM0C 98.25	B	1250	0.07	OA
01/17/2019	7573	EDM0C 98.25	B	1250	0.07	OA
01/17/2019	7574	EDM0C 98.25	B	250	0.07	OA
02/04/2019	7659	EDM0C 98.25	B	1250	0.06	OA
02/04/2019	7660	EDM0C 98.25	B	250	0.06	OA
02/04/2019	7663	EDM0C 98.25	B	1500	0.06	OA
02/05/2019	7692	EDM0C 98.25	B	10000	0.06	PCP
06/03/2019	8903	EDM0C 98.25	S	400	0.32	COA
06/03/2019	8904	EDM0C 98.25	S	100	0.32	COA
06/03/2019	8905	EDM0C 98.25	S	100	0.32	COA
06/03/2019	8881	EDM0C 98.25	B	1775	0.29	JL
06/03/2019	8883	EDM0C 98.25	S	1775	0.29	JL
10/14/2019	11947	EDM0C 98.25	S	200	0.295	OA
10/14/2019	11945	EDM0C 98.25	S	500	0.295	OA
10/14/2019	11946	EDM0C 98.25	S	200	0.295	OA
03/04/2020	18447	EDM0C 98.25	S*	9326	1.04	CJL
03/04/2020	18449	EDM0C 98.25	S*	1475	1.04	CJL

As of Date	Ticket	Security Description	B/S	Amount	Price	Type
03/04/2020	18449	EDM0C 98.25	S*	1475	1.04	CJL
03/04/2020	18451	EDM0C 98.25	S*	950	1.04	CJL
06/15/2020	27217	EDM0C 98.25	S	5749	1.451	PCJ

The Entire Trade Log[17] of June 2020: Eurodollar future call options with strikes 98.375 and 98.25 transacted by HonTe.

Having started the year strong gave me the leverage to weather the volatility. Even with that cushion, I ended up stretched pretty thin around the Ides of March.

The disjoint price action that occurred as the world fell into the black hole was daunting. Below you will find the chart of the five-day rolling average annualized volatility of my portfolio. One easily spots the singularity that occurred during the week I labeled The Dark Days.

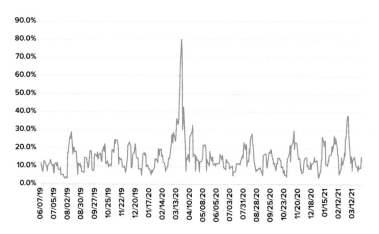

Annualized 5d Rolling Net Return Volatility

Five-Day Rolling Volatility of HonTe LH Macro Fund Net Return Since Inception Date, May 1, 2019.

---

17 S stands for "sell" trades. The ones marked with an * are not actual sell trades. These are options being exercised early. These exercises were mentioned in the March 4 Slacks.

By the end of March 2020, I could clear my head and weigh the opportunities ahead. The weather was getting better, and when the beaches reopened, I would be able to spend many afternoons by the ocean, contemplating my strategies by the sound of the waves. My family was adjusting to lockdown conditions and homeschooling. I coped with the stress and, eventually, managed to get my health scares under control.

Throughout the year, pandemic anxiety waxed and waned. The uncertainty was still high throughout the world, but my shield held up and my confidence increased.

I was in a better position than most to ride the storm of liquidity coming from the white hole. The *Shield against Uncertainty* had helped me survive, and now the *Magic Sword of Necessity* was unsheathed.

THE BEANIE BABY THEORY

What stood out about our performance in 2020 was that we did very well in the first quarter before the crisis unfolded and as the crisis was unfolding, but we also continued to do well during the rest of the year, when the recovery in risk assets surprised many investors with its speed and magnitude.

A poker player on a winning streak is more likely to make good decisions and pyramid their gains. I was not only able to stay in the game, but I also formulated a thesis that would carry me through the rest of the year. Here is what I tweeted in April:

I call it The Beanie Baby Theory. I laid it out in my next quarterly report, which summarized the performance of the first half of 2020:

> What I do know and what I have talked about for years is that for a money manager to move into cash for safety during the times of uncertainty is a PROFOUND and CATASTROPHIC fallacy. Indeed, the greatest bubble I have witnessed in my career was not beanie babies, or internet stock, or mortgage securities, or ICOs; it was USD cash in March 2009. Everything was cheap in terms of cash - from homes being auctioned on the steps of courthouses - to stocks of companies which had no debt like eBay or Google - to bonds of banks which would not be allowed to fail anymore after the Lehman disaster - to foreign currencies - to... pick your asset.
>
> Cash has only an aspect of safety for a consumer who has immediate cash needs. Over longer periods of time, cash has been demonstrably less safe because of persistent inflation. This is not to say cash cannot be a holding at certain junctures - the point is that it must be viewed as an asset which can be cheap or expensive at a given time.
>
> So, if you are tempted to sell a stock short - remember - you are buying cash. You are, in fact, going to the Fed, which is

a monopolistic and costless producer of cash, and telling them: "I want your product. And I will give you this other asset for it."

So, when evaluating statements from managers imagine replacing the word "cash" with another cheaply produced asset: the aforementioned beanie babies.

How do you feel about:

"We have strengthened our balance sheet by converting some of our risky bonds into beanie babies."

"Our Var-At-Risk levels measured in terms of beanie babies are very conservative."

"Beanie babies are king."

"The global shortage of beanies babies and the unfunded beanie baby liabilities are bound to cause a beanie baby squeeze."

And my personal favorite:

"During these times of uncertainty, we will stay invested in beanie babies. When other assets will stabilize and establish an upward trend, we will have plenty of opportunity to sell our beanie babies and convert them into gold, real estate, or shares of operating companies."

I was poking fun at investors who insisted on giving back their first quarter trading profits by holding on to short risk-asset positions because the pandemic recession was so bad.

The hapless sellers of Tesla (TSLA) and GameStop (GME) were blindsided by focusing on the numerator—the intrinsic value of the company they were shorting. Instead, they faced a localized collapse of the Beanie Babies in the denominator (thus, an explosion in the listed share price). It is not that GME became so much more valuable in January 2021; rather, the market just stopped accepting dollars in exchange for GME shares.

Indeed, stocks had gone down in previous recessions, and the ensuing bear markets were usually long and painful. But one has to ask the question: why do stocks go down during a recession at all? Of course, certain crises hit certain sectors severely. Banks and mortgage companies came under pressure during the GFC; travel and hospitality were devastated by the pandemic.

We all know that every recession ends, and all companies, which are ongoing concerns, will only benefit in the long run from lower interest rates and higher valuations. So why sell stocks at all?

The origin of market fluctuations is liquidity. When the economy goes into a slowdown, cash becomes scarce. Some investors have to sell to raise cash; others fail to raise the cash needed to buy. This has nothing to do with rational long-term outlook.

This pattern has been so persistent over decades, and possibly centuries, that traders have started to think of it as some sort of divine valuation metric prescribing how the stock market should act.

Fortunately, I have long been aware of the fallacy of such thinking and questioned the relationship between recessions and bear markets. So when I observed that in this particular crisis the liquidity problem would be very transitory, I was prepared to discard the old stock metrics. I went from hoarding the Beanie Babies (also known as US dollars) when they were in demand to selling them when the supply exploded and exchanging them for any assets I could lay my hands on.

Social media often portrays central banks as the villains who distort and manipulate markets, eventually exacerbating societal problems. I see them as market players like any others. Their product is domestic currency, and they provide it when there is a demand. In the last two decades, they simply became more adroit at producing when the demand increased.

In this sense, the Federal Reserve was the true protagonist of this story, for they turned the black hole into a white hole. I rode the storm of liquidity they created for the rest of 2020.

The Big Bang launched our known universe by outpouring pure energy, which gradually started to find formations first as small particles and atoms and then as galaxies and filaments.

The cash created by the Beanie Baby Big Bang is now swirling in search of structure. We are in a new universe, but it is still governed by economic gravity. Good trades are abundant, but I always keep the promise I made at the end of my first book and look for *The Next Perfect Trade*.

ACKNOWLEDGMENTS

THE SUCCESS AND VALUE OF THIS BOOK IS INSEPARABLE FROM the success and value of HonTe Investments. In order to write *The Trades of March 2020*, I first had to *execute* the trades of March.

The success of our business hinged on the efforts of all our team members. They include Joann Shie-Chen (Head of Operations), Kushan Balasooriya (Director, Controller), and Tony Peng (Quantitative Research Analyst). I would especially like to thank my longtime partners and associates, Chris Lutton and Qin Zhu, who have been with me every step of the way, from the founding of this firm (and long before that) to the writing of my first book and all the way through this new project. Chris Kelley joined the firm more recently, but he was there for the sleepless nights of the pandemic, putting in tremendous effort gathering data and editing *The Trades of March 2020*.

The two team members who joined during the pandemic, Jessica Carvin and Melanie Jordan, have been working very hard on publishing a book of the highest possible quality.

Besides employees, an investment firm has another key constituency: investors. I am thankful to our clients (many of whom are personal friends) for entrusting their savings to our stewardship and for their support during the challenging times in the market.

The banks, brokerages, and exchanges met the challenge of operating in an unprecedented environment, standing by their clients, including HonTe, to allow transactions to be executed without interruption.

My success in the markets was facilitated by my bosses, mentors, and colleagues who generously shared their market experience. Those include David Puth, John Anderson, Jeff Bosland, Even Berntsen, Mark Zarb, Sheldon He, and Greg Parr.

Over the years, I have benefited from bouncing my thoughts about investment strategies off market colleagues and friendly competitors. Among those are Jim Leitner, John Burbank, Raoul Pal, Michael Green, and Brent Johnson.

My other guides were my math professors and teachers, who provided me with the intellectual training that became the foundation of this book. These include my thesis advisor Prof. Carlos Kenig, Prof. Robert Fefferman, Maria Yurievna Filina, and Nikolai Moiseevich Kuksa.

When it comes to getting the words out, I owe much to my closest friends who are passionate about writing. Mary Salome, my weekly writing partner, sat with me in-person or virtually throughout most of this effort; she helped me brainstorm and held me to my writing plan. Years ago, my high school friend Eugene Fink became a writer and gave me no option but to follow suit. Mary Anne Mohanraj inspired me with her own journey through the world of words and was always generous with her advice. Minal Hajratwala, my writing coach, helped me develop my craft.

Many others helped me obtain the requisite knowledge, experience, and skills. Most of the writing workshops I attended were led by established writers, who volunteered their time to beginners like myself to help us hone our craft. I am thankful for their structured exercises as well as the countless casual conversations on trading floors or at a writing convention.

As always, I am grateful to my wife, Christa, for constantly supporting and encouraging my creativity, as well as my children, Anabelle and Joseph, whose very presence is a continuous inspiration.